ANCHORAGES
AND MARINE PARKS

Peter Vassilopoulos

A coastal guide to Anchorages in the Pacific Northwest
Featuring the San Juan Islands, the Gulf Islands, Desolation Sound
and the West Coast of Vancouver Island
Marine Parks and Anchorages on major routes
from Victoria, B. C. to Ketchikan, Alaska
Plus a comprehensive list of Launching Ramps

By the Same Author:

Mariner Artist John M. Horton
Published by Heritage House

Docks and Destinations
Marinas Guide: Olympia to Ketchikan

North of Desolation Sound
The Broughton Islands

Gulf Islands Cruising Guide

Antiques Afloat
from the Golden Age of Boating in British Columbia

Pacific Marine Publishing • Vancouver

Photographs, maps, drawings and text copyright Peter Vassilopoulos 2008
Pacific Marine Publishing, Vancouver, PO Box 1312, Delta, B.C. V4M 3Y8
USA: PO Box 984, Point Roberts, WA. 98281-0984
Prepress graphics and typesetting–Peter Vassilopoulos
Printed in Canada.
All photographs by author unless otherwise indicated.
Aerial photography by author, special thanks to Heinz Bold, Justin Taylor and the late
Henry Karcz.

The information in this book is correct and accurate as far as can be determined. All
cautions and anchoring information is provided without guarantee and it is up to the boat
operator to ensure the proper technique in anchoring and careful attention to reading of
tide and current tables, monitoring weather and wind and using of hydrographic service
charts. Depths, shallows, hazards and other features are approximate where shown and
should be verified by use of authorized maritime publications including charts, BC Sailing
Directions and Small Craft Guide. The publisher and author are not liable for marine
operations leading to accident, damage or injury in any way connected with reference
to this guide. It is intended purely as a reference to popular moorings, anchorages and
marine parks on the coast.

First printing 1998. Second Printing 2000. Third printing (Revised) 2008.

Library and Archives Canada Cataloguing in Publication

Vassilopoulos, Peter, 1940-
    Anchorages and marine parks / Peter Vassilopoulos. -- 2nd ed.

Includes bibliographical references and index.
ISBN 978-0-919317-44-4

1. Marinas--British Columbia--Pacific Coast--Guidebooks. 2. Marinas--
Washington (State)--San Juan Islands--Guidebooks. 3. Marine parks and
reserves--British Columbia--Pacific Coast--Guidebooks. 4. Marine parks
and reserves--Washington (State)--San Juan Island--Guidebooks. 5. Pacific
Coast (B.C.)--Guidebooks. 6. San Juan Islands (Wash.)--Guidebooks. I. Title.

FC3845.P2V38 2008   917.11'1045   C2007-906119-2

*Copies are available from marine stores, marinas and book stores. Distribution and
acquisition enquiries to Pacific Marine Publishing, Box 1312, Delta, BC. V4M 3Y8.*

Contents

Weather

For weather information listen to the weather channel on VHF radio, or phone

Vancouver 604-666-3655

Cover: A busy but peaceful anchorage at Winter Cove in the southern Gulf Islands.

Introduction

*"One ship drives east and another drives west
With the selfsame winds that blow.
'Tis the set of the sails
And not the gales
Which tells us the way to go."*

–Ella Wheeler Wilcox

Confined to our allotted living space; buildings of wood, brick, and stone, we peer out to the ocean. A hidden world of dynamic and challenging beauty. A world of ebb and flows, of serenity and solitude. A world waiting to be explored.

Steep fjords and hidden passages, beckon to the traveller. Clouds and mist mould the landscape. The sounds of whales and eagles are heard, muted, off in the distance. Virgin wilderness rises to greet the ones bold enough to challenge the waters of Canada's west coast. It is a wilderness that can offer the traveller immense comfort with "safe harbour", or conversely incredible calamity.

Many times I have walked along the beaches of some deserted island, and searched for the ones who travelled unaware and unprepared. The hills and cliffs offering only silent comment as to the circumstances of my being there.

Preparation is the key to an enjoyable and safe marine passage.

Professional mariners rely on a complex web of sometimes confusing government publications to plan and execute safe marine travel. As necessary as these publications are, nothing can take the place of well prepared and documented observations of a first hand nature. Such is a document you now hold in your hands.

I first met Peter Vassilopoulos, while he was on his boat at anchor in a small cove near the south end of Vancouver Island. He peered suspiciously over the top rim of his sun glasses at the young R.C.M.P. (Royal Canadian Mounted Police) marine officer who was coming alongside, somewhat cautiously, in an inflatable craft.

We talked, and I learned that he was doing research for some writing he was planning on doing. Some research I thought. Sun, sand, surf and a very impressive vessel in which to experience this research.

Peter glanced into my small boat and noted the scuba diving gear piled haphazardly in the bow. It turned out that he was a bit of a dive enthusiast. We talked boating and scuba diving, travelling and writing. When it came time to leave I opened my briefcase to retrieve a business card and some marine information. A somewhat crumpled copy of Diver Magazine had to be moved to get at the required publications.

"You have excellent choice in reading material." Peter commented.

I discovered sometime later that Peter Vassilopoulos was the editor and publisher of Diver Magazine. A bit of a dive enthusiast indeed, I thought.

As we parted that summer day, he extended his hand, and I realized that I was lucky. For that day I had made a friend.

Anchored in Glenthorne Passage, Prevost Island, the old Balladeer *in which the author and his wife Carla began their discovery of the B.C. coast.*

Over the years my marine training and travel has taken me throughout the coastal waters of British Columbia and the San Juan Islands of Washington State.

As captain of the R.C.M.P. patrol vessel *Lindsay* for many years, I planned and initiated coastal patrols. Such patrols involve travel between and into the safe harbours identified within the following pages.

Few things bring me greater pleasure than travelling into one of these areas and meeting old friends, with the prospect of making new ones. The uncommon camaraderie and fellowship among mariners is truly unique.

Often I have ventured into these natural harbours and destinations, to find Peter and Carla Vassilopoulos sketching, photographing, and making notes of the area. Coastal cruising has become their passion. The information they gather and prepare is timely and accurate. Peter has an uncanny ability to answer the questions we as mariners want to know. Photographs and sketches make the information clear and enjoyable to view.

This material will help the traveller prepare for safe and enjoyable coastal cruising. ***Anchorages and Marine Parks*** together with Peter's companion book, ***Docks and Destinations***, are must-have guides for boaters travelling the San Juan Islands and Canada's west coast.

—Kenneth K. Burton
Captain–RCMP Voyage of Rediscovery patrol vessel Nadon (St Roch II) *2000.*

Acknowledgements

The author wishes to thank all who have participated in providing input for this book, and to my wife Carla who shared a lot of her time on this project.

Thanks to those who have helped with the photography and for proofreading the text. Special thanks to John Horton, Sharon Allman, Iz Goto and Norman Elliot, and to others who have helped in the acquisition and provision of photographs, illustrations and information. John Horton's paintings used in this guide, and others can be seen on his website at *www.johnhorton.ca*. Thanks also to Dan Parker and the crew at Monaro Marine for building a fine boat that has enabled us to rediscover many of the areas included in this book, and to John De Jong for helping maintain it in functional condition. And a special thank you to *Pacific Yachting Magazine* for many years of collaboration.

Foreword

The anchorages described in this book have been selected for their value as popular destinations to spend quality time enjoying your boat, as well as preferred places to stop en route to those and other destinations. Such anchorages are where people gather to spend weekends or brief holidays, extended vacations or just to find protected overnight shelter. Their inclusion in this book is based on their popularity and relative safety from weather conditions. While it is the intention of the author to provide information that will enable the mariner to readily pull into a cove or bay and drop anchor confident in knowing what is in store during the night there can be no guarantee that any anchorage will not be adversely affected by wind, weather or tidal currents.

Even the best of anchorages can be subject to wind. Those most highly recommended are, therefore, not excluded from the possibility of discomfort during a blow. Do not assume that because an anchorage is described in this book it is immune to conditions that will cause the anchor to drag. There are few places on the British Columbia and Washington coast that can provide total protection from all weather at all times. The anchorages included have been selected as the ones considered by most mariners to provide the best possible shelter. Notes accompanying the diagrams advise mariners generally if weather effects are felt in the anchorages wherever that information is available. Most anchorages included have been visited by the author and therefore personal experience in weather conditions has been included. Some anchorages include additional information supplied by fellow mariners in conjunction with reference to official coast guides and the observations of other authors.

Please use official CHS and NOAA charts for all navigation and marine operations, and use the official and other guides referred to elsewhere in this book for more information about coastal passages, places to anchor, tides and currents, docks and protected marinas. The list of launch ramps provided at the end of the book is intended to help trailer boat users find the closest launching point to reach some of the anchorages and marine parks described in this book.

Larger boats cannot always manoeuvre easily in all constricted waterways, so be courteous and help rather than hinder them. Also be aware of private property and private businesses. While laws governing waterfront allow access, respect property owners' privacy, on remote islands in particular. When anchoring off privately owned marinas or docks, respect the rights of the owners and operators and paying mooring customers. For example you cannot expect to go ashore and use any of their facilities if you are not a bonafide guest. This includes the dumping of garbage—and the purchasing of fuel usually does not provide exception.

Some anchorages other than in popular cruising areas and marine parks, and those beyond the major connecting waterways, are not necessarily included in this guide. In areas mostly used in transit, such as Grenville Passage en route north to Prince Rupert, or along the west coast of Vancouver Island, the guide includes reference to primary and some secondary anchorages and leaves out others that are suitable but off the beaten path. Cruising yachtsmen looking for anchorages other than adjacent to main passages should consult reference books such as Robert Hale's **Waggoner** and other extensive local cruising guides including **Docks and Destinations, Gulf Islands Cruising Guide, North of Desolation** and others by this author. For a list of recommended books see page 315.

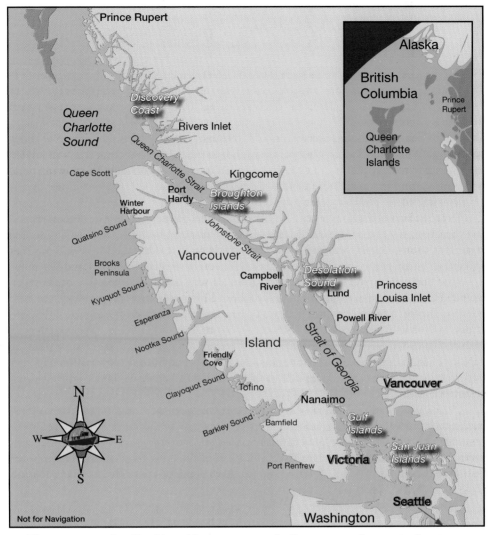

Not for Navigation

The maps contained in this guide are not to scale (hence my reference to them as maps or diagrams rather than charts) nor are they precise tracings from hydrographic charts. They are all hand-drawn renditions of coastal features intended solely for the purpose of illustrating approximate locations of anchorages and marine installations, such as mooring buoys, docks and shelter. The drawings should not be used for navigation but only in conjunction with official hydrographic marine charts.

The information on the maps includes shaded areas–green shows marine parks' approximate park area. The amber shows land mass, the blue shows ocean and the lighter blue tones indicate reefs, rocks and shallow non-navigable waters. They are only for general reference and are not necessarily accurate nor is the placement of the shallows precise, and use should be made of the largest scale charts available at all times, especially whenever entering small coves and anchorages. Mooring buoys are not always as described, as changes to number and location can take place without notice. The author assumes users of this guide are capable navigators. Anchorages are indicated by placement of icons of sailboats anchored or anchors or both, as space has allowed.

Using This Guide

The diagrams, photographs and information contained in this guide are laid out to make it the most user-friendly publication available for its purpose. The easy reference to anchorages is achieved where possible, by having large and small scale diagrams as well as photographs on or adjacent to the same two-page spreads as the information for each anchorage or marine park. This saves having to page back and forth looking for area maps showing where the locations are. Additional information for your recreational enjoyment includes reference to marinas, fuel stops and nearby activities such as diving and kayaking. For specifics on marinas it is recommended you use **Docks and Destinations** and other appropriate guide and reference books as listed on page 315.

Scuba diving is possible practically anywhere on the coast. But currents and extreme depths require special training, and recreational divers are advised to exercise caution in selecting their dive sites. Stay shallow, keep out of currents, time your depth and duration conservatively, maintain your comfort level and always dive with a buddy or an organized group.

Where scuba diving is indicated on diagrams by the presence of the diagonal striped dive flag emblem it means there is good diving nearby or in the vicinity. Placement of the flag emblem adjacent to shorelines and locations of artificial reefs indicates reference to actual dive sites. For specific information consult Betty Pratt-Johnson's *151 Dives* or visit a local dive store. Use a reputable charter boat or dive shop service to safely dive the many wonderful sites of British Columbia and the San Juan Islands.

Kayaking and canoeing are popular pastimes on the coast. While kayaking is possible on practically any body of water the kayaking emblem shown on the diagrams is merely an indication of where kayaking is known to be most popular. And in some cases where there are good natural or man-made features for launching, look for the underlined K_ indicating a kayak launching area. Wherever reference is made to good available small craft recreational areas, they are indicted by the emblem of a kayak. General launch ramps are indicated by an underlined R_. Refer to the *Sea Kayak* guide series from Heritage House.

LEGEND	
⊓	Water
Λ	Camping
⚓	Anchoring
⚓	Mooring
🚻	Toilets
⊼	Picnic Tables
◣	Scuba sites
🛶	Kayaking

Key above shows icons used in marine park diagrams.

The legend shown at left is for reference to facilities at marine parks and anchorages. Key symbols have been included in diagrams throughout this guide. Some of them are well known and used universally to indicate the availability of amenities such as camping, toilets, anchoring and mooring. Their appearance on the diagrams serve to advise the user of the guide of the probability of such amenities existing where shown and in the approximate location of the symbol. The legend is included periodically throughout the guide as a reminder of the meaning of the key items.

Boat launching symbols for kayaks and boats are: **K** and **R.**
For Marine Parks Information phone: 250-387-5002.
Lower Mainland district 604-924-2200. South Vancouver Island district 250-391-2300, Strathcona (North Vancouver Island) district 250-954-4600, Garibaldi Sunshine Coast district 604-898-3678, North Coast–Hakai Cariboo district 250-398-4414, Queen Charlottes Skeena district 250-847-7320.

Summer Places

There are many coves and harbours to anchor in when cruising the waters of British Columbia and the San Juan Islands. Scattered throughout the area are hundreds of marinas offering services–from moorage and fuel to groceries, overnight guest rooms, restaurants, adjacent pubs, and various forms of entertainment. But the intrepid yachtsman looking for places away from busy commercial centres can find many alternatives to escape the crowds and find tranquility where few others congregate.

Anchorages described in this book include many that are located where there is a variety of interesting coastal features to please everyone in search of idyllic nearby cruising, nature viewing, spectacular scenery and a close proximity to marine services. For it is generally a combination of these elements–the interesting passages coupled with the bays and anchorages beyond–that provides mariners the greatest joy of boating on the west coast.

Cruising through Tahsis Narrows on the west coast of Vancouver Island.

Anchoring

Anchoring skills help make boating experiences happy ones. Dropping the hook in shallow water with lots of swinging room is usually a simple process, and if the wind conditions are mild, and tidal exchanges not too dramatic, overnight rest is seldom interrupted. But in some of the more remote areas of the coast, with deeper waters in which to anchor, the skills you have developed for setting the anchor can make a big difference to your state of peace of mind.

There are several syles and many makes of anchors. These include Bruce, Delta, Northill and Danforth. The most reliable anchors are made of high quality steel. For decades fishermen's choice of anchor was the Northill. Nowadays a very popular anchor is the Bruce or variations of it. When choosing the right anchor weight or size for your boat, use an anchor chart that reflects the amount of wind it is designed to hold in. While most anchors come in sizes for 20 or 30 knot winds, the Bruce is categorized to 42 knots. Then decide on all chain or chain and rope. Some mariners carry all chain. This is a good idea, but not practical if you are operating a smaller boat, especially if you have no windlass or capstan and have to haul the anchor back up manually. If your boat is large enough to accommodate all chain, then do so.

Generally, the rule of using length of rode for deployment at 5:1 scope, can be applied to the most severe conditions. In calmer, shallower water, a ratio of 3:1 is more appropriate. First and foremost, check that your anchor chain or rode is secured at the bitter end. Then ensure all connections, shackles and splices, are in good condition. Make sure, on a small boat, the amount of chain you have attached to the anchor, is equal to at least the overall length of your boat.

Newcastle Island is a well know destination where facilities include moorage at docks serving the well known marine park. The park, one of the largest marine parks, and with most ameni-

When coming into an anchorage, assess tidal factors as well as currents, wind, other boats already anchored and space for later arrivals. Anchor in consideration of others. In relation to where you want your boat to be, allow for the spot in which your anchor will lie and where it is likely to grab. Do not throw your anchor overboard. Lower it steadily until all the chain and rode you want in the water is paid out. Gently back up to set the anchor, carefully monitoring the line, until it becomes taut and begins to swing sideways. The line should not angle down too sharply, as then the anchor will not grip well. A gentle angle will more likely give you a good hold.

Keep an anchor watch as the tide changes. Sometimes the initial set may break free, depending on the type of bottom and obstructions that could cause the anchor to slide. Best bottoms for the average anchor are mud, sand and shale. Avoid rocky or kelp-covered bottoms.

When stern-tying in an anchorage make sure you have a very long stern line. If you can, it is gratifying to approach the shore and turn as close as you can get to the land and, if it is deep enough inch the swimstep right up to the shoreline, have a crew member step off and loop your stern line around a tree and pass it back to someone in the cockpit. In some anchorages there are tie rings in the bank. Pay out the line as the boat moves forward, until you have reached the point where you want to drop the anchor. Drop it and then back up until you reach the point where you want the boat to lie, bringing in the line as the boat is backed up. Tie it to a heavy cleat. If the cove shallows off near shore, drop the anchor and back up as close to shore as you can. Have someone take one end of the stern line ashore, pass it around a tree and row back to the boat. If the line you have used is long enough and you have simply slipped it around a tree or through a tie ring, when it comes time to leave the anchorage, all you have to do is untie one end on the boat and pull the other side to retrieve it from shore.

ties on the coast, offers trails for walking, places to picnic, campsites and other facilities. The large anchorage is somewhat exposed and is occasionally beset by wind.

1

Marine Parks
and Anchorages in the
San Juan Islands

The San Juan Islands
For expanded information on marinas and facilities in the San Juan Islands, refer to the author's cruising guide: *Docks and Destinations*. See also *Gunkholing in the San Juans*, and *A Cruising Guide to Puget Sound and the San Juan Islands*.

Boats at Sucia Island's Fossil Bay. This is one of the larger marine parks on the coast and very popular among mariners from the USA and Canada alike. Opposite: The landing at Olga on Orcas Island.

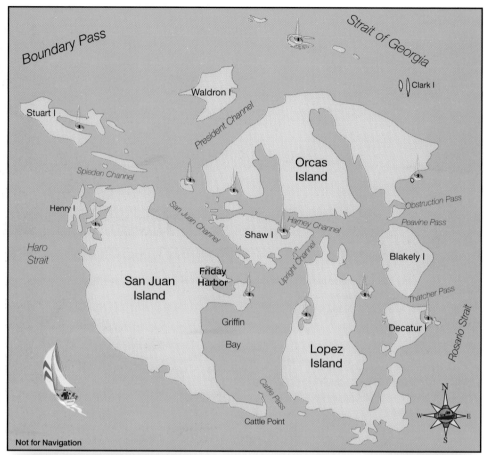

Boundary Pass

Strait of Georgia

Clark I

Waldron I

Stuart I

President Channel

Spieden Channel

Orcas
Island

Henry I

San Juan Channel

Obstruction Pass

Peavine Pass

Harney Channel

Shaw I

Haro
Strait

Blakely I

Upright Channel

Friday
Harbor

San Juan
Island

Thatcher Pass

Griffin

Decatur

Rosario Strait

Bay

Lopez
Island

Cattle Pass

N
W   E
S

Cattle Point

Not for Navigation

Washington State's Beautiful San Juan Islands

The San Juan Islands–State Parks

Fisherman Bay and other tranquil anchorages

Most yachtsmen travelling out of British Columbia waters into the San Juans cruise into Roche Harbor or nearby Friday Harbor, declare customs and go on a shopping spree for groceries, marine supplies and gifts or souvenirs. However, many have learned also the joys of other nearby islands and their tranquil natural beauty, or character of bygone years that thrives today.

Lopez Island is one such place where the local islanders and much of their lifestyles have been almost forgotten by time. Only the presence of modern facilities at some of the marinas reminds one that we are living in a new age. Lopez Village is one of those places that time has almost forgotten. It was one of the sleepiest places in the islands but is now evolving in keeping with the times, and yet seems to be retaining its old-time charm and character. It's a place where you can sit and watch the passing of pleasure boats as they wend their way through the narrow opening that is the entrance to Fisherman Bay. This

Above: 'The Encampment' from a painting by John M. Horton, shows this landing near the entrance to Puget Sound, in the late 1700s, much as it is today. Right: An anchorage in the nook of Turn Island just off San Juan Island. This tiny State Marine Park is located a short way south of Friday Harbor. It makes a pleasant stop away from the hustle and bustle of a busy anchorage but one must arrive early if it's a mooring buoy you want.

Marine Parks Phone 360-902-8844
Customs (Pleasure Boat Reporting System) Phone 1-800-562-5943

bay is one of my favourite places in that it offers a huge shallow anchorage as well as optional mooring at marinas. It also provides access to the island with its rural community, easy walking and access to its delightful village and nearby vineyards.

The escape in the San Juans from today is so complete at some places that even one marina, on Blakely Island, offers no access to anything but its own facility. The fascination of these American islands is complete with typical shore access at Orcas Landing where you can watch the ferries coming and going, disgorging their loads of summer holidaymakers who descend on the ice cream stands, the cafes and restaurants, flow into the local hotel or wheel their bicycles up the hill for a start to a riding tour of Orcas island. Or at East Sound with its fascinating and quaint old town and nearby historic Mansion at Rosario. Or the historic sites of the near-war between the British and the Americans on San Juan Island–over a dispute concerning a pig. Stops of interest such as West Sound can lead you to picturesque walks along rural roads lined by gnarled arbutus (madrona) trees and abutted by farms and homesteads, some of which have dominated the scene since the earliest settlement. And the beauty of the San Juans is that they lie within minutes of the southern Gulf Islands making it easy to slip in, clear customs, stay a short while and return home if time constraints are an issue.

James Island and Decatur Head viewed from the east. Mooring buoys are located either side of the narrow, low isthmus on James Island as well as in the curve of the bay beyond Decatur Head.

James Island

Charts 18429, 18421

Access

The park is located in Rosario Strait near Thatcher Pass. It lies just off the east side of Decatur Island where Decatur Head protrudes into the Strait. Vessels arriving at James Island have usually come from Anacortes across Rosario Strait or up the Strait from Puget Sound.

The Park and Anchorage

Features of the park include a float and four mooring buoys as well as about a dozen campsites ashore. There is a strong current along the west side of the island. Take care on the approaches to the harbor. If mooring buoys are full, anchor nearby or in the north lee of Decatur Head, which offers some shallow temporary anchorage. But the currents and constant boat traffic make this anchorage and mooring area less than ideal.

The park has no water but there are toilet facilities, picnic tables and a shelter as well as fireplaces. Trails on the island are not all recorded and care should be taken when exploring as some trails could take you close to a dropoff at the edge of a cliff.

Nearby

Anacortes is only a few miles from the park and is a large community with all facilities including marinas, service, airport, shops and hospital. Spencer Spit Marine Park is also nearby. It has mooring buoys, sheltered anchorage and somewhat better protection from weather, sea conditions and passing traffic. Launch small boats at Flounder Bay, Fidalgo Island or at Spencer Spit (hand launching only–see Spencer Spit Marine Park).

Small boat operators beware of a two knot current in Thatcher Pass.

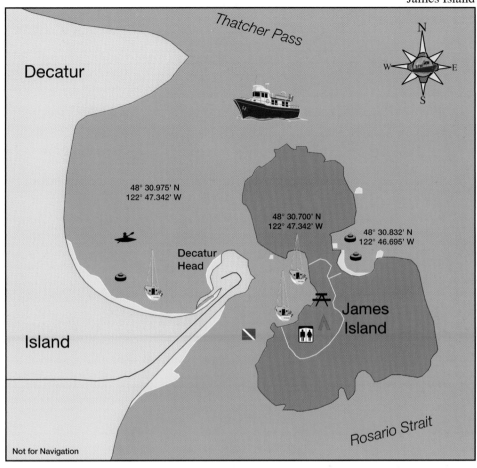

James Island Marine State Park

Features of James Island include a float and mooring buoys. There are more buoys beyond the north side of Decatur Head on Decatur Island.

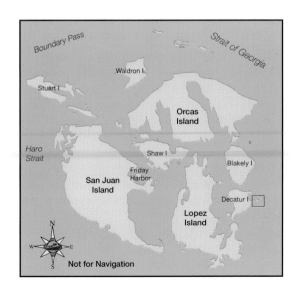

Park facilities

4 mooring buoys, dock, toilets, campsites, picnic shelter, fireplaces. No water.

There are many mooring buoys, mostly to the south of the Spit. The passage between the tip of the Spit and Frost Island is deep and safe. Stay center channel and use the proper chart.

Spencer Spit

Charts 18429, 18421

Access

This park can be reached by road or by water. It lies on the east side of Lopez Island and has mooring buoys located on either side of the spit. There is a fairly narrow passage between Lopez Island and Frost Island at this point, but the water is deep enough for safe transit. Lopez Island is serviced by ferry from Anacortes.

The Park and Anchorage

Facilities ashore include toilets, picnic tables, fireplaces, telephone and picnic shelters. There is no dock but sandy beaches make it easy for small boats (canoes, kayaks, car toppers) to launch or land. Sixteen mooring buoys provide overnight, protected tie up for boats and there is temporary anchorage in the lee of the spit. Watch the wind direction and tidal currents for comfortable overnight anchoring. If you are going into the park with an overload of passengers there is bunk-style accommodation available. Birdwatching is a popular activity in the park and paddlers will find lots of nooks and crannies to explore and marine life and birds to view. Good hiking and walking trails provide an opportunity for exercise as well as breathtaking views on good days.

Nearby

There are anchorages in the coves along the shores of Lopez Island to the south and a marina at the top end of Blakely Island to the north. The Anacortes ferry lands at the top of Lopez Island providing road access to Spencer Spit.

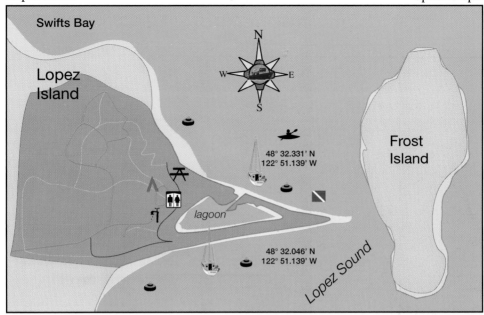

Not for Navigation

Spencer Spit Marine State Park

Park facilities

16 mooring buoys. Anchorage. Walking trails. Drinking water. Toilets. Camping. Picnicking. Fireplaces. Good scuba diving and kayaking in the vicinity. Ranger on duty. Ph. 360-468-2251.

Below: Overview of the San Juan Islands with Patos Island in the foreground.

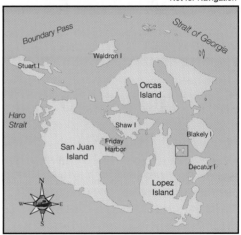

Lopez Island

Charts 18434, 18421

Fisherman Bay

Just across San Juan Channel from Friday Harbor, the large bay on the west side of Lopez Island is a shallow basin that affords good and plentiful anchorage, preferred at the head of the bay. The entrance to Fisherman Bay is narrow but well marked. Vessels should mind the shallows at the entrance during low tides, but there is usually little to prevent vessels coming and going at all times. Enter past the outer marker then #4 to your starboard, through the narrows and then beyond, keeping markers #5 and #7 to your port and #8 to your starboard. Use the local chart for precise navigation. Cartoppers, rowboats and kayaks should be used with extreme caution beyond the confines of the bay due to tidal currents in San Juan Channel.

Nearby

Lopez village is quaint and attractive. It is less than a one-mile walk from the marinas to the village and then a short way beyond are the Lopez Island Vineyards. These are open to the public, and wine tasting is available daily from June to early September. During the remainder of the year they are open on Fridays and Saturdays. At the marinas located on the east side of the bay, accommodations, moorage, meals, charters, kayak and bicycle rentals are available.

Hunter Bay

Strong north winds may be all that disturb the anchorage in Hunter Bay. It is the more protected of anchorages in the area and is chosen over others for a secure mooring. There are private waterfront properties around the bay and these should be respected. Careful use of small boats can provide good recreation in the area.

Nearby

There is a park at Mud Bay but it is without any services or facilities. A small public dock between Hunter Bay and Mud Bay provides walking access ashore.

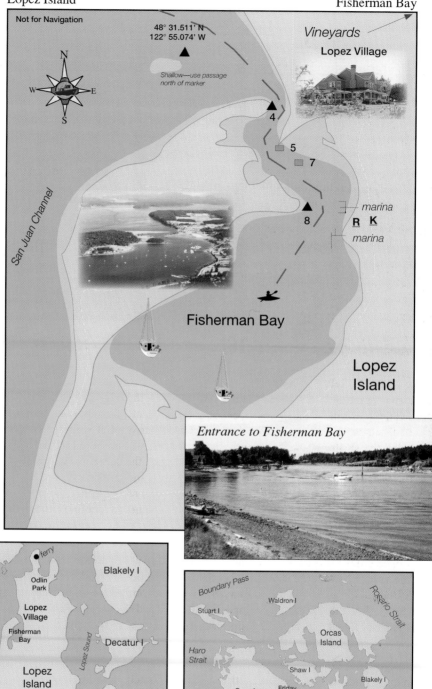

Not for Navigation

48° 31.511' N
122° 55.074' W

Vineyards

Lopez Village

N
W *E*
S

Shallow—use passage
north of marker

4

5

7

San Juan Channel

marina

R **K**

marina

8

Fisherman Bay

**Lopez
Island**

Entrance to Fisherman Bay

ferry

Blakely I

Odlin
Park

**Lopez
Village**

Fisherman
Bay

Decatur I

San Juan Channel

Lopez Sound

**Lopez
Island**

Hunter Bay

Mud Bay

Not for Navigation

Boundary Pass

Waldron I

Rosario Strait

Stuart I

Orcas
Island

Haro
Strait

Shaw I

Blakely I

San Juan
Island

Friday
Harbor

Decatur I

**Lopez
Island**

N
W *E*
S

Not for Navigation

Turn Island
Charts 18434, 18421

Access
This island lies near San Juan Island in San Juan Channel not far from Friday Harbor. The moorage can be approached from the south or the north, the former with caution for Turn Rock which is well marked with a navigational aid. Mind also the strong currents in the passage. Buoys at the park are mostly missed by the strong current.

The Park and Anchorage
It is a relatively undeveloped park with limited facilities including campsites (no water), picnic tables and toilets. Three mooring buoys are located off the north shore and it has gravel beaches and hiking trails for those going ashore. Overnight moorage is safe but can be uncomfortable when the wind blows strongly from the north.

Kayak launching from the beach on the shore of San Juan Island provides access to the waters around Turn Island as well as to Turn Island itself where shore facilities provide overnight comforts and camping pleasure. Moor in the anchorage on the west side of the island. Boats tied up at Friday Harbor are sometimes left there while the crew takes the tender and travels the short distance to the park. Caution is advised for small boats using the adjacent waterways, which are subject to strong tidal currents and washes from passing vessels.

Nearby
The port of Friday Harbor is a thriving community of permanent residents and sees a large influx of visitors during summer. Shops, restaurants, theater and a variety of tourist attractions include auto and motor cycle rentals. Alternative mooring and anchoring is available in the harbor and protected waters behind Brown Island (also knows as Friday Island).

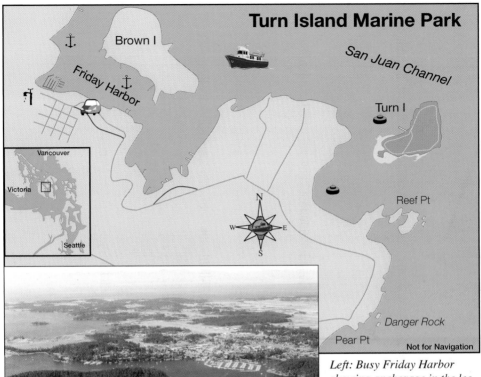

Turn Island Marine Park

Brown I

Friday Harbor

San Juan Channel

Turn I

Reef Pt

Vancouver

Victoria

Seattle

Danger Rock

Pear Pt

Not for Navigation

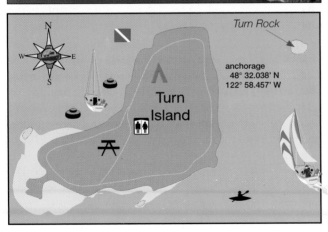

Turn Rock

anchorage
48° 32.038' N
122° 58.457' W

Turn
Island

*Left: Busy Friday Harbor
showing anchorage in the lee
of Brown Island.
Opposite: Turn Island from the
south. Friday Harbor beyond.
Inset shows it from the north.
There are several marine
park-maintained buoys at Turn
Island. Some vessels anchor
in the curve of the bay. Be
mindful of the strong currents
that wash through the area, as
they can cause some anchor
dragging. Usually if you anchor close enough to shore in
such situations you are fairly
protected from the force of the
currents.*

Boundary Pass

Strait of Georgia

Waldron I

Stuart I

Orcas
Island

Shaw I

Blakely I

Haro
Strait

San Juan
Island

Lopez
Island

Park facilities

3 mooring buoys, toilets, picnic tables, campsites, stoves, no water, kayaking, scuba diving
in the vicinity.

Blind Island is seen top, center of Blind Bay. There are mooring buoys south of the island and anchoring is preferred near the head of the bay. Occasional winds from the north cause a slight chop in Blind Bay. Orcas Landing can be seen across Harney Channel, upper left corner.

Blind Island
Charts 18434, 18421, CHS 3462

Access
This park is a small island in Blind Bay. It lies at the north end of Shaw Island just inside the bay opposite Orcas Landing.

The Park and Anchorage
There are four mooring buoys and anchorage in the lee of the island as well as deeper in the bay. However, caution should be exercised as winds can make it uncomfortable at times while anchored in Blind Bay. Facilities on the island are spartan. Beware of the rocks around Blind Island and across Blind Bay. They lie just where you are likely to go when entering the bay. Check your chart for the locations of hazards around and opposite the mooring area.

Larger craft can ride at anchor deeper in the bay. Smaller vessels are more secure, but not necessarily more comfortable in a blow, at a mooring buoy (located in the lee of Blind Island). Paddlers arriving by ferry can launch at the marina adjacent to the ferry dock. For campers there are about a dozen campsites on Shaw Island and a couple on Blind Island–popular among visiting paddlers.

Nearby
Two ferry landings. Orcas Landing across Harney Channel is a lovely spot among the islands. It is the ferry landing that serves the island of Orcas and has a small community of businesses and tourist attractions.

The ferry to Shaw Island lands not far from the park's anchorage at the north eastern end of Blind Bay on Harney Channel. Temporary anchorages may be found in West Sound, East Sound or Deer Harbor.

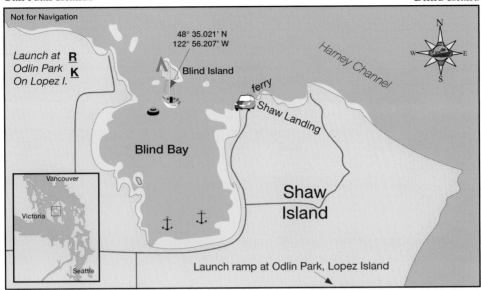

Blind Island
Marine State Park
(Shaw Island)

Park facilities
4 mooring buoys, campsites, re-commended kayaking–launch ramp at Odlin Park, Lopez Island. Scuba diving in area.

Below, left: Orcas Landing is a convenient place to stop for arts, meals and supplies. The dock allows short stops while shopping. Below, right: In the village of East Sound on Orcas Island.

Doe Island   Charts 18430, 18421

Access
This secluded island lies just off the southeastern side of Orcas Island. There are toilets, but no water and no mooring buoys. A 30 foot float is located at the park in summer months only.

The Park and Anchorage
The park consists primarily of wooded uplands with some clearings and several camp-sites. A trail rings the island and this provides a scenic walk for those wishing to go ashore and stretch their legs. There are no facilities for boats other than a small dock with limited use. Anchor with care off the north east end of Doe Island or in the shelter of Doe Bay. Use a good large scale chart for navigating in the area and mind the shoal off Orcas Island on the northwest side of Doe Island. Mooring buoys are private.

Nearby
Orcas Island. Doe Bay and Doe Bay Resort and campground. Around the southeast point of Orcas Island you enter East Sound. A nearby activity is kayaking, ever popular in most areas of the San Juan Islands.

Rosario Resort

Half way up East Sound is the historic and charming Rosario Resort. The anchorage and mooring buoys are adjacent to the marina, alongside the resort. It is exposed to winds from the south but many vessels stop there for brief periods during sum-mer. It is worth the stop to pay a short or overnight visit to Rosario Resort, whose magnificent history has been told countless times in many publications and is retold frequently to visitors viewing the fascinating interior of the historic building.

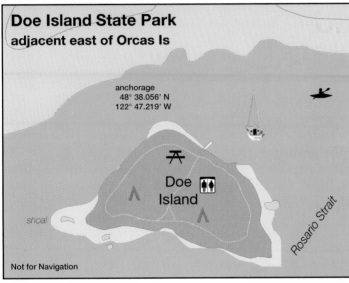

Doe Island State Park
adjacent east of Orcas Is

anchorage
48° 38.056' N
122° 47.219' W

Doe Island

shoal

Rosario Strait

Not for Navigation

Above: Rosario. This is a popular marina and resort destination. Its anchorage becomes quite busy in summer. But it is exposed to winds from the south which sometimes come up in the afternoon. Close weather monitoring will provide information on expected blows.

Rosario Resort
48° 37.060' N
122° 49.950' W

Park facilities

Private mooring buoys nearby–use anchorage. Campsites, trails, picnic tables, beachcombing. Toilets, recommended fishing, scuba diving, kayaking. No garbage disposal, no drinking water.

Vancouver

Victoria

Seattle

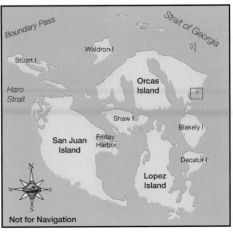

Boundary Pass

Strait of Georgia

Waldron I

Stuart I

Orcas Island

Haro Strait

Shaw I

Blakely I

San Juan Island

Friday Harbor

Decatur I

Lopez Island

N
W E
S

Not for Navigation

Jones Island Charts 18434, 18432, 18421

Access
This is a popular marine park, lying just off the southwest side of Orcas Island. There is a reef at the top of the island and care should be taken approaching the cove. Use a large scale chart when navigating the area. The cove is exposed to north winds.

The Park and Anchorage
There are mooring buoys on either side of the island with the majority located in the north side cove. Facilities on the island include a float, toilets and campsites as well as water. Kayaking is popular in the vicinity and campsites provide overnight stays. There is a float in the north cove. Hiking the trails on the island will probably include friendly encounters with deer and other wildlife.

Nearby
Proceeding eastward to West Sound you will find two state parks that are left unnamed in marine park guides. They are Victim Island and Skull Island. These two undeveloped marine parks are of historic interest only and offer no amenities. The nearest anchorage to Victim Island is just south in the lee of **Double Island**. West Sound Marina and adjacent public dock offer protected moorage in the north east corner of West Sound. Another undeveloped state park with no facilities is Freeman Island. It lies farther north along the Orcas Island shore.

Left: The nearby alternative anchorage at Deer Harbor lies just off the marina. This anchorage can be subject to wind.

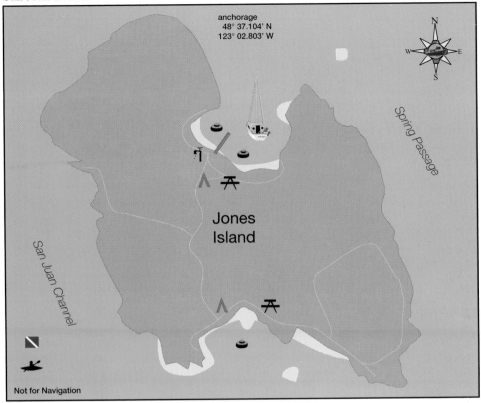

anchorage
48° 37.104' N
123° 02.803' W

Not for Navigation

Jones Island Marine State Park

Park facilities
7 mooring buoys, walk-in campsites, trails, picnic tables, drinking water, beach, hiking, recommended kayaking, scuba diving.

anchorage
48° 37.284' N
123° 00.195' W

Deer Harbor
Deer Harbor and West Sound Marina are popular stops for those seeking moorage at a dock. They have overnight moorage and facilities. West Sound has chandlery facilities and a short walk takes you past rows of beautiful arbutus (madronas) to a fine rural setting overlooking the bay.

Anchorage
Possible off Deer Harbor Marina or in the lee of Double Island in West Sound.

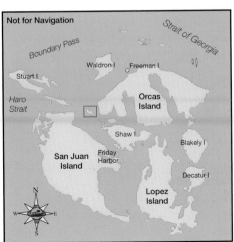

Anchorage at Garrison Bay just down Mosquito Passage from Roche Harbor (photo opposite).

Roche Harbor and Garrison Bay

Roche Harbor Access   Chart 18433

From the north via Spieden Channel, entrance to Roche Harbor is preferred west of Pearl Island–from the south, via Mosquito Passage. Use a large scale chart and follow the passage carefully.

Garrison Bay and Westcott Bay Access

Access to Garrison and Westcott is by way of Mosquito Pass around White Point.

The Anchorages (attractions)

Mariners arriving in Roche Harbor are usually looking for a comfortable overnight place to moor their boat. This long established boating destination has a large, modern marina with all amenities and shallow water anchorage off the end of the marina docks. It is a customs port of entry and has long been a primary arrival point for visiting vessels from Canada or returning vessels to the United States. Today there are alternative ways to clear customs. But this has not made Roche Harbor any less popular. Its famous Hotel de Haro attracts visitors for overnight accommodations as well as fine dining in an elegant restaurant. The grounds are picturesque and summer sees numerous visitors milling about admiring the flower beds, gardens, covered pathway and adjacent spectacle of boats anchored in the bay. Garrison Bay is a preferred anchorage for those wishing to escape the congestion that sometimes occurs at busier harbors which have large marinas and ferry stops. Go ashore and hike up Young Hill or visit the site of the British Camp where troops were encamped during the Pig War. Just to the north of Garrison Bay lies the alternative anchorage of **Westcott Bay**. Your large scale chart 18433 will help you determine adequate depth for anchoring.

Nearby

In the nearby inlets and waterways protected from the open waters of Haro Strait by Henry Island, there are anchorages and places to go ashore including a marina, at Mitchell

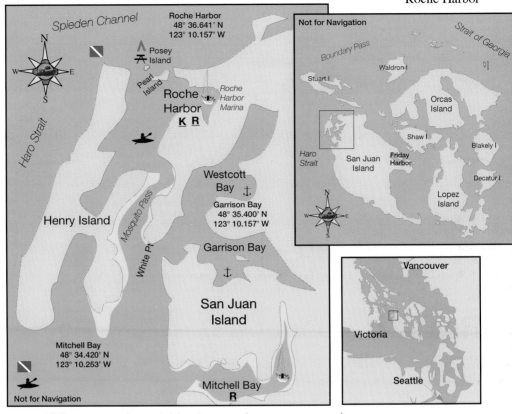

Bay, which accommodates visiting boats and permanent mooring customers.

The area is not without a marine state park. The tiny **Posey Island** just off Pearl Island at the northern entrance to Roche Harbor is one, although it has no boat docking facilities. It does, however, attract many kayakers and people in small boats who go ashore and enjoy the spectacle of passing vessels in Spieden Channel.

Clark Island

Charts 18431, 18430, 18421

Access

Clark is part of a series of islands north of Orcas Island. It lies east in the group. There are some facilities for camping and mooring and there are nine mooring buoys but no float and no water on shore.

The Park and Anchorage

There are campsites, fireplaces and picnic facilities on the island. Mooring buoys provide tie up for up to nine boats, one boat per mooring. The anchorages are exposed so prefer a forecast of calm weather when planning a night on a mooring buoy.

Nearby

The popular islands/marine parks: Matia Island, Patos and Sucia. Also Orcas Island with Rosario Resort around the south east end and up into East Sound. Parts of the islands are known for their excellent tidepools and birdwatching. There is good scuba diving in the vicinity, and kayakers enjoy this area throughout summer. Look out for these small craft when cruising in the vicinity. Many birds gather on the rocks just off Clark Island. Nearby Barnes Island is private property.

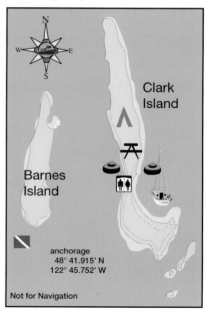

Clark Island Marine State Park

Park facilities

9 mooring buoys, walk-in campsites, trails, picnic tables, toilets, beach hiking, recommended kayaking, scuba diving, fishing.
Note: Strong currents make it dangerous to paddle in the area.

Recommended for experienced small-boat operators.
No garbage disposal.

Matia Island

Charts 18431, 18430, 18421

Matia Island Marine State Park

Access

Matia Island lies almost top centre north of Orcas Island abutting the Strait of Georgia.

The Park and Anchorage

The actual park area is a small section of Matia Island as most of it is designated a wildlife refuge. There are trails to hike and lots of bird life to watch. It has a fairly substantial float as well as a couple of mooring buoys. Trails and several old campsites are features of the island, which is part of the National Wildlife Refuge.

Some vessels anchor at the entrance to Rolf Cove, but regard this as temporary anchorage only. Beware of anchor holding surfaces on the rocky bottom. Tidal currents flowing through the moorage area should be monitored. The park is open year round but the dock is removed for winter.

Nearby

Sucia and Patos Islands marine parks with mooring and park facilities.

Park facilities

2 mooring buoys, walk-in campsites, trails, picnic tables, toilets, trail hiking, kayaking, scuba diving, wildlife sanctuary.

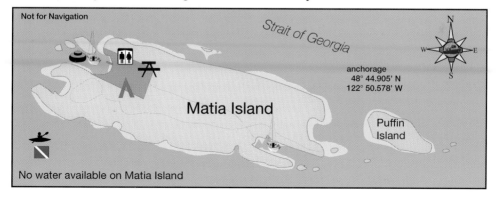

Not for Navigation

Strait of Georgia

anchorage
48° 44.905' N
122° 50.578' W

Matia Island

Puffin Island

No water available on Matia Island

Sucia Island

Charts 18431, 18430, 18421

Access

Enter the island's anchorages from the Strait of Georgia minding Danger Reef off Ewing Island. Enter Fossil Bay or Fox Cove from the south and east.

The Park and Anchorage

Sucia Island, one of the most popular of marine parks in the San Juans, is well known among mariners for its protected bays and many mooring buoys, docks and anchorages. The bays around this island have no less than four dozen mooring buoys, numerous campsites and many amenities. Anchor in all bays near the location of buoys, preferring nooks that are not exposed to open water.

There are 16 mooring buoys and two docks in Fossil Bay. Shallow Bay has 8 mooring buoys. Echo Bay has 14 buoys but no dock and is known to be subject to easterly winds. There are two buoys in Snoring Bay and 4 at Ewing Cove. Fox Cove has 4 buoys and is entered east or southwest of Little Sucia Island. Mind the currents in the entrance.

Small craft tend to favour the float at the head of Fossil Bay. Some are even beached to land campers for overnight visits. On shore the facilities include water and toilets.

Sucia Island has many walk-in campsites and facilities for camping, picnics and shore activities. There are porta potti dump stations located near the various landings.

Trails wind around the island with easy to moderate walks up to three miles. All trails are well signposted complete with distances to the trail heads. Numerous viewpoints take in the panoramic vistas towards Mount Baker, across the Strait of Georgia and towards the rest of the San Juans. Chinaman Rock on the north side of Shallow Bay is a weather-sculptured sandstone edifice. For diving, there is an artificial reef off Ewing Island comprising three sunken boats. If you are looking for a nice beach try Shallow Bay.

Nearby

Matia and Patos Islands marine parks with limited mooring and camping facilities. Orcas Island lies just two miles from Fossil Bay and East Point on Saturna Island in the Gulf Islands is not far to the northwest. Point Roberts, on the mainland, is just a short distance across the Strait of Georgia from this group of outer San Juan Islands.

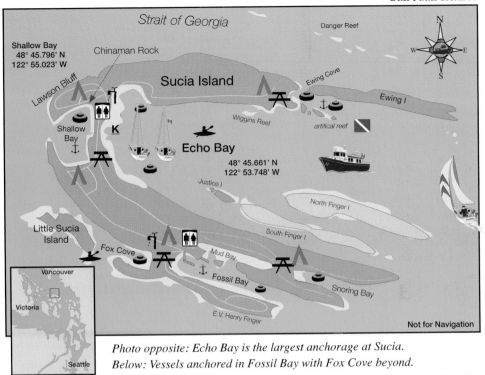

Strait of Georgia

Danger Reef

Shallow Bay
48° 45.796' N
122° 55.023' W

Chinaman Rock

Sucia Island

Ewing Cove

Ewing I

Lawson Bluff

Shallow
Bay

K

Wiggins Reef

artifical reef

Echo Bay

48° 45.661' N
122° 53.748' W

Justice I.

North Finger I

Little Sucia
Island

Fox Cove

South Finger I

Mud Bay

Fossil Bay

Snoring Bay

E.V. Henry Finger

Vancouver

Victoria

Seattle

Not for Navigation

Photo opposite: Echo Bay is the largest anchorage at Sucia.
Below: Vessels anchored in Fossil Bay with Fox Cove beyond.

Sucia Island Marine State Park

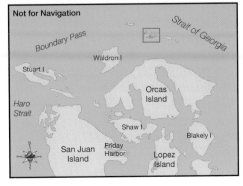

Not for Navigation

Boundary Pass

Strait of Georgia

Waldron I

Stuart I.

Orcas
Island

Haro
Strait

Shaw I.

Blakely I

San Juan
Island

Friday
Harbor

Lopez
Island

Park facilities

48 mooring buoys, walk-in campsites, trails, view points, picnic
tables, drinking water, toilets,
beach hiking, recommended
kayaking, swimming, fishing and
scuba diving.

Pictured Above: Shallow Bay with its mooring buoys and lots of room for anchoring. It is a popular and attractive anchorage. Some wave action can be felt in the bay when winds are from the west, but it is one of the more sheltered anchorages in the islands. It is a good place to stop for shelter on the edge of the Strait of Georgia.

Sucia Island is one of the most attractive and busiest islands in the region. It was bought by the Puget Sound Coalition of Yacht Clubs and given to the state as a park in 1960. It has been developed as a fine recreational area over the years. Today it boasts well maintained campsites, picnic sites, hiking and biking trails and facilities including shelters, firepits, picnic tables, toilets and water. The mooring buoys in all of its bays and coves provide relatively protected mooring for overnight and two docks in Fossil Bay accommodate a fair number of boats for limited three night stays. Paddlers should stay clear of larger vessels operating in conditions where currents dictate restricted ability to manoeuvre.

The trails lead around the island taking in access to some fine beach areas as well as cliff top viewpoints. The cliffs are sheer and drop-offs steep. One should take great care hiking the upper trails as the cliffs are precarious. It is dangerous to venture too close to the edges.

In Shallow Bay stroll the beaches and visit photogenic Chinaman Rock, a large sandstone cliff that has been carved by wind and water erosion of many centuries.

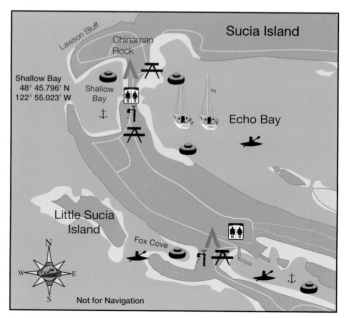

Shallow Bay
48° 45.796' N
122° 55.023' W

Sucia Island

Lawson Bluff

Chinaman Rock

Shallow Bay

Echo Bay

Little Sucia Island

Fox Cove

N
W — E
S

Not for Navigation

Top: Anchorage in Fossil Bay, near the dock that is frequented mostly by smaller craft. Some tend to favour the other dock, pictured above. Small boats slide up to the beach to offload overnight campers. Beyond the beach and its narrow isthmus is the anchorage at Fox Cove.

Patos Island

Charts 18431, 18432, 18421

Patos Island Marine State Park

Access

Another, smaller marine park in the San Juans is Patos Island. It lies to the north of its neighbours, Sucia and Matia, on the edge of the Strait of Georgia and only about five miles from Orcas Island. It can be reached from Point Roberts on the Mainland in half an hour in a fast boat and one to two hours sailing. From the area of Anacortes it is a landmark en route to the north when entering the lower Strait of Georgia.

The Park and Anchorage

Patos Island is a breeding ground for birds, and many bird watchers from near and far, are known to frequent the island.

The island does not afford a great deal of protection from the open sea. Active Cove in the lee of the island, protected from the Strait of Georgia, provides the little shelter available. There are two mooring buoys in this cove. The anchorage, which is quite subject to the strong tidal currents, is minimal with two to three spots available depending on how the vessels swing. There are some camping facilities available; campsites, picnic tables and pit toilets. A picnic site with table, located at the curve of the bay provides a very picturesque setting. There is no garbage disposal on the island.

Nearby

Sucia and Matia Islands with their mooring buoys and anchorages, trails and camping facilities. The nearest landfall across the Strait of Georgia is Point Roberts with its many facilities, marina, shipyard and moorage.

Opposite: Patos Island looking towards East Point on Saturna Island. Little Patos is located top left in photo. It provides a breakwater for the anchorage.

Above: Across Sucia Island towards Patos.

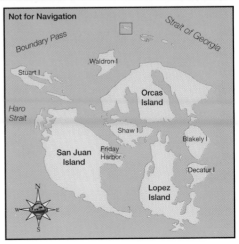

Park facilities

2 mooring buoys, walk-in camp-sites, trail, points of interest, picnic tables, toilets, beachcombing, recommended fishing. Some good scuba diving off the island.

Stuart Island

Stuart Island Marine State Park

Charts 18432, 18421

Access

Stuart is the island that most mariners pass after leaving Bedwell Harbour to enter the USA by water. Or that is passed by those travelling north via Bedwell Harbour when leaving the San Juans. The island is washed by Haro Strait and Boundary Pass to the northwest end of Orcas Island. Enter Prevost Harbor around Charles Point when approaching from Haro Strait, or east of Satellite Island, being very cautious of submerged rocks and a shoal off Satellite Island. The anchorage in Prevost Harbor is best entered between Satellite Island and Charles Point.

The Park and Anchorage

Reid Harbor and Prevost Harbor have docks and mooring buoys. Both bays are suitable for anchoring. There are walking and hiking roads and trails on Stuart Island linking the parks to other points of interest. There are toilets, marine pumpout stations, campsites, picnic tables, drinking water and beaches to walk on. It is open year round with fees in effect during summer.

Nearby

Haro Strait where killer whales are often sighted at times in summer, abuts Stuart Island's southwest side. The island is located only three-and-a-half miles from Roche Harbor. Use large scale charts when navigating in the area, and beware of the hazards in Spieden Channel including reefs, shoals and especially strong tidal conditions.

Above: The dock and anchorage in Prevost Harbor. Opposite page: Looking down onto Reid Harbor (left) and Prevost Harbor. Both anchorages are fairly well protected from the wind.

Park facilities

Reid Harbor

15 mooring buoys, 219 feet of dock, marine pumpout, toilets, campsites, picnic tables, fireplaces, stoves, drinking water.

Prevost Harbor

7 mooring buoys, 539 feet of dock, marine pumpout, toilets, campsites, picnic tables, fireplaces, stoves. Drinking water.

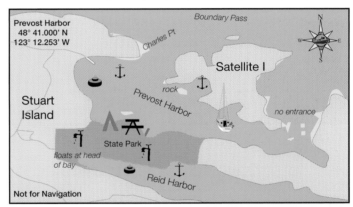

Prevost Harbor
48° 41.000' N
123° 12.253' W

Boundary Pass

Charles Pt

Satellite I

rock

Prevost Harbor

no entrance

Stuart Island

State Park

floats at head of bay

Reid Harbor

Not for Navigation

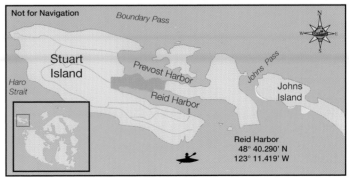

Not for Navigation

Boundary Pass

Stuart Island

Prevost Harbor

Johns Pass

Haro Strait

Reid Harbor

Johns Island

Reid Harbor
48° 40.290' N
123° 11.419' W

41

British Columbia's captivating coast, its waterways and islands.

Evening falls on a calm summer's day in Princess Cove on Wallace Island, one of the prime marine park anchorages in the Southern Gulf Islands.

2

Vancouver Island South
and the
Gulf Islands

The Gulf Islands
For expanded information on the waterways, islands, marine parks and facilities in the Gulf Islands, refer to the author's cruising guide: *Gulf Islands Cruising Guide*.

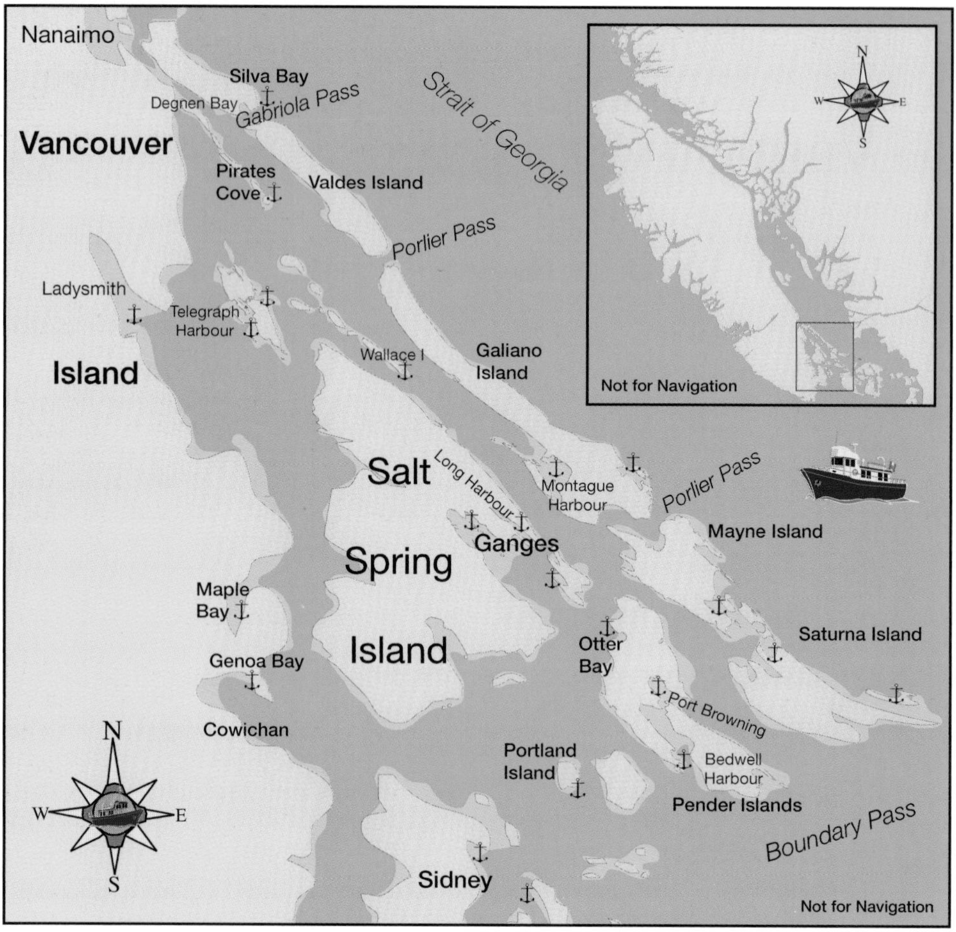
Nanaimo
Silva Bay
Degnen Bay
Gabriola Pass
Strait of Georgia
Vancouver
Pirates Cove
Valdes Island
Porlier Pass
Ladysmith
Telegraph Harbour
Island
Wallace I
Galiano Island
Not for Navigation
N
W
E
S
Salt
Long Harbour
Montague Harbour
Porlier Pass
Ganges
Mayne Island
Spring
Maple Bay
Island
Otter Bay
Saturna Island
Genoa Bay
Port Browning
Cowichan
N
W
E
S
Portland Island
Bedwell Harbour
Pender Islands
Boundary Pass
Sidney
Not for Navigation

The Jewel of British Columbia Boating

Anchorages in the Gulf Islands– Marine Parks Phone 250-387-5002
Many bays, coves and snug overnight moorings.

Beginning at Victoria and travelling northwards, the cruising mariner will find numerous anchorages and safe havens en route through the inside passage all the way to a final destination in Alaska. And back. The single most popular destination for most mariners is the Gulf Islands with strong competition from Desolation Sound. These popular destinations attract thousands of boats every summer, from local marinas as well as from farther afield. Some mariners travel from points in Puget Sound and some trail smaller boats to the area from the Interior of BC as well as Alberta. Others cruise up the west coast of the USA, from San Francisco and Los Angeles.

Although there are numerous coves and bays in the Gulf Islands, few offer totally sheltered overnight anchorage. As you travel up the coast from Sidney you have the option of moving slightly eastward and stopping at Princess Margaret Marine Park's Princess Bay or at Royal Cove, the tiny anchorage on the north end of Portland Island. The south anchorage is popular and can become very crowded in summer. The cove shallows

*Anchorages in bays and coves attract hordes of mariners to British Columbia every summer.
Looking west over Ganges Harbour, the busiest centre in the Gulf Islands.*

out as you approach the beach, and when anchoring at high tide be mindful of the tidal drop, so that you don't end up touching bottom. The wind has been known to cause a great deal of discomfort in this cove, when blowing from the southeast. If there is a wind forecast that dictates you think twice about staying overnight at Princess Bay, move up to the north end, or continue to one of the anchorages at South or North Pender Island, Otter Bay or Bedwell Harbour. Then to Winter Harbour, Horton Bay or Cabbage Island if that is the direction you intend to go.

To the west of these anchorages you could drop the hook in Long Bay, or Ganges Harbour on Salt Spring Island, or the beautiful, sheltered Annette Inlet or Glenthorne Passage on Prevost Island. Continue around the east side of Salt Spring Island to Montague Harbour or to Wallace Island's Princess Bay or Conover Cove, Clam Bay, Degnen Bay or Silva Bay, the latter of which can be open to north winds at times.

When you are travelling around the western side of Salt Spring Island, a safe anchorage can be found in Genoa Bay or Maple Bay or farther north at Thetis Island (Preedy Harbour), or at Pirate's Cove (Marine Park).

If you are trying to cross the Strait of Georgia from Active Pass but weather conditions hold you back, try for the anchorage in Whaler Bay. You can reach it by passing through Active Pass and turning to port just before Gossip Island. Mind the reefs either side of the passage. Pass straight through the narrows and find anchorage up against the Galiano shoreline.

Many mariners travelling north through the Gulf Islands, end up at Newcastle Island. This is a popular destination because it not only has reasonably good anchorage but also a fairly large dock. And just across the way is the city of Nanaimo which is a large centre for all types of stores, marine service, entertainment and restaurants.

Beyond Nanaimo mariners cruise across the Strait to Vancouver and Howe Sound, or to the waters of Jervis Inlet and Princess Louisa Inlet. Many continue up to Desolation Sound taking in Denman and Hornby Islands along the way. Mind the restricted military area WG north of Nanaimo.

Victoria
Charts 3313, 3440, 3412

Anchorages *–or not*

In the immediate area of Victoria anchoring is not readily possible. There are many alternative marinas and docks where mariners can find moorage for stays of a few hours, to permanent moorage (see ***Docks and Destinations***). For people in transit, Victoria offers customs clearing, many forms of shoreside entertainment, sightseeing and an opportunity to provision the boat for the trip north or to the west coast. The mariner cruising towards the west coast will find anchorage at Sooke or Port San Juan en route.

Those travelling north up the inside passage will be in search of sheltered coves such as in the beautiful Gulf Islands. Look for the anchorage you want in the pages ahead. Or stay awhile at a dock in Victoria and enjoy the many attractions this British style city has in store for tourists. Do a slow scenic cruise up The Gorge. It is shallow but adequate for small craft. Watch for narrows and currents.

Nearby

If you want a place to anchor near Victoria the favoured coves are at **Cadboro Bay** or at **Esquimalt Harbour**–anchor in **Thetis Cove** or at the head of the harbour. In a southbound direction try **Fleming Bay, Albert Head** or **William Head**. The latter two are temporary, while Fleming Bay has a dock and launch ramp. Be prepared to be checked by naval security officials when entering Esquimalt Harbour.

Esquimalt Lagoon and Fisgard Light are scenic places to visit, with beach access or by land. The lagoon is a sanctuary for birds and wildlife.

The cove in the northern nook of Albert Head is a good anchorage from conditions other than a northerly blow, which seldom affects it in summer. William Head has limited anchorage in **Quarantine Cove**. This is due to security restrictions imposed by the adjacent prison. Use the western part of the cove for anchoring and keep a weather watch for strong winds in the forecast. Farther south at **Becher Bay** anchorage should be considered temporary. See page 306.

The Gorge

Thetis Cove

Inskip I

Esquimalt
Harbour

West Bay

Inner Harbour

lagoon

Fisgard Light

48° 25.464' N
123° 26.876' W

R

Victoria

Royal Roads

Flemming Bay

breakwater
Ogden Point

48° 24.803' N
123° 23.740' W

Not for Navigation

While there is no place designated to anchor at Victoria, check nearby anchorages southwest of Victoria at Esquimalt (above), Becher Bay and Sooke or east of the city at Oak Bay (opposite page). For more information on Sooke, Pedder Bay and Becher Bay see **The Gulf Islands Cruising Guide** *by this author.*

Inset above: Off Thetis Cove, Esquimalt Harbour.

Customs:

In Victoria's Inner Harbour, the Customs dock is to the left as you approach the Empress Hotel (dock). Phone 1-888-226-7277

Not for Navigation

Vancouver

**Gulf
Islands**

Sidney

**San Juan
Islands**

Becher Bay

Pedder Bay

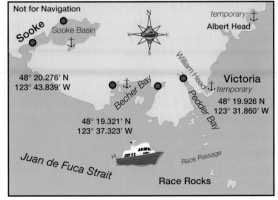

Not for Navigation

temporary
Albert Head

Sooke

Sooke Basin

William Head

Victoria
temporary

48° 20.276' N
123° 43.839' W

Becher Bay

Pedder Bay

48° 19.926 N
123° 31.860' W

48° 19.321' N
123° 37.323' W

Juan de Fuca Strait

Race Passage

Race Rocks

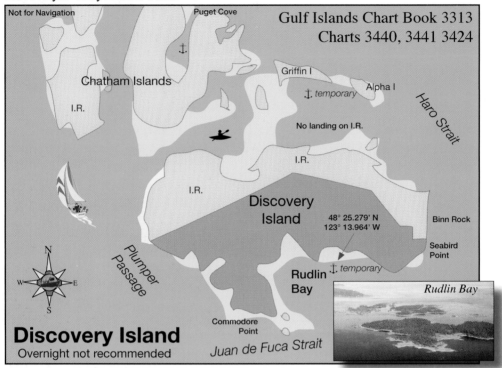

Not for Navigation
Puget Cove

Gulf Islands Chart Book 3313
Charts 3440, 3441 3424

Griffin I

Chatham Islands

Alpha I
temporary

I.R.

Haro Strait

No landing on I.R.

I.R.

I.R.

Discovery Island
48° 25.279' N
123° 13.964' W

Binn Rock

Seabird Point

Plumper Passage

temporary

Rudlin Bay

Rudlin Bay

N
W E
S

Commodore Point

Discovery Island
Overnight not recommended

Juan de Fuca Strait

Gulf Islands

Discovery Island Marine Park

Access

Discovery Island is located at the south end of Haro Strait which forms the border between Canada and the United States, with the Saanich Peninsula on the western side and the San Juan Islands to the east. Discovery Island looks out onto Juan de Fuca Strait and is located a mere two miles from Oak Bay, Victoria. The park area can be entered from Plumper Passage to the west or through Rudlin Bay from the south. Beware of rocks and shallows in Rudlin Bay and Virtue Rock in Plumper Passage.

The Park and Anchorage

There is no totally protected anchorage at this park. But it is a beautiful natural island that justifiably forms part of the marine parks system.

The island is not developed but has some trails for walking. The park has limited facilities such as toilets and wilderness camping but no potable water. Fees are payable. Kayaking is popular in the area and the wilderness camping is used largely by visiting paddlers.

The northern part of Discovery Island and nearby smaller islands are Native Reserves and should be respected as such. The public should not access the private roads on these lands.

Discovery Island was formerly owned by Captain E.G. Beaumont who donated the property to the Parks Branch. An important lighthouse is located on the island for navigation in the tidal waters of the adjacent channels.

Nearby

The closest safe harbour to Discovery Island is Oak Bay. Also nearby is Victoria with its multitude of marinas and docks, commercial and private.

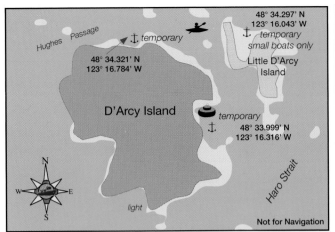

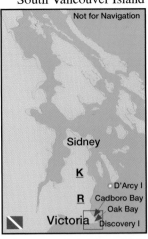

D'Arcy Island and Little D'Arcy.

No services at these marine parks. Nearest facility is at Oak Bay. Suitable anchorage at Cadboro Bay.

Cadboro Bay

While occasional south easterly blows will cause some disturbance in the bay, the anchorage is not subject to much danger of dragging. The best anchorage is at the head of the bay over a muddy bottom. Use the south passage to enter the bay when approaching from the east or north, via Jemmy Jones Island. Royal Victoria Yacht Club is located at Cadboro Bay.

D'Arcy Island Marine Park

Access.

The island is north of Discovery Island to the south of James and Sidney Islands in Hughes Passage, Haro Strait. Enter from the west to the south of the lighthouse with great caution, as there are numerous reefs and shoals in the vicinity.

The Park and Anchorage

This small island is not for mariners in search of facilities. There are mooring buoys. The island is prefered by campers who will find nothing more than wilderness camping facilities. Camp fees are in effect. No water. D'Arcy Island was once a leper colony.

Nearby.

Those looking for protected overnight mooring should try Sidney Spit. Little D'Arcy Island is private, but temporary, small boat anchorage may be found at its north end.

Marine parks such as Discovery and D'Arcy are for nature lovers. Birds, marine mammals and other wildlife can be observed close up in these parks. Scuba divers will see some of British Columbia's unique and rare marine creatures in local waters.

Discovery Island

beach hiking, fishing, recommended kayaking, scuba diving, viewpoint. Both parks open year round.

D'Arcy Island

3 mooring buoys, beach hiking, fishing, recommended kayaking, scuba diving, viewpoint of interest.

Sidney Spit

Charts 3313, 3476, 3441

Access

The park is situated at the northern tip of Sidney Island between Miners Channel and Sidney Channel. The anchorage is entered from Sidney Channel and although very shallow at places, especially during a low tide, all but very large pleasure boats should be able to slip well into the lee of the spit without any danger of touching bottom. Larger vessels should consult the large scale chart for the anchorage, to avoid the shallow spots.

The Park and Anchorage

Swimming is a popular pastime at Sidney Spit. There are literally thousands of metres of sandy beach areas, and summertime sees beachcombers, scores of sunbathers, day visitors and overnight campers arriving at the park for weekends or longer periods. There are numerous mooring buoys throughout the anchorage, and a dock (which is removed off season) with space for a limited number of small craft and dinghy mooring. Anchoring in the area is safe and fairly protected although some winds cause discomfort, especially early in the season. It is recommended that you monitor wind forecasts for the area before settling in for a night's sleep at anchor.

There is a lot of activity, small boats and children in the anchorage so be careful when navigating through the moorings.

A foot passenger ferry from Sidney, lands at a designated dock regularly at weekends, carrying campers and other visitors back and forth.

The island has some pleasant walking trails that traverse open uplands and picturesque meadows, cool forests of Douglas fir and arbutus trees. The circuitous trail provides many panoramic views of the surrounding waterways and nearby islands.

There are camping and picnic facilities including some for groups.

Nearby

The town of Sidney is a popular tourist destination. It is picturesque with waterfront hotel, restaurants, a museum and uptown shopping. A large, modern marina near the foot of the town's main road, and another in Tsehum Harbour serve mariners seeking overnight moorage with power, water, cable TV hook-up and access to service and supplies. Canoe, kayak and small boat rentals are available. Other marinas are located a short distance

Not for Navigation

Forrest I

Sidney Island
Nearby: At Sidney–
Launch ramps, marinas,
charter vessels, canoe/
kayak rentals, sales,
repairs, hotels, restau-
rants, sporting goods,
shops and services.
Medical facilities.

48° 38.201' N
123° 20.012' W

Sidney Spit
Marine Park

Private

Miner's Channel

Sidney

Channel

Sidney

Island

N
W   E
S

Photo opposite: Sidney Spit attracts many campers and day visitors as well as boaters. There is lots of room to anchor and many mooring buoys at this marine park.

north at Tsehum Harbour and Canoe Cove where fuel and marine services are available. Customs docks are located at primary marina locations.

Park facilities
35 mooring buoys, boat/dinghy dock, 24 walk-in campsites, park host, picnic tables, drinking water, toilets, beach hiking, fishing, recommended kayaking, viewpoint/point of interest.

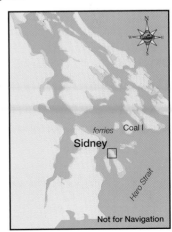

N
W   E
S

ferries Coal I

Sidney

Haro Strait

Not for Navigation

Canoe Bay with anchorage to the west of Kolb Island.

Canoe Bay

Charts 3313, 3476, 3441

Access

The anchorage should be reached by passage between the marina and Kolb Island. There are some obstacles in the adjacent Page and Iroquis Passages when approaching Canoe Cove. Use a large scale chart and exercise great caution. The passages are good between some of the rocks and reefs but be mindful of the currents during tidal exchanges.

Anchorage

Just south of Canoe Cove Marina is the anchorage known as Canoe Bay. It is sheltered from most conditions year round, but winter winds can cause some discomfort at times. Mooring buoys in the bay are private. Anchor in locations away from obvious boat passages accessing the marina. Mind the private mooring buoys and anchor in two to seven metres (chart reading).

Nearby

Canoe Cove Marina, located in Canoe Bay, is a long-established facility for resident and some transient mariners. The Cove has been associated also with the manufacture of pleasure boats which bear its name.

Facilities at Canoe Cove include restaurants, yacht brokerage, service and chandlery. There is a resident artist located in an A frame on the property, Morgan Warren, whose work is widely known. A fuel dock supplies gas and diesel as well as oils and some other items for mariners. Toilets are located at the head of the fuel dock for customers and the marina office, located across the parking lot, will be able to allocate moorage, if there is any available, to visiting yachtsmen.

Tsehum Harbour lies just to the south of Canoe Bay with access via Page Passage and around Curteis Point. There are marinas, boat works, restaurants and a public dock as well as semi exposed anchorage just off the large Van Isle Marina. Here too is the well-known, long-established Philbrooks Shipyard, adjacent to the marina.

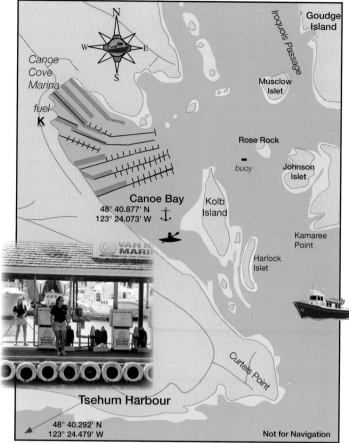

N
W E
S

Canoe
Cove
Marina

fuel
K

Iroquois Passage

Goudge
Island

Musclow
Islet

Rose Rock
–
buoy

Johnson
Islet

Canoe Bay
48° 40.877' N
123° 24.073' W ⚓

Kolb
Island

Kamaree
Point

Harlock
Islet

Curteis Point

Tsehum Harbour

48° 40.292' N
123° 24.479' W

Not for Navigation

Tsehum Harbour

N
W E
S

Strait of Georgia

Salt
Spring
Island

Not for Navigation

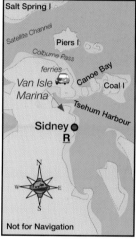

Salt Spring I

Satellite Channel

Piers I

Colburne Pass

ferries

Van Isle
Marina

Canoe Bay

Coal I

Tsehum Harbour

Sidney
R

N
W E
S

Not for Navigation

Top: Diagram of Canoe Cove. There is room to anchor in Canoe Bay and at nearby Tsehum Harbour. Photo below: Tsehum Harbour anchorage. These sheltered coves have many slips at available marinas, as well as occasional room at the Tsehum Harbour public dock.
At locations such as Van Isle Marina (fuel dock shown above) and Canoe Cove Marina, overnight guests have access to facilities including showers, laundry, garbage disposal, service and repairs.

The anchorage at Fulford Harbour, quiet when this photo was taken, can become fairly busy at times in summer. Note the shallows, and avoid anchoring if easterly winds are forecast.

Fulford Harbour

Access

Fulford Harbour opens into Salt Spring Island off Satellite Channel.

Anchorage and nearby

In summer months the long inlet with its shallow head provides temoporary anchorage. Monitor wind and weather forecasts before settling in for the night. Easterly winds can cause some discomfort and you may be better off tied up at the nearby marina (1). Another temporary anchorage is in the lee of **Russel Island** (2). Overnight winds can blow towards the island or away from it, but are not usually severe enough in summer to cause any problems.

Genoa Bay

Access

If you travel via Satellite Channel around the south of Salt Spring Island you may want to look for anchorage in the shelter of Genoa Bay. When entering, steer clear of the shallows, rocks and reefs in the en-

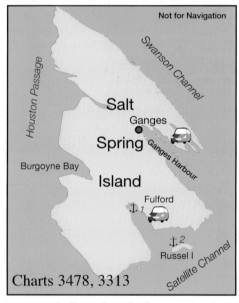

Not for Navigation

Houston Passage

Swanson Channel

Salt

Ganges

Spring Ganges Harbour

Burgoyne Bay

Island

Fulford

Russel I

Satellite Channel

Charts 3478, 3313

trance as indicated on the large scale chart.

Anchorage and nearby

There is lots of room to anchor in the bay although the marina will be pleased to have you as a mooring customer. The marina's Genoa Bay Cafe offers breakfast, lunch and dinner. There is a launch ramp at Genoa Bay and another at Cowichan on the opposite side of **Cowichan Bay**. Anchorage in the harbour is temporary. Local docks offer overnight moorage and access to town.

The anchorage at Genoa Bay lies beyond the marina. It is usually well protected from wind, but always check weather reports.

Not for Navigation

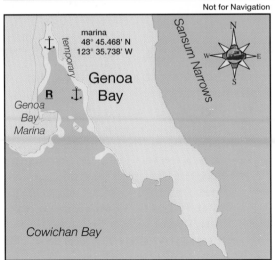

marina
48° 45.468' N
123° 35.738' W

temporary

Genoa
Bay

Sansum Narrows

R

Genoa
Bay
Marina

Cowichan Bay

Salt
Spring
Island

Fulford

Strait of Georgia

R
Genoa Bay
Cowichan Bay
R   K

Satellite Channel

Sidney

Charts 3313, 3478, 3441

Anchoring adjacent to the marinas at Maple Bay. Inset: Anchorage (temporary) and dock in Burgoyne Bay–map page 54. Opposite: At anchor in Royal Cove, Portland Island–see page 58.

Inset: Anchorage (temporary) and dock in Burgoyne Bay–map page 54. Opposite: At anchor in Royal Cove, Portland Island–see page 58.

Maple Bay

48° 47.743' N
123° 36.010' W

Charts 3313, 3478, 3441

Access

From the south via Satellite Channel the entrance to Maple Bay is just north of Sansum Narrows. From the north out of Houston Passage Maple Bay lies against the east coast of Vancouver Island before entering Sansum Narrows. As you enter the anchorage you pass Maple Bay public dock at a distance off to starboard and Birds Eye Marina and fuel dock.

Anchorage

The anchorage is in **Birds Eye Cove**, a tapering inlet which runs southwards from Maple Bay and houses a yacht club and marinas along the shore to starboard, from its entrance to its narrow head. There is a large buoy at the entrance cautioning mariners to observe a no wash speed. Anchor in Birds Eye Cove, on the approaches to the last marina down the inlet, which is Maple Bay Marina, a large facility with fuel dock, overnight moorage and many dockside facilities. Boats generally anchor off between the northern arms of the marina and the opposite shore. Several larger vessels make the cove their permanent mooring. There are times when winds gusting into the cove down Maple Bay from the north can make it uncomfortable, particularly in the off season.

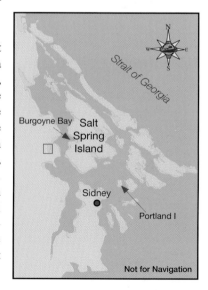

56

Portland Island

Charts 3313, 3476, 3441

Access

The island is southeast of Salt Spring Island off Satellite Channel and adjacent to Moresby Passage. It is only minutes out of Sidney travelling north.

The Park and Anchorage

Princess Margaret Marine Park on Portland Island has been a popular day or overnight destination for southern Vancouver Island boat owners for a very long time. It became a marine park after the island was acquired by the province from Princess Margaret who received it as a gift in 1958.

Middens located near Kanaka Bluff reveal that the island was once used extensively by coastal natives. It was farmed until its transfer to the province, and apple and plum trees can still be found ashore in Princess Bay.

At low tide there is not much depth in the bay near the shore so check your depth before anchoring during a receding tide. The presence of shoals and reefs around the island, particularly on the east and northeast sides, requires a cautious approach. Use a large scale chart. The northwest and southwest shores have sandy beaches. Anchorage in fair weather conditions is best at **Princess Bay** and **Royal Cove**. Temporary anchorage can be taken behind **Brackman Island**.

There are camping and picnic facilities on the island including water and toilets.

Nearby

The first vessel sunk by the Artificial Reef Society of British Columbia resides in waters off the east side of the island in Moresby Passage. It is the 56 metre *GB Church*, placed in 1991. Its location is well marked with fixed, permanent buoys for easy diving access. Tortoise Islets just off Princess Bay also provide some promising scuba diving.

Park facilities

20 walk-in campsites, picnic tables, drinking water, toilets, park host, beach hiking, fishing, recommended kayaking, scuba diving, viewpoint/point of interest. Park host.

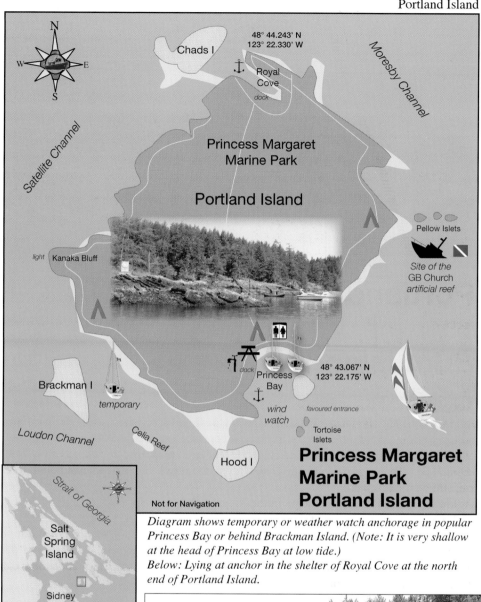

48° 44.243' N
123° 22.330' W

Chads I

Royal Cove

dock

Moresby Channel

Princess Margaret
Marine Park

Portland Island

Satellite Channel

Pellow Islets

light Kanaka Bluff

Site of the
GB Church
artificial reef

Brackman I

temporary

Loudon Channel

Celia Reef

clock Princess Bay

wind watch

favoured entrance

48° 43.067' N
123° 22.175' W

Tortoise Islets

Hood I

Not for Navigation

**Princess Margaret
Marine Park
Portland Island**

Strait of Georgia

Salt
Spring
Island

Sidney

*Diagram shows temporary or weather watch anchorage in popular
Princess Bay or behind Brackman Island. (Note: It is very shallow
at the head of Princess Bay at low tide.)*
*Below: Lying at anchor in the shelter of Royal Cove at the north
end of Portland Island.*

*Opposite: Princess
Bay. Entrance is south
or north of the rocks,
but keep clear. In the
background, Fulford
Harbour opens into
Salt Spring Island.
Russel Island lies just
off the entrance to
Fulford Harbour.*

Rum Island (Isle de Lis)   Charts 3313, 3441

Access

Rum Island and its attached neighbour, Gooch Island, lie east of the town of Sidney. From Sidney to Rum Island passage may be made around the top of John Island or to the south of it taking care to use a large scale chart for reef and submerged rock avoidance. Most are marked by buoys and other navigational aids, but some reefs close to protruding rocks are dangerous, especially at low tides. The island is adjacent to Haro Strait and Prevost Passage and can be reached via Haro Strait quite easily.

The Park and Anchorage

The entire island is a park, known as Isle de Lis Marine Park. It has a walking trail, toilets and beaches. Apart from tenting and relaxing on the island scuba divers are visiting the area in large numbers since the sinking off Rum Island in September 1995 of the decommissioned HMCS *MacKenzie*, a 366 foot former escort ship of the Canadian Navy.

The adjacent anchorage is best used temporarily during daylight. Most mariners drop the hook just north or south of the drying passage between Rum Island and Gooch Island. Scuba divers exploring the *MacKenzie* use mooring buoys at the site while diving. Watch for the red and white divers' flag, indicating underwater activity.

Nearby

Good cruising in the area, being mindful of reefs such as South and North Cod Reefs. Sidney Spit Marine Park a few miles to the west is a popular anchorage.

Not far from Rum Island is the border between Canadian and US waters with interesting points in the San Juan Islands within easy reach. Mind the open stretch of water crossing Haro Strait during windy periods, especially when there is a large tide change. Best passages are at slack or near slack tides.

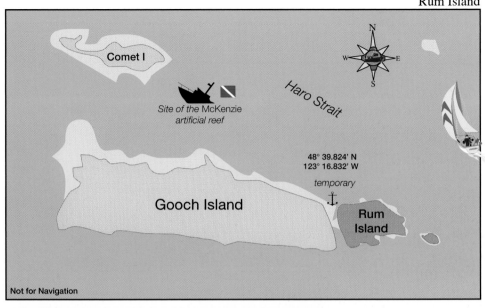

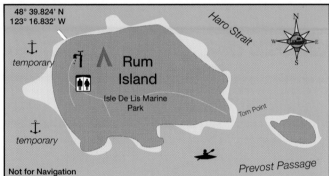

Rum Island
Park facilities
3 walk-in campsites, park host, trails, points of interest, toilets, drinking water, hiking, kayaking, fishing, scuba diving.

Opposite: Rum Island (Isle de Lis), appears attached to Gooch Island (centre of photo). Domville Island lies in the foreground. Haro Strait and the San Juan Islands are in the distance.
Above: MacKenzie, *pictured at its sinking for divers, lies between Gooch and Comet Island.*

The anchorage, and vessels on mooring buoys in Bedwell Harbour. Opposite inset: Marina seen in the curve of the bay. This is a Canada Customs port of entry.

Bedwell Harbour

Charts 3313, 3477, 3441

Access

Bedwell Harbour can be entered via the Pender Canal (clearance under the road bridge is 28 feet) north of the park or from Swanson Channel to the south.

Nearby

Bedwell Harbour has long been known as an entry point for American visitors arriving in Canada and Canadians returning from cruising in the waters of Washington State. South of the park and its adjacent anchorage, Poet's Cove Marina provides a range of facilities and services, including fuel, moorage, some supplies and books. Poet's Cove Resort has a restaurant and pub, and a convenience store on the property. The customs dock is situated adjacent to the marina. *Marine Park details pages 63 & 64.*

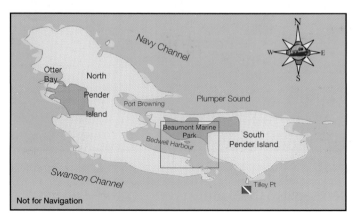

Diagram showing the location of Beaumont Marine Park and its proximity to the Pender Canal which cuts between North and South Pender Islands linking Bedwell Harbour with Port Browning.

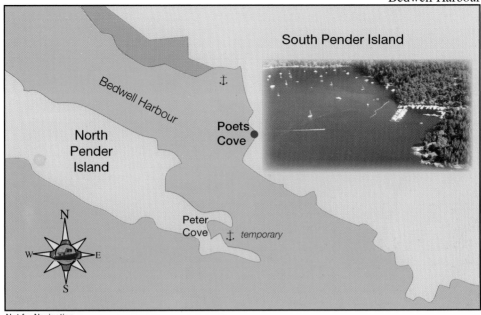

South Pender Island

Bedwell Harbour

Poets Cove

North Pender Island

Peter Cove ⚓ *temporary*

N
W E
S

Not for Navigation

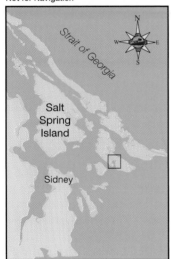

Strait of Georgia

N
W E
S

Salt Spring Island

Sidney

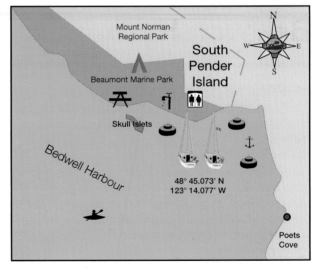

Mount Norman Regional Park

Beaumont Marine Park

South Pender Island

Skull Islets

Bedwell Harbour

48° 45.073' N
123° 14.077' W

Poets Cove

Bedwell Harbour
Beaumont Marine Park, South Pender Island

Diagrams are for reference only and should Not be Used for Navigation

🚰	Water
⛺	Camping
⚓	Anchoring
⬤	Mooring
🚻	Toilets
⛩	Picnic Tables
◼	Scuba sites
🛶	Kayaking

Beaumont Marine Park facilities

15 mooring buoys, 11 walk-in campsites, trails, points of interest, picnic tables, drinking water, toilets, park host, beach hiking, recommended kayaking.

Port Browning. The bay is open to southeasterly winds, which are not the prevailing winds in summer. But once in a while anchored vessels may be disturbed by such winds. Monitor weather reports. The marina offers sheltered overnight moorage. Also seen inset opposite.

Beaumont Marine Park and Anchorage

Beaumont Marine Park is situated at Bedwell Harbour on South Pender Island. Its west facing location provides long daylight hours. It enjoys the protection from open water of the southern tip of North Pender Island, which forms a natural breakwater for the bay.

An expansive beach provides good access from the water for kayakers.

In the park there are camping and daytime facilities with picnic tables, toilets, drinking water and scenic trails to walk to points of interest. Immediately adjacent to the park is Mount Norman Regional Park where hiking opportunities are favoured and panoramic vistas are abundant. Serious hikers will find ready access to the 890 foot Mount Norman with its splendid trails and vistas.

Mooring buoys are located off the south end of the park southeast of Skull Islets, providing safe overnight mooring for vessels of all types and sizes, and anchoring is safe and comfortable in almost all weather conditions. Medicine Beach is an attractive park on the west side of Bedwell Harbour. Anchor off temporarily while going ashore to explore. Southeasterly winds can cause discomfort to boats anchored in parts of the bay.

Small boat access to Port Browning from Bedwell Harbour is via the Pender Canal. This is a scenic waterway that separates the two Penders. It is narrow and has some reefs but the channel is quite well marked. The canal passes beneath a road bridge that has been featured in many photographs of the area. It opens into a small bay with a white sandy beach where you will usually see people sunbathing or children fishing from shore. This passage and the adjacent shoreline makes a most picturesque and scenic side trip when taken slowly and cautiously. The large scale chart should be referred to when transitting the passage.

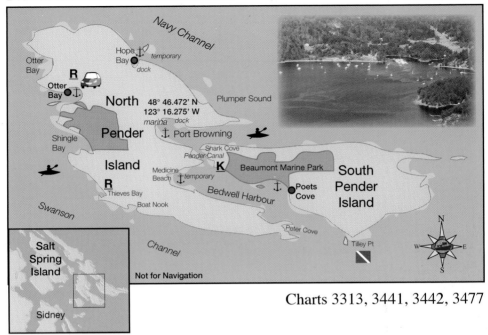

Charts 3313, 3441, 3442, 3477

Port Browning

Anchorage is fair in the bay, but southeast winds can blow in summer time giving some discomfort to anchored boats. The public float in Port Browning is mostly used by local boats. It is a small float adjoining the northern shore of the bay and if space is available it affords a good temporary stop with the possibility of walking along the adjacent road up to the shopping centre or around to Port Browning Marina. Between these two centres you will find grocery shops, post office, bakery, liquor store, restaurant and pub, book and gift shops and a variety of other businesses that tend to change from time to time. An automotive service station is located near the main shopping centre. There are marine services available on South and North Pender Islands.

Port Browning is connected to Bedwell Harbour by way of the Pender Canal. See previous pages and photograph opposite.

Port Washington

This is an historic spot on North Pender Island. The old general store which served the community and passing vessels for decades has undergone changes from time to time, but somehow manages to retain its original countenance.

The 147 foot dock for accessing land is located in Grimmer Bay on the west side of North Pender Island. Some paddlers launch their boats at the Port Washington dock.

Launch Ramps If you are launching a small boat, having driven onto the islands via the ferry service, you will be able to launch at ramps at Otter Bay or Thieves Bay or by hand at Port Washington, Bedwell Harbour, Hope Bay or at Shark Cove's white, sandy Mortimer Spit where the two islands almost meet at Pender Canal. Beware of tidal currents in all passages between and around the Pender Islands.

Otter Bay

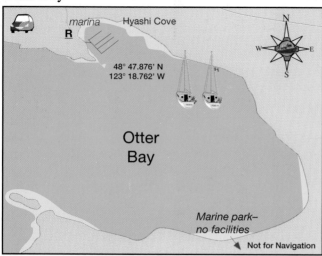

marina
R
Hyashi Cove

48° 47.876' N
123° 18.762' W

Otter
Bay

Marine park–
no facilities

Not for Navigation

Strait of Georgia

Salt
Spring
Island

Sidney

*Anchor in the lee of the
point protecting the marina
in Hyashi Cove.*

Otter Bay

Charts 3313, 3442

Access

Otter Bay opens off Swanson Channel, the route taken by the BC Ferries between Swartz Bay, Sidney and Tsawwassen via Active Pass. The ferry landing at Otter Bay serves the Pender Islands. It is passed on the approaches to the bay.

Anchorage

There is a popular, busy marina in Otter Bay and sheltered anchorage in depths from 40 to 60 feet that protects boats from most conditions at most times. The only disturbance is the regular but much diminished swell from passing ferries that wash into the cove. Most of the swell is dissipated by the time it rounds the curve of the bay and reaches the anchorage. It is a busy spot in summer, so make sure you allow a reasonable amount of scope in your anchor line, and don't swing onto a neighbouring boat. Keep the rise and fall of the tide in mind when anchoring.

When the marina is full with moorage customers, mariners anchored off are welcome to go ashore by dinghy and visit the facility, which provides groceries, snacks, cappuccino, books, gifts and other items. If there is space, check into the marina and enjoy all of its facilities, including the pool. A small fee will be charged for brief stops or docking a dinghy at the marina.

This is a marina well worth advance booking into for weekend stays and overnight visits during the week. It is very busy in peak summer periods. On the island there are many interests from craft stores to fine restaurants, overnight accommodations and services for the many permanent and holiday residents.

Please note that marinas in the Gulf Islands generally have very limited water supplies and restricted garbage disposal. Do not expect them to supply water, showers or laundry services other than to their paying moorage guests and then on a limited conservation basis.

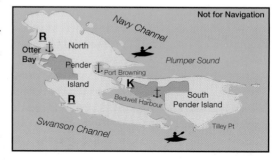

Not for Navigation

Navy Channel

R
Otter
Bay
North

Pender

Port Browning

Island

K

Plumper Sound

South
Pender Island

R
Bedwell Harbour

Swanson Channel

Tilley Pt

Above: From the air, looking north, Otter Bay Marina is located in the northwest corner of the cove, adjacent to where anchoring is most sought. It becomes shallow near the shore, to the right as you approach the marina. Anchorage within the exposed bay is also possible most times in summer provided there is no wind forecast for westerly blows. Going ashore to access the marina facilities during busy summer periods when the docks are full is acceptable, but check with the operators first, as a fee for landing may be in effect.

Below: Slowly easing through the Pender Canal. Watch for boats approaching from the opposite direction. Observe the five knot speed limit and navigate carefully as close to mid channel as possible. The 28' low tide height of the bridge limits the passage of sailboats. Shark Cove lies beyond.

Horton Bay anchorage with the public dock in lower, centre foreground.

Horton Bay

Charts 3313, 3477, 3442

Access

Access to Horton Bay is through Bennett Bay from the Strait of Georgia or via Georgeson Passage past Lizard Island from the south. Mind the current and a reef marked by kelp at the south entrance. There is a public float in Horton Bay which is often filled with boats of all types, derelict to functional. If you want to go ashore and access the island this is a good point to do so, although there are no facilities at the head of the dock. Anchorage in the bay is safe, but be mindful of the currents, especially during the off slack periods and in the passages approaching the anchorage. Best anchorage away from the current, is to the northwest in the shallows. Use a large scale chart for safe passage into the bay. It is also possible to find temporary anchorage in **Campbell Bay**. This bay is sheltered from northerly and northwesterly winds, but avoid it in southerlies and southeasterlies.

Irish Bay

Charts 3313, 3477, 3442

Access

The bay forms a major indentation into Samuel Island. Nearby at Winter Cove, Saturna Island, is a route through Boat Passage from the Strait of Georgia. This is not a passage to be taken lightly. It is suitable for small craft only and navigation should be done in keeping with the right chart and tidal and current information.

Irish Bay is a good but open anchorage exposed to southerly winds. Anchorage is temporary in the southeast section with the northern portion providing daytime stopping in good conditions. The anchorage can be suitable in summer for overnight or prolonged stays.

Irish Bay and adjacent waters. Beware of Minx Reef (centre right) on approach to the bay. Boot Cove entrance can bee seen at upper right.

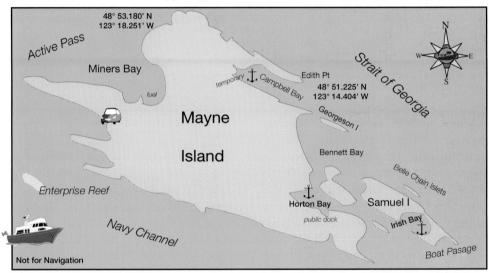

48° 53.180' N
123° 18.251' W

Active Pass

Miners Bay

fuel

Mayne

Island

Enterprise Reef

Navy Channel

temporary — Campbell Bay

Edith Pt
48° 51.225' N
123° 14.404' W

Georgeson I

Bennett Bay

Horton Bay

public dock

Samuel I

Belle Chain Islets

Irish Bay

Boat Passage

Strait of Georgia

N
W — E
S

Not for Navigation

Not for Navigation

Strait of Georgia

Salt
Spring
Island

Sidney

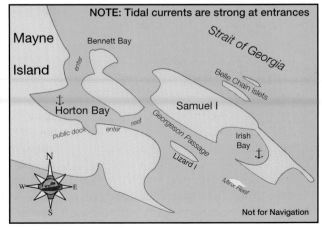

NOTE: Tidal currents are strong at entrances

Mayne

Island

enter

Bennett Bay

Horton Bay

public dock   enter

reef

Strait of Georgia

Belle Chain Islets

Samuel I

Georgeson Passage

Lizard I

Irish
Bay

Minx Reef

N
W — E
S

Not for Navigation

Winter Cove. Boat Passage at centre, top. Inset: The lamb barbecue. Opposite, centre: Boot Cove and anchored in Winter Cove during the annual lamb barbecue on Canada Day.

Winter Cove
Charts 3313, 3477, 3422

Access
Easiest access is from inside the Gulf Islands rather than from the Strait of Georgia. Vessels cruising to Winter Cove on Saturna Island are advised to use Active Pass or other waterways into the islands when entering from the Strait as Boat Passage entrance is tricky and intimidating, especially to new mariners. The large scale chart should be referred to when transitting the passage. Mind the reefs on the outside.

The Park and Anchorage
Although Winter Cove is exposed to winds from the northwest, and is extremely shallow at places it affords protected anchorage for limited periods. Open grassy stretches and shady adjacent woods provide a picturesque setting for this park. It is used frequently as a picnic spot by ferry passengers, cyclists and kayakers. Overnight anchoring should be planned carefully according to wind forecasts. No camping.

Nearby
Lyall Harbour is an open anchorage preferred by larger vessels. Saturna Landing has fuel and short visits are permitted while going ashore for post office, general store or restaurant/pub. Temporary anchorage can be found in **Irish Bay** or **Boot Cove** (strong winds enter the cove). Stop at the dock or anchor off in Plumper Sound to visit the Saturna Vineyards.

Park facilities
Anchorage, picnic tables, drinking water, toilets, hiking, kayaking. Walking trails.

Boot Cove
At the west end of Saturna Island Boot Cove offers protected anchorage, although strong gusts of wind are known to cause some anxiety. The limited fetch within the cove reduces any sizeable waves, making overnight stays potentially comfortable. Many private docks surround the cove.

Samuel
Island

Strait of Georgia

Russel Reef

Boat Passage

Winter Cove

Winter Cove
Marine Park

Saturna Island

anchorage
48° 48.564' N
123° 11.680' W

Winter Cove, Saturna Island

Not for Navigation

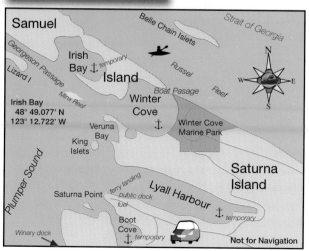

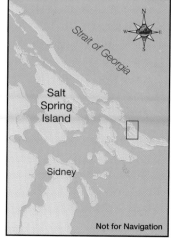

Samuel

Belle Chain Islets

Strait of Georgia

Georgeson Passage

Lizard I

Irish
Bay ⌑ temporary

Island

Russel Reef

Boat Passage

Minx Reef

Irish Bay
48° 49.077' N
123° 12.722' W

Winter
Cove

Veruna
Bay

King
Islets

Winter Cove
Marine Park

Plumper Sound

Saturna
Island

ferry landing

Saturna Point

Lyall Harbour

public dock

fuel

⌑ temporary

Boot
Cove

⌑ temporary

Winery dock

Not for Navigation

Strait of Georgia

Salt
Spring
Island

Sidney

Not for Navigation

Above: Cabbage Island with Tumbo Island, Tumbo Channel and East Point beyond. The anchorage lies in the lee of Cabbage Island. Patos and Sucia islands in the San Juans are close by.

Cabbage Island

Charts 3313, 3441

Access

The island is located off Tumbo Island to the northeast and Saturna Island to the east. Entrance to the anchorage in Reef Harbour is from the Strait of Georgia or Tumbo Channel. Regular visitors use the channel and cut between the kelp patches at the northwest tip of Tumbo. Do so with much caution and use the large scale chart. *Waggoner* reports easy access to the anchorage by crossing the reef on the Tumbo Channel side and passing between two patches of kelp near the north end of Tumbo Island.

The Park and Anchorage

It is safe to stop in fair weather on the south side of the island where mooring buoys have been placed. The anchorage is somewhat exposed to winds from the east and northwest, but the sandy beaches, swimming and sunbathing makes this park a popular one. There are facilities for camping and picnics. Camp fees are in effect.

Nearby

Saturna Island has interesting features and, at the north end, a dock for fuel and access ashore where there is a general store, post office, restaurant and other facilities. The BC Ferry Service has a landing at Saturna Island.

Park facilities 10 mooring buoys, camp sites, picnic tables, toilets, beach, fishing, kayaking, scuba diving. No water available.

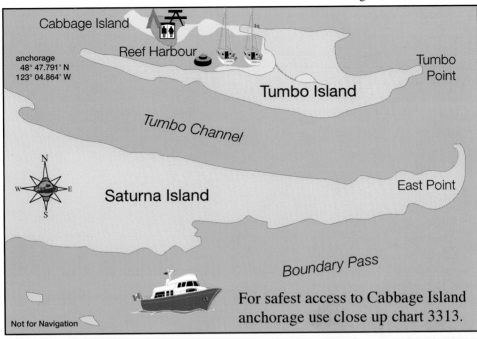

Cabbage Island

anchorage
48° 47.791' N
123° 04.864' W

Reef Harbour

Tumbo Island

Tumbo Point

Tumbo Channel

N
W E
S

Saturna Island

East Point

Boundary Pass

For safest access to Cabbage Island anchorage use close up chart 3313.

Not for Navigation

Nanaimo

Silva Bay

Degnen Bay
Gabriola Pass

Vancouver

Pirates
Cove

Valdes Island

Porlier Pass

Ladysmith

Telegraph
Harbour

Wallace I

Island

Galiano Island

Strait of Georgia

N
W E
S

This diagram shows the location of Cabbage Island.
It is just off the southern tip of Saturna Island. See the
author's *Gulf Islands Cruising Guide* for more information. Other popular anchorages in the Gulf Islands
covered in the preceeding and following pages are shown
on this overview diagram.

Not for Navigation

Long Harbour

Montague
Harbour

Active Pass

Salt
Spring
Island

Ganges

Mayne Island

Maple
Bay

Saturna Island

Genoa Bay

Otter
Bay

Port Browning

Strait of Georgia

Salt
Spring
Island

Cowichan

Portland
Island

Bedwell
Harbour

Sidney

Pender Islands

N
W E
S

Sidney

Boundary Pass

73

Montague Harbour

Gulf Islands

Access

The harbour is located on the west side of southern Galiano Island. Entrance is from Trincomali Channel from the south through the passage between Julia Island and Phillimore Point, or from the north on the Galiano side of Parker Island.

BC Ferries operates a regular stop at Sturdies Bay in Active Pass on Galiano Island. Ferries run from Swartz Bay on Vancouver Island and from Mayne, North Pender and Saturna Islands as well as from Tsawwassen south of Vancouver.

The Park and Anchorage

Montague Harbour Marine Park is one of the most popular anchorages in the Gulf Islands. It has moorage and anchoring in a well protected bay, and a dock for small boats and dinghies. A marine interpretive centre is located on the water, with summer viewing of marine life and park staff on hand at weekends in July and August. Sunbathing and swimming are ideal at the sandy beaches in the harbour and on the north side of Gray Peninsula. This latter promontory is a fairly heavily forested piece of land connected to Galiano Island by a narrow isthmus, with trails to scenic locations.

Campsite reservations: 1-800-689-9025 or 604-689-9025.

Nearby

A full service marina is located a short distance across the harbour. It has fresh produce, groceries and other supplies as well as a coffee shop and patio. There are also books, gifts and souvenirs. At the dock, moorage, fuels and oils, and kayak rentals are available. Good scuba diving (by charter boat is recommended) in Active Pass and at nearby Enterprise Reef. Whaler Bay–see following pages.

Park facilities 26 mooring buoys, boat/dinghy dock, 15 walk-in and 14 vehicle accessible campsites, picnic tables, drinking water, toilets, park host, beach hiking, kayaking, scuba diving, viewpoint/point of interest, boat launching, swimming.

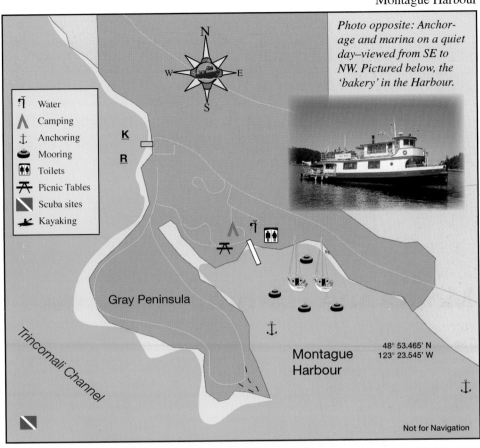

Photo opposite: Anchorage and marina on a quiet day–viewed from SE to NW. Pictured below, the 'bakery' in the Harbour.

🚰	Water
🏕	Camping
⚓	Anchoring
⚓	Mooring
🚻	Toilets
🏓	Picnic Tables
🚩	Scuba sites
🛶	Kayaking

K
R

Gray Peninsula

Trincomali Channel

Montague Harbour

48° 53.465' N
123° 23.545' W

Not for Navigation

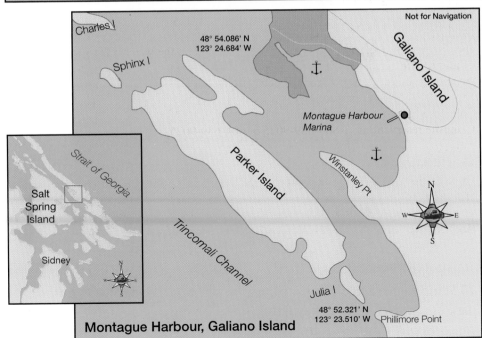

Not for Navigation

Charles I

Sphinx I

48° 54.086' N
123° 24.684' W

Galiano Island

Montague Harbour Marina

Parker Island

Winstanley Pt

Strait of Georgia

Salt Spring Island

Sidney

Trincomali Channel

Julia I

48° 52.321' N
123° 23.510' W

Phillimore Point

Montague Harbour, Galiano Island

Ganges Harbour at the end of a summer weekend–marinas are emptying and the anchorage is less crowded.

Ganges

Charts 3313, 3478, 3442

Access and Anchorage

Ganges Harbour is entered from Trincomali Channel between Salt Spring Island and Prevost Island, when coming from points such as Porlier Pass or Active Pass (or from Montague Harbour). Coming from points south it is entered after rounding Beaver Point on the east of Salt Spring Island. It faces North Pender Island across Swanson Channel. The harbour is a windy piece of water and although many vessels moor there it is a place to anchor temporarily. During summer there can be many tranquil nights anchored in the harbour, but just as many windy nights, with the breeze picking up in the afternoons. Best bet is to book moorage at one of the marinas or stay at a nearby more protected cove, perhaps at Prevost Island, for the night and visit Ganges in the morning. Monitor the weather for the wind prediction, and if you have a comfortable boat with good gound tackle, stay in the harbour overnight, but be mindful of the potential for a disturbed sleep. The town has much to offer and it is a most worthwhile place to visit.

Madrona Bay

Chart 3313

If you cannot find moorage at a suitable marina on Salt Spring Island you may want to anchor out in the harbour, or for more protection, around the corner in **Madrona Bay**. Across the harbour, **Walter Bay** offers some limited anchorage sheltered from southeast winds. Beware of rocks when navigating through Madrona Bay.

Long Harbour

Chart 3313

Opening into the southeast end of Salt Spring Island this harbour accommodates a ferry terminal as well as a yacht club facility. Farther up the inlet from these two entities is a widening bay with a good protected anchorage in shallow water. Consideration should be given to the boats and homes of local residents.

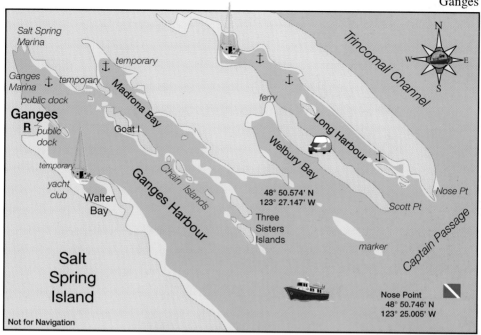

Salt Spring
Marina

Ganges
Marina
temporary

public dock

Ganges

R public
dock

temporary

yacht
club

Walter
Bay

temporary

Madrona Bay

Goat I

Chain Islands

Ganges Harbour

Trincomali Channel

ferry

Long Harbour

Welbury Bay

48° 50.574' N
123° 27.147' W

Three
Sisters
Islands

marker

Scott Pt

Nose Pt

Captain Passage

**Salt
Spring
Island**

Nose Point
48° 50.746' N
123° 25.005' W

Not for Navigation

*There are anchoring
sites near Ganges such
as Selby Cove (Prevost
Island) or Walter Bay
(Salt Spring Island), that
are not protected from all
winds. Ganges Harbour
itself is subject to occasional severe wind condi-
tions and when they come
in from the southeast you
could be in for a night of
anchor watch duty.
There is good anchor-
age at Prevost Island
in Annette Inlet or at
Glenthorne Passage (see
following pages).*

Strait of Georgia

Salt
Spring
Island

Sidney

Looking across Annette Inlet and, to its right, Glenthorne Passage on Prevost Island. This is a convenient anchorage for excursions to Ganges in a small runabout.

Prevost Island

Charts 3313, 3442, 3478

Access

Captain Passage lies across the west side of Prevost Island and grants access to the protected anchorages of Annette Inlet and Glenthorne Passage. They are among the most protected anchorages in the Gulf Islands.

Annette Inlet

The large opening into Prevost that is Annette Inlet is gained after passage past an unmarked drying rock at the entrance. Mild winds blow through Annette Inlet sometimes and it is most comfortable to anchor in the lee of the land where possible. There is a drying bay at the far eastern end of Annette Inlet.

Glenthorne Passage

This popular overnight mooring has good anchorage in the muddy shallows in the cove at its eastern end. Anchoring is also possible between Prevost Island and Secret Island.

The entrance is via the opening between Owl Island and Secret Island or from the northwest of Owl Island. Anchoring here will not impede the passage of boats as this is not actually a through route for boats. An alternative for reaching the east cove is by squeezing between Glenthorne Point and the rock just west of it. This is passable at high or low tides but it is best only for smaller boats and during slack water. Although we have always experienced complete protection, some mariners have reported windy conditions in Glenthorne Passage have kept them up at night.

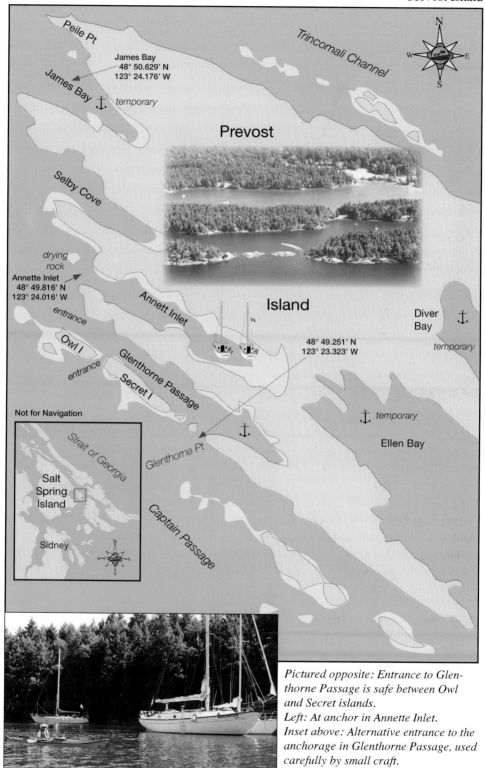

Peile Pt

James Bay
48° 50.629' N
123° 24.176' W

Trincomali Channel

N
W   E
S

James Bay ⚓ *temporary*

Prevost

Selby Cove

drying rock

Annette Inlet
48° 49.816' N
123° 24.016' W

Annett Inlet

Island

Diver
Bay ⚓

entrance

48° 49.251' N
123° 23.323' W

temporary

Owl I

Glenthorne Passage

entrance

Secret I

⚓ *temporary*

Ellen Bay

Not for Navigation

⚓

Glenthorne Pt

Strait of Georgia

Salt
Spring
Island

Sidney

N
W   E
S

Captain Passage

Pictured opposite: Entrance to Glenthorne Passage is safe between Owl and Secret islands.
Left: At anchor in Annette Inlet.
Inset above: Alternative entrance to the anchorage in Glenthorne Passage, used carefully by small craft.

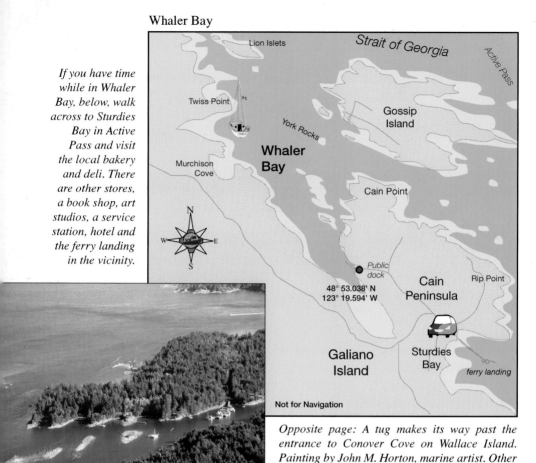

If you have time while in Whaler Bay, below, walk across to Sturdies Bay in Active Pass and visit the local bakery and deli. There are other stores, a book shop, art studios, a service station, hotel and the ferry landing in the vicinity.

Lion Islets

Strait of Georgia

Active Pass

Twiss Point

Gossip Island

York Rocks

Whaler Bay

Murchison Cove

Cain Point

N

W — E

S

Public dock

48° 53.038' N
123° 19.594' W

Cain Peninsula

Rip Point

Galiano Island

Sturdies Bay

ferry landing

Not for Navigation

Opposite page: A tug makes its way past the entrance to Conover Cove on Wallace Island. Painting by John M. Horton, marine artist. Other works by John M. Horton are featured in the 2007 art book Mariner Artist John M. Horton.

Charts 3313, 3473, 3442

Whaler Bay

Access

Entrance off the Strait of Georgia is between Gossip Island and Lion Islets just northwest of Active Pass. It can be entered also from Active Pass between Gossip Island and Cain Peninsula.

Anchorage

If you are trying to cross the Strait of Georgia from Active Pass but are delayed due to sea conditions, you have several choices: Go back through the pass to Montague Harbour, Prevost Island, Pender Island or Salt Spring Island, or remain on the Strait of Georgia side of the Pass and linger at Whaler Bay on Galiano Island.

This bay has a small public dock which is often occupied by commercial vessels, as well as those belonging to local residents. But there is protected anchorage in the north part of Whaler Bay. It is generally taken in a curving bight on the Galiano shore, opposite the top end of Cain Peninsula. There are reefs and rocks throughout the bay, and a large scale chart is necessary for safe passage and for finding a suitable mooring spot. Space is sometimes available at the public dock.

Wallace Island

Charts 3313, 3442

Access

Cruising northwards up Trincomali Channel from the direction of Active Pass you arrive at Wallace Island, lying between Galiano Island and Salt Spring Island. From Porlier Pass, travel south between Reid and Hall Islands, pass between Norway and Mowgli Islands north of the Secretary Islands, and down Houston Passage past Jackscrew Island. There are rocks and reefs to beware of in the vicinity. A large scale chart is recommended. Reefs running parallel to Wallace Island form a breakwater to the entrances of **Princess Cove** and **Conover Cove.** Use caution entering these coves, minding the drying reefs at the entrance to Princess Cove. Good anchorage for a fair number of boats can be found at Princess Bay, while Conover Cove is a tight squeeze for only a few.

The Park and Anchorage

An extremely popular and desirable stop in the Gulf Islands, Wallace Island Marine Park is a superb place for those wanting to go ashore and walk. It has pathways winding through the woods to either end of the island with magnificent views over Trincomali Channel and Houston Passage. Grassy landings, camping and picnic sites are prominent features of this idyllic island. No fires are allowed on shore and some private waterfront property is located near or adjacent to the landings. Camping and mooring fees are in effect.

Nearby

Thetis Island has marinas and services which can be accessed by voyaging north around Thetis or south around Kuper Island, or through the shallow passage known as The Cut off Clam Bay between the two islands. Another anchorage that many favour, can be found opening onto Trincomali Channel, in the **Secretary Islands.**

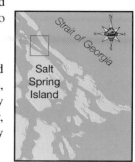

Strait of Georgia

Salt Spring Island

Above: The dock and anchorage at Conover Cove. Below: Anchored in Princess Cove.

Conover Cove

Charts 3313, 3442

Conover Cove with its historic landing and walking paths was once the private home of writer David Conover whose novels *Once Upon an Island* and *One Man's Island* have intrigued readers for decades. The docks in the cove are limited in space but assure access ashore by dinghy, if you are anchored in the cove. Trails run the length of the island and provide good walking and exercise. The grounds and docks are maintained by K2 Park Services, and the park is visited regularly by a member of the Parks Branch staff. Visit the historic Conover Cabin built in 1889. Visitors make use of a picnic shelter built in the 1930s and now adorned with driftwood art.

Park facilities

Boat/dinghy dock, 20 walk-in camp-sites, picnic tables, drinking water, toilets, park host, beach, hiking, fish-ing, recommended kayaking, scuba diving, viewpoint/point of interest.

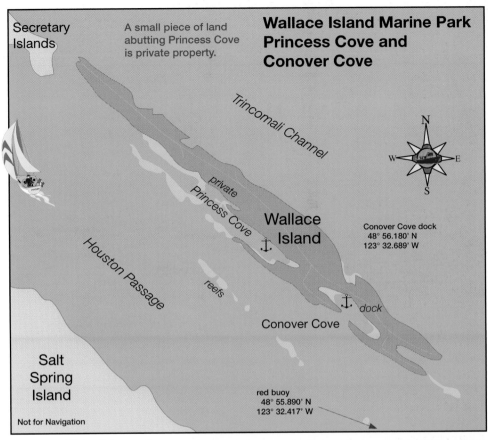

Secretary Islands

A small piece of land abutting Princess Cove is private property.

Wallace Island Marine Park Princess Cove and Conover Cove

Trincomali Channel

N
W E
S

Conover Cove dock
48° 56.180' N
123° 32.689' W

private
Princess Cove

Wallace Island

Houston Passage

reefs

Conover Cove

dock

Salt Spring Island

red buoy
48° 55.890' N
123° 32.417' W

Not for Navigation

Right: Princess Cove. There are reefs extending beyond the entrance. North of the reef in Houston Passage, align abeam of the point at the entrance to Princess Cove to enter. Allow for the shallows off the point.

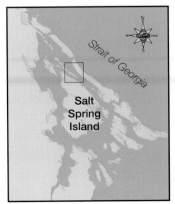

N
W E
S

Strait of Georgia

Salt Spring Island

Opposite: Wallace Island. Above: Trincomali Channel looking southeast over the Secretary Islands and Wallace Island. There is a small anchorage between the Secretaries, far right. Princess Cove on Wallace Island lies beyond. In the foreground is the tip of Hall Island with Galiano Island to the left.
Left: North Cove on Thetis Island is sheltered from south and southwesterly winds.
Below: Preedy Harbour on Thetis Island.

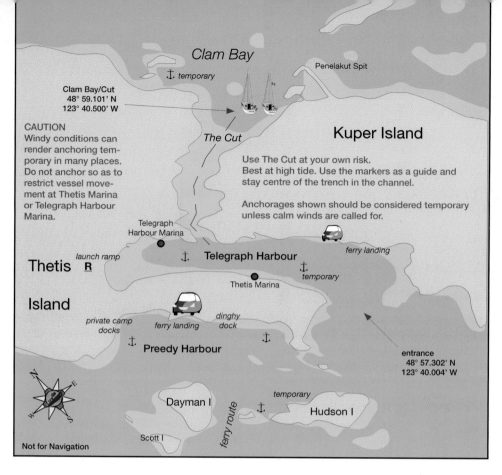

Clam Bay

Penelakut Spit

Clam Bay/Cut
48° 59.101' N
123° 40.500' W

⚓ temporary

CAUTION
Windy conditions can
render anchoring tem-
porary in many places.
Do not anchor so as to
restrict vessel move-
ment at Thetis Marina
or Telegraph Harbour
Marina.

The Cut

Kuper Island

Use The Cut at your own risk.
Best at high tide. Use the markers as a guide and
stay centre of the trench in the channel.

Anchorages shown should be considered temporary
unless calm winds are called for.

Telegraph
Harbour Marina

ferry landing

launch ramp

Thetis **R**

⚓ Telegraph Harbour

⚓ temporary

Thetis Marina

Island

private camp
docks

ferry landing

dinghy
dock

⚓ Preedy Harbour

⚓

entrance
48° 57.302' N
123° 40.004' W

temporary

Dayman I

⚓

Hudson I

ferry route

Scott I

Not for Navigation

Telegraph Harbour

Charts 3313, 3477,
3442, 3443

Access

Vessels approaching the anchorage at Telegraph Harbour from the direction of Porlier
Pass can use The Cut, which is very shallow, as a short cut, or travel around the north end
of Thetis or the south end of Kuper. The latter is the longer route. No matter which way
you go, beware of rocks, reefs and shallows. Use a large scale chart.

Anchorage

Sheltered moorage in Telegraph Harbour is excellent. There are boats at private mooring
buoys throughout summer. The two local marinas offer moorage with services which
include power, limited water, showers, laundry, pub, general store, fuel, post office, restaurant and much more. These are available to guests mooring overnight at the marinas.
Mariners anchored out may access Thetis Marina or Telegraph Harbour Marina by dinghy in order to visit the stores, pub/restaurant and '50s style cafe. Please note that the
Gulf Islands have limited water supplies and restricted garbage disposal. Do not expect
marinas to supply water, showers or laundry services other than to their paying moorage
guests and then on a limited basis. There is a regular ferry service from Thetis Island to
Chemainus where you will find banks, groceries, restaurants, all in a quaint tourist town
renown for its exquisite murals. Refer also to ***Docks and Destinations***.

Arriving in Preedy Harbour, there is temporary anchorage near the reef that runs alongside the ferry passage between Dayman and Hudson Islands. Or anchor near the dock northwest of the ferry landing. There is a dinghy dock nearby with more temporary anchorage southeast of it.

Preedy Harbour

Often overlooked due to the better known shelter of Telegraph Harbour, Preedy is a good anchorage with spectacular scenery. There are some hazards to be mindful of when entering Preedy Harbour so consult a large scale chart. The ferry from Chemainus lands in the harbour so expect the occasional but mild wash from passing vessels. The best anchorage is located in the north end of the harbour, but another caution: read the signs ashore for submarine cables.

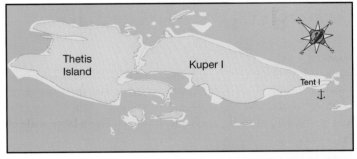

Not for Navigation

Clam Bay

Some vessels will stop and anchor in Clam Bay while waiting for the tide to rise to enable safe passage through The Cut to Telegraph Harbour. Many use Clam Bay as a destination. It is subject to some wind conditions but summertime breezes rarely cause difficulty for boats at anchor. Favour the southeast shore of the bay. It is shallow with a sandy bottom adjacent to Kuper Island. I have seen small vessels beached on Kuper, but it is a reserve and should be respected as such.

Above: Clam Bay, its sandy beach at Penelakut Spit, and the entrance to The Cut, tidal passage to Telegraph Harbour from Clam Bay.
Left: Boats anchored in Tent Island off the south end of Kuper Island. This is a sheltered anchorage in most conditions in summer.
Below: Preedy Harbour showing ferry landing and dinghy dock, and approaches.
Bottom: Telegraph Harbour looking west, with anchorage east of Thetis Marina. Telegraph Harbour Marina lies beyond.

Opposite page: Sibell Bay, on the approaches to Ladysmith Harbour. Anchorage is taken behind the islands in the foreground, seen also in the inset photograph. Many mariners make their way into the harbour and moor at the public and private docks.

Ladysmith Harbour

Charts 3313, 3475, 3443

Access

The harbour opens off Stuart Channel which washes the east shore of Vancouver Island and the western shores of Thetis and Kuper Islands.

Anchorage

Although windy, there are several spots that are somewhat protected. These are in the lee of some of the rocky islets and reefs that run close along the outer shores of the harbour. Enter the anchorage through **Sibell Bay** and tuck in next to the most southern of the Duns-vmuir Islands. Take care and use a large scale chart for navigating into the cove. Respect private and native reserve property. For secure overnight stays in this harbour try for moorage at Page Point Lodge or the public dock at Ladysmith.

There is a great deal to see and do at Ladysmith. To go ashore and readily reach the town it is easiest to tie up at the substantial public dock to port as you pass the narrows at the harbour entrance. Up town you will find all services from banks to post office, supermarket, bakery, hardware and marine, some located in historic buildings dating back to the turn of the century (19th-20th). The town was named for Ladysmith in South Africa and has seen the days of the importance of coal mining in the early part of the century give way to the lumber industry.

There are beach areas along the substantial shores of the harbour, a couple of launch ramps and park areas with walking paths. The island highway runs along the shore between the harbour and the town so take care crossing the road to reach the shopping centres.

Whaleboat Island

Charts 3313, 3443

Access

This island is tucked in behind the south end of Ruxton Island. It is in the northern section of Whaleboat Passage and appears unnamed on charts up to recent editions. The group of islands in which it is located, lies between Stuart Channel and Pylades Channel. There is limited anchorage in the shelter of Whaleboat Island and a fair number of boats use the passage to travel between Pylades and Stuart Channels. The location is a short distance north inside Porlier Pass, or south of Gabriola Island.

The Park and Anchorage

This is an undeveloped marine park but has been maintained in its pristine condition, representing the best of the natural state of the Gulf Islands. Some mariners use the narrow pass between Ruxton Island and Whaleboat for anchorage while others prefer the more open area south of a shallow reef nearby. The anchorage is temporary.

Nearby

Pirates Cove Provincial Marine Park is a short distance north and beyond Ruxton Island on De Courcy Island. This is a popular anchorage and a good preferred alternative to Whaleboat Marine Park. Beyond Pirates Cove one can easily reach Silva Bay with its many facilities, or Degnen Bay for a good anchorage. In good weather there is also suitable anchorage at Herring Bay at the north tip of Ruxton Island.

Park facilities

Recommended kayaking. No Mooring. No anchorage. Temporary stop in sheltered passage and adjacent cove. Watch currents and wind conditions. There are no facilities at this park.

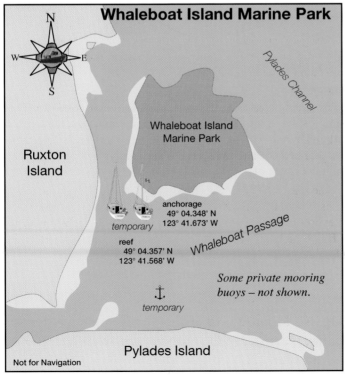

Whaleboat Island Marine Park

N
W • E
S

Whaleboat Island
Marine Park

Pylades Channel

Ruxton
Island

anchorage
49° 04.348' N
123° 41.673' W

temporary

reef
49° 04.357' N
123° 41.568' W

Whaleboat Passage

*Some private mooring
buoys – not shown.*

⚓
temporary

Pylades Island

Not for Navigation

*Above and opposite:
Views of the anchorage
at Whaleboat Island. The
one above shows Whale-
boat Passage that passes
from Stuart Channel to
Pylades Channel west to
east. The anchorage is
considered temporary but
is used readily when wind
forecasts are favourable.*

N
W • E
S

Strait of Georgia

Salt
Spring
Island

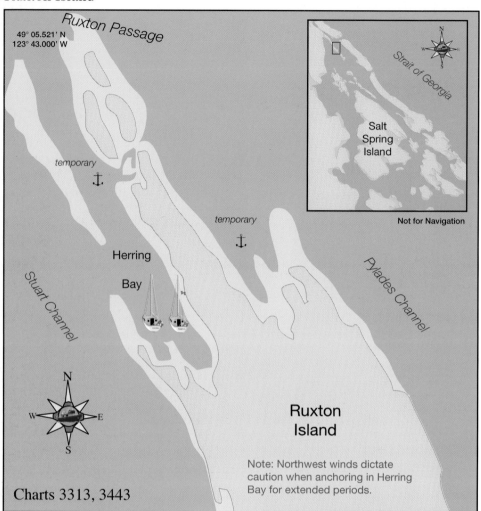

49° 05.521' N
123° 43.000' W

Ruxton Passage

temporary ⚓

Salt
Spring
Island

Strait of Georgia

Not for Navigation

Herring

Bay

temporary ⚓

Stuart Channel

Pylades Channel

N
W E
S

Ruxton
Island

Note: Northwest winds dictate
caution when anchoring in Herring
Bay for extended periods.

Charts 3313, 3443

Herring Bay

Access and Anchorage

Anchor in the bay at the north end of Ruxton Island. It faces onto Ruxton Passage south of De Courcy Island and can be reached from Stuart Channel or Pylades Channel.

Nearby

Anchorages are available at Pirates Cove Marine Park on De Courcy Island, or Degnen Bay off Gabriola Passage to the north at the north end of Pylades Channel. Just beyond Degnen Bay and through Gabriola Pass is Silva Bay where facilities are available for fuel, moorage and supplies.

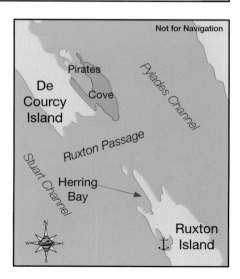

Not for Navigation

De
Courcy
Island

Pirates

Cove

Pylades Channel

Ruxton Passage

Stuart Channel

Herring
Bay

N
W E
S

Ruxton
⚓ Island

Ruxton Island

Herring Bay, at the north end of Ruxton Island, is not only a popular anchorage but also it is considered overflow anchorage for the nearby Pirates Cove. The photos show the anchorage from the water (above) and the east (below). The entrance faces northwest onto Ruxton Passage. Right: Another anchorage lies south of Herring Bay on the west side of the island.

A busy anchorage, Pirates Cove is a popular destination for mariners. It is one of the better known anchorages and marine parks and includes dinghy docks for shore access.

Pirates Cove

Charts 3313, 3443, 3475

Access

The cove is located at the southeast end of De Courcy Island facing onto Pylades Channel. This is also the point of entry into the cove, but care should be taken as there is a reef extending beyond the breakwater. In summer this usually has a telltale covering of kelp. A white marker on shore also reveals where the reef ends. In the entrance, as the narrow passage widens, there is another reef to starboard. Ensure that you pass this submerged rock before turning into the cove, keeping slightly east of centre channel. Directly ahead is where anchorage is popular and where a dinghy dock is located. There are private docks in the cove. Use a chart and watch your depth as well as the waters ahead of you as you navigate.

The Park and Anchorage

It is deeper in the east side of the cove and it is best for boats with a deeper draft not to anchor in the shallows. If you do so at high tide you may wind up touching bottom at low water. The small dinghy docks allow access ashore. These docks should not be used for moorage other than for dinghies. If the anchorage becomes crowded additional anchorage is available at nearby Whaleboat Island, which is also a marine park. Pirates Cove Marine Park itself is extensive and includes walking trails. It has drinking water and there are toilets. Picnicking and camping are popular. There is a trail to a beach area facing Ruxton Passage, and amenities for camping and picnicking. This has been a major marine park

continued on page 96

Park facilities

Dinghy dock, 12 walk-in campsites, picnic tables, drinking water, toilets, park host, beach, hiking, recommended kayaking, viewpoint/point of interest.

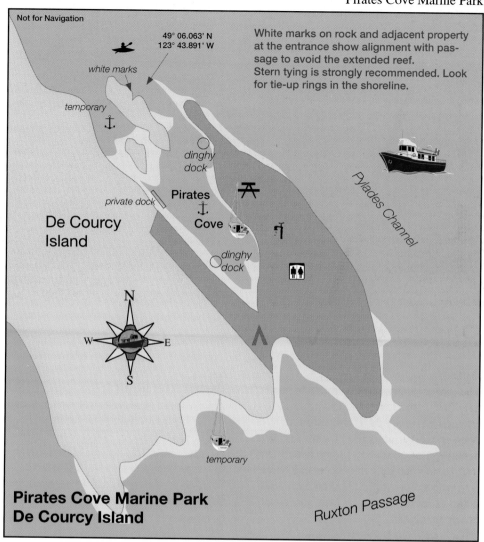

Not for Navigation

49° 06.063' N
123° 43.891' W

white marks

temporary

dinghy dock

Pirates

Cove

private dock

De Courcy
Island

dinghy dock

White marks on rock and adjacent property at the entrance show alignment with passage to avoid the extended reef.
Stern tying is strongly recommended. Look for tie-up rings in the shoreline.

Pylades Channel

N
W   E
S

temporary

Pirates Cove Marine Park
De Courcy Island

Ruxton Passage

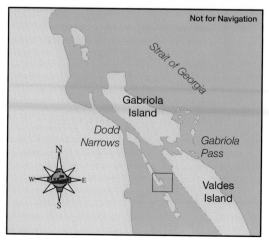

Not for Navigation

Strait of Georgia

Gabriola
Island

Dodd
Narrows

Gabriola
Pass

N
W   E
S

Valdes
Island

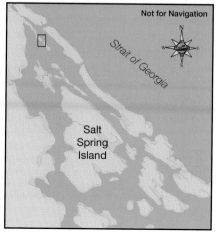

Not for Navigation

Strait of Georgia

N
W   E
S

Salt
Spring
Island

Degnen Bay

Charts 3313, 3475, 3443

After leaving Pirates Cove Marine Park your northbound choices are Dodd Narrows and the city of Nanaimo or Gabriola Passage and the community of Silva Bay. Many mariners travel through to Silva Bay taking Gabriola at the slack and completely miss the protected anchorage at Degnen Bay. That's perfectly acceptable as it leaves it less crowded for those who prefer to keep it that way.

Degnen Bay is near Silva Bay by road as well as through Gabriola Pass by boat. It's a good, sheltered but small anchorage surrounded with private docks. There is not a great deal of room in the bay for anchoring and most yachtsmen simply forego stopping there in favour of the larger anchorage at Silva Bay.

If you do get to stop at Degnen Bay, however, go ashore by dinghy and dock at the public wharf. There is quick and easy access to the road on the island for walking.

Nearby

Two anchorages which range from fair to good are at **Wakes Cove** on the inside of Gabriola Pass and **Dogfish Bay** in the lee of Kendrick Island. Wakes Cove is quite open and therefore somewhat exposed to the wind and some passing traffic wash. A dinghy dock is located in the curve of the bay for shore access. Dogfish Bay is small and subject to a fair amount of current due to the opening at the south end of Kendrick Island.

Pirates Cove *from page 94*

from page 94

for a long time. The cove's chequered history includes the settlement on the island of the infamous Brother Twelve who was known to have coerced crew, and especially wives, to remain on the island leaving their vessels to sail off without them.

Nearby

Anchorages at Herring Bay on Ruxton Island, just off Ruxton Passage to the south of De Courcy Island, or at Degnen Bay off Gabriola Passage to the north at the top end of

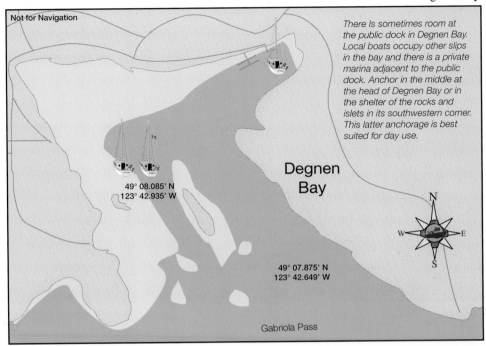

There Is sometimes room at the public dock in Degnen Bay. Local boats occupy other slips in the bay and there is a private marina adjacent to the public dock. Anchor in the middle at the head of Degnen Bay or in the shelter of the rocks and islets in its southwestern corner. This latter anchorage is best suited for day use.

Charts 3313, 3475, 3443

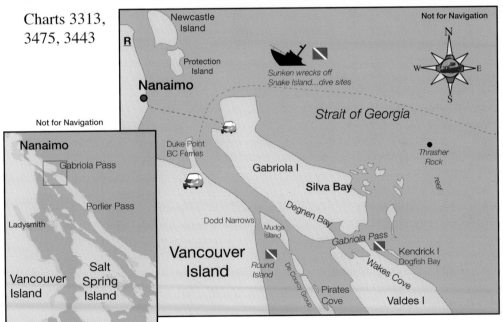

Pylades Channel. Just beyond Degnen Bay and through Gabriola Pass is Silva Bay, a popular anchorage, where facilities include moorage, fuel and supplies.

Visitors are fascinated to learn of the dubious history of Pirates Cove.
Read *Canada's False Prophet* by H.E. Wilson.

Silva Bay

Charts 3313, 3475, 3443

Access

Silva Bay is reached by mariners crossing the Strait of Georgia from the Lower Mainland (Vancouver) via Thrasher Rock on the outside of Tugboat Island. The entrance to the bay is usually through the passage between Tugboat Island and Acorn Island, although passage can be made between Acorn and Gaviola around Vance Island. Vessels approaching from Gabriola Passage (Degnen Bay) can slip into Silva Bay via the narrow, shallow waterway between Gabriola Island and Sear Island.

When entering Silva Bay through the Tugboat route be mindful of Shipyard Rock just inside the entrance. It needs to be cleared before turning into the bay. Many have turned too soon and run aground. It is marked and clearly shown on local charts.

Anchorages

When headed across the Strait of Georgia in the direction of Howe Sound or Vancouver, or if you are continuing straight up the coast of Vancouver Island you might want to stop on the edge of the Strait to await suitable weather. Degnen Bay or Silva Bay are the usual places to anchor. Most people know Silva Bay, as it is also the first anchorage you arrive at when crossing the Strait in the opposite direction. It is also known for its marinas and stores, craft shops and historic shipyards. The Royal Vancouver Yacht Club has a station in Silva Bay on Tugboat Island. There is a fuel dock at Page's Marina as well as one at Silva Bay Marina.

Anchor anywhere in the bay clear of obstructions and a reasonable distance away from the marinas. But keep a careful wind watch as it has been known to blow strongly in Silva Bay, enough to cause alarming instances of anchor dragging.

Stop for fuel at Page's Marina at the south end of Silva Bay and visit their quaint store.
At the larger marina there is a pub and sometimes other facilities, depending on the time of the year. Nearby, a waterfront store at Silva Bay Inn sells groceries and other supplies for mariners. Across the bay at Tugboat Island is the Royal Vancouver Yacht Club's private facility.

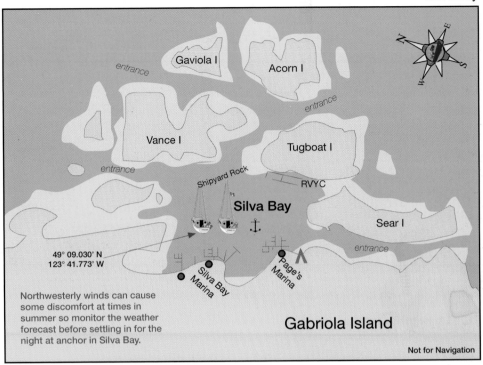

Gaviola I

Acorn I

entrance

entrance

Vance I

Tugboat I

Shipyard Rock

RVYC

Silva Bay

Sear I

entrance

49° 09.030' N
123° 41.773' W

Silva Bay Marina

Page's Marina

Northwesterly winds can cause
some discomfort at times in
summer so monitor the weather
forecast before settling in for the
night at anchor in Silva Bay.

Gabriola Island

Not for Navigation

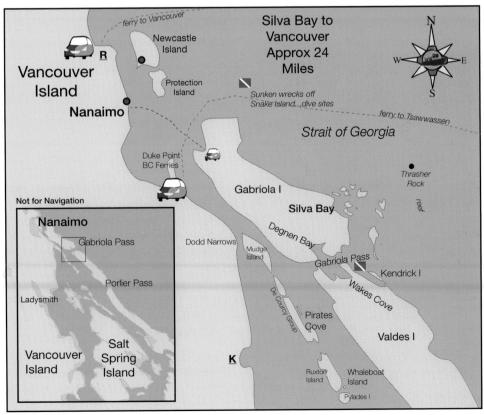

ferry to Vancouver

Newcastle Island

Silva Bay to Vancouver Approx 24 Miles

Vancouver Island

R

Protection Island

Nanaimo

Sunken wrecks off
Snake Island...dive sites

ferry to Tsawwassen

Strait of Georgia

Duke Point
BC Ferries

Thrasher
Rock

reef

Not for Navigation

Gabriola I

Silva Bay

Nanaimo

Gabriola Pass

Dodd Narrows

Mudge
Island

Degnen Bay

Gabriola Pass

Kendrick I

Porlier Pass

Wakes Cove

Ladysmith

De Courcy Group

Pirates
Cove

Vancouver Island

Salt Spring Island

K

Ruxton
Island

Whaleboat
Island

Valdes I

Pylades I

Newcastle Island

Charts 3313, 3457,
3458, 3443

Access

Opposite Nanaimo and located in the harbour, Newcastle Island Marine Park can be reached from across the harbour or by entrance to the harbour from the south or the north. Vessels arriving in Nanaimo Harbour from the Strait of Georgia may travel into Departure Bay where the BC Ferry terminal is located, and cruise slowly down Newcastle Island Passage via Brechin Point. Or enter by way of Meakin Channel around the south end of Protection Island.

The Park and Anchorage

This is one of the busiest parks in or near the Gulf Islands. There is a substantial boat dock at the south end of Newcastle Island for day and overnight use. Anchoring is possible in the cove to the northwest of the docks. Some vessels anchor in the shallows off the drying passage between Newcastle and Protection Islands. Some winds can cause discomfort at anchor at times. Facilities ashore include a social centre with dance floor, restaurant, gift shop and snack bar. There are facilities for groups, camping, showers, tenting and an adventure playground. Around the island there are bays, beaches and playing fields and over 20 kilometres of trails for walking and some for bicycling.

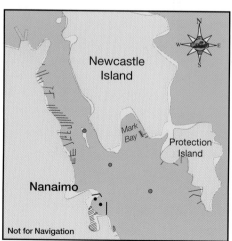

Nearby

All services and marinas are located across the harbour at the city of Nanaimo. The BC Ferry terminals are located at Departure Bay and Duke Point. On the west, northwest shore of Protection Island there is a floating marine pub with dock space for customers.

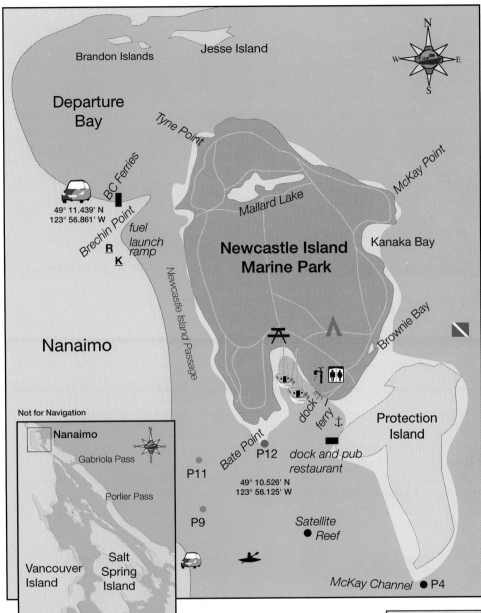

Brandon Islands

Jesse Island

N
W E
S

Departure
Bay

Tyne Point

McKay Point

BC Ferries

49° 11.439' N
123° 56.861' W

Brechin Point

fuel
launch
ramp

R
K

Newcastle Island
Marine Park

Mallard Lake

Kanaka Bay

Nanaimo

Newcastle Island Passage

Brownie Bay

Protection
Island

Bate Point

P12

dock and pub
restaurant

ferry

49° 10.526' N
123° 56.125' W

Not for Navigation

Nanaimo

N
W E
S

Gabriola Pass

Porlier Pass

P11

P9

Satellite
● Reef

Vancouver
Island

Salt
Spring
Island

McKay Channel ● P4

Park facilities

Boat/dinghy dock, 18 walk-in campsites, showers, restaurant, passenger ferry service, pay phones, picnic tables, drinking water, toilets, beach, hiking, bicycling trails, playground, gift shop, recommended kayaking, viewpoint/point of interest. Go by dinghy to Nanaimo. Charts and books are available from Harbour Marine, or The Chart Shop on Church Street, uptown.

🚰	Water
A	Camping
⚓	Anchoring
⬤	Mooring
🚻	Toilets
⛩	Picnic Tables
◣	Scuba sites
🛶	Kayaking

Newcastle Island and Protection Island with the adjacent anchorage across Nanaimo Harbour seen from the waterfront at Nanaimo. The Dinghy Dock Pub is located on Protection Island.

Interesting and historic sites are found at places on Newcastle Island. Coal was mined there from 1853 to 1887, but the area was inhabited by the Coast Salish people long before the arrival of the first settlers from Europe. In 1869 sandstone was quarried on the island and columns manufactured for export were shipped abroad. An ornate sandstone column is displayed at a site on Newcastle Island. It was one of a pair bound for San Francisco for use in the construction of the new city hall but ended up at the bottom of the Strait of Georgia when the freighter which was transporting it sank off Mayne Island. The column was recovered by scuba divers in the 1980s.

From 1910 to 1941 a Japanese boat yard and salter plant was in operation near Shaft Point and in 1931 there was a resort on the island for the Canadian Pacific steamships that cruised there out of Vancouver.

The present social centre on the island was once a pavilion for the entertainment of passengers off the cruise ships.

Penny's Palapa Restaurant on the docks at Nanaimo serves authentic Mexican dishes.

102

3

Vancouver area to Desolation Sound

Indian Arm, Howe Sound, the Sunshine Coast and Princess Louisa Inlet.

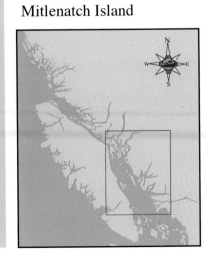

Crescent Beach

Charts 3463, 3311

Access and anchorage

From the Strait of Georgia south of Point Roberts there is a long, marked route into Boundary Bay. It curves around Crescent Beach into the mouth of the Nicomekl River, passes beneath a railway trestle with a clearance of 12 feet (9 feet at swing span) and enters the cove that shelters Crescent Beach Marina. Beyond the marina, up the river (following centre channel and preferably at high tide) is a large curved bay which serves as a protected anchorage. It lies in an open area with pastoral lands surrounding it. Because of the low nature of the terrain strong winds can be felt in the anchorage. It is a muddy bottom and in the event of dragging anchor, the potential for damage is minimal.

Nearby

Marine facilities, supplies and boat repairs at Crescent Beach Marina. Long nature walks on the nearby beach or Boundary Bay dike. Launch ramps at Crescent Beach Marina and **Ward's Marina** nearby. Restaurants and shops at Crescent Beach.

Above: Crescent Beach and entrance to the river. Left: Anchorage in the Nikomekl River.

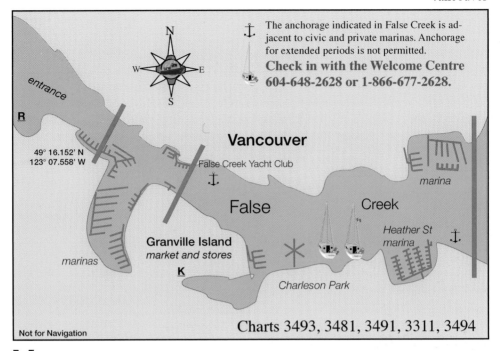

The anchorage indicated in False Creek is adjacent to civic and private marinas. Anchorage for extended periods is not permitted.
Check in with the Welcome Centre 604-648-2628 or 1-866-677-2628.

Vancouver
False Creek Yacht Club

49° 16.152' N
123° 07.558' W

False   **Creek**

marina

Heather St
marina

Granville Island
market and stores

marinas

Charleson Park

Not for Navigation   Charts 3493, 3481, 3491, 3311, 3494

Vancouver Cowards Cove and False Creek

Cowards Cove. After crossing the Strait of Georgia from Silva Bay, Active Pass or Porlier Pass, if the seas are rough and you need a break there is a safe spot to stop on the approaches to Vancouver. It is just inside the entrance to the North Arm of the Fraser River. Cowards Cove (also known as Boat Basin) is located immediately behind the breakwater that extends from Wreck Beach. There is usually some log boom activity in the vicinity of the cove but tying to a boom or anchoring in the cove seldom presents a problem. Many go there from Vancouver or from upriver, just to anchor for the day and bask in the sun, or perhaps to join the naturalist sunbathers on Wreck Beach.

False Creek. Vessels are allowed limited time at the anchorage, which lies along the shallows off Charleson Park, as well as beyond Heather Street Marina.

There is a small amount of additional anchorage space at the head of the inlet as well as just beyond the False Creek Yacht Club floats.

In **Vancouver Harbour**, east of the First Narrows (Lions Gate Bridge) there is no anchoring available due to shipping movements and harbour activities. But move on east beyond the Second Narrows and you will find a boating playland in Indian Arm where overnight anchorage is available.

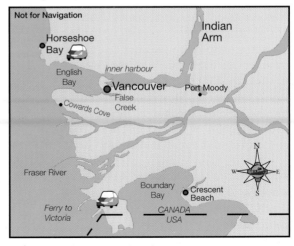

Not for Navigation

Indian Arm

Horseshoe Bay

English Bay

inner harbour

Vancouver   Port Moody

False Creek

Cowards Cove

Fraser River

Boundary Bay   Crescent Beach

Ferry to Victoria

CANADA
USA

South Coast

Not for Navigation

⚓

Croker I

Indian

Arm

Indian Arm
Provincial
Park

Marine
Park
Twin
Islets
dinghy dock
park facilities

Racoon I

N

W   E

S

49° 19.710' N
122° 56.128' W

Deep
Cove

K

Bedwell
Bay

Belcarra Park

R

Cates
Park

Reed Point   R

Not for Navigation

Horseshoe Bay

Indian
Arm

English
Bay

inner harbour

Vancouver

Port Moody

False
Creek

Cowards Cove

Captain's
Cove

Steveston

N

W   E

S

Fraser River

Boundary
Bay

Crescent
Beach

Ferry to
Victoria

CANADA
USA

If you are travelling up the Strait of Georgia and decide to put into the Fraser River, there is a place to anchor temporarily at Steveston. It is at the very far end of the harbour in a narrowing waterway that almost continues through back into the river. At low tide the river drops so that a bar across this north end of **Steveston Harbour** is mostly exposed. Anchor in the shallows but be mindful of the movement of boats and the possibility of underwater snags. You could continue about seven miles up the river and anchor more securely off **Captains Cove** Marina located opposite the BC Ferries work yards. See *Docks and Destinations*.

Top: View of Indian Arm from the south, with Belcarra Park to the right, centre. Opposite: Bedwell Bay is a popular anchorage in the summertime.

Anchorage in Bedwell Bay. This is a popular anchorage where sheltered conditions usually prevail in summertime.

Indian Arm
Charts 3311, 3495

Access
From Vancouver it is a safe and simple cruise eastward into Indian Arm–provided you have checked the tide tables first. Entering Vancouver Harbour from English Bay one should exercise caution when passing beneath Lions Gate Bridge. The currents there can be treacherous as can be the coming and going of large ships. Continuing east, passage under Second Narrows Bridge can be wild if it is windy and the currents are running at full speed. Indian Arm is a sheltered cruising area in the summer. It is a busy waterway, used extensively by small boats. Watch for kayaks.

The Park and Anchorage
The best anchorage is in **Bedwell Bay** and the summer wind directions seldom cause discomfort. Winter winds are far worse and great care should be taken when anchoring in the Arm during wintertime. **Twin Islets Marine Park** is located just north of Bedwell Bay.

Nearby
The city of Vancouver with several marinas downtown and in False Creek has a wide choice of cultural events and many social activities and attractions.
Port Moody farther east of the entrance to Indian Arm has a large marina at Reed Point and a launch ramp adjacent to a popular park. Or go west into Howe Sound.

Park facilities at Twin Islets
Dinghy dock, walk-in campsites, picnic tables, drinking water, toilets, hiking, recommended kayaking, scuba diving.

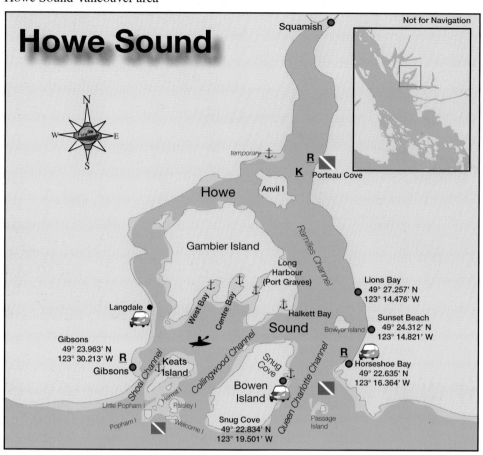

Howe Sound

Squamish

Not for Navigation

temporary

R
K Porteau Cove

Howe

Anvil I

Gambier Island

Long
Harbour
(Port Graves)

Ramillies Channel

West Bay

Centre Bay

Langdale

Halkett Bay

Sound

Bowyer Island

Lions Bay
49° 27.257' N
123° 14.476' W

Sunset Beach
49° 24.312' N
123° 14.821' W

Gibsons
49° 23.963' N
123° 30.213' W

R

Gibsons

Shoal Channel

Keats
Island

Hermit I

Little Popham I

Popham I

Raisley I

Welcome I

Collingwood Channel

Snug
Cove

Bowen
Island

Snug Cove
49° 22.834' N
123° 19.501' W

Queen Charlotte Channel

R

Horseshoe Bay
49° 22.635' N
123° 16.364' W

Passage
Island

South Coast

Charts 3311, 3534, 3526, 3512

Go west of Vancouver into the varied coves of Howe Sound. It is a popular cruising area with moorage, marinas and marine parks to fill the needs of Vancouver and nearby mariners. Visitors travelling north from the USA and southern Vancouver Island frequently stop in the Sound when time permits en route up the coast. It is a good place to tuck into also when the weather is up while travelling south down the Sunshine Coast.

Located near Vancouver and with a ferry service catering to an otherwise isolated Sunshine Coast, services and facilities are always close at hand. The town of Gibsons has a large marina and all services including boat repairs. This town serves the Sunshine Coast as does Horseshoe Bay the West Vancouver boating communities. Anchorages are found at Bowen Island and on Gambier Island, with marine parks located at the latter as well as Keats Island opposite Gibsons. The marine park at Halkett Bay is becoming increasingly popular as the boating community becomes familiar with its tree-lined forest walks and gentle shore.

There are not many shallow, protected anchorages in Howe Sound, the most popular being at West Bay and Centre Bay on Gambier Island and at Plumper Cove on Keats Island. One of the popular destinations in Howe Sound is Snug Cove with its large marina, nearby Killarney Lake, and quaint village where restaurants, bakeries, general stores and gift shops cater to locals and the many summer visitors.

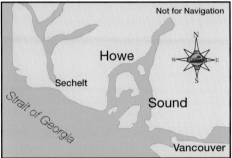

Top: Snug Cove and Mannion Bay. There is temporary anchorage in Mannion Bay (also known as Deep Bay).
Above: Union Steamship Marina.
Right: Boats can be seen anchored in Mannion Bay from this high altitude photograph,

The beauty of Howe Sound is its close proximity to Vancouver yet with a remote wilderness about the islands that is comparable to those in more isolated areas that require long distances to travel, and the towering, often snow-capped peaks that rise loftily above its northern and eastern shoreline.

Above: Centre Bay. Anchorage can be found in the lee of the point at left. The island nearby is property of the Royal Vancouver Yacht Club. Facility at the head of the bay is private.

Charts 3311, 3534, 3526, 3512

Howe Sound Anchorages

The most popular anchorages for restful overnight visits in Howe Sound are at **Plumper Cove, West Bay** and **Centre Bay** (and some say **Port Graves**–which is known to be uncomfortable in windy weather). There are other places to anchor but none as sheltered as these. However, even these can be subject to uncomfortable conditions in varying degrees. I have known strong winds to gust into Plumper Cove, one of the most sheltered anchorages in the Sound, that have kept me at anchor watch all night. They are rare in summer, come in from the southwest and have been known to cause boats to drag anchor.

If you are snugly anchored in the tuck of Centre Bay or in West Bay you are more likely to have a completely restful overnight stay in Howe Sound. As for Mannion Bay, you will be able to relax, as long as you are not hit by an easterly blow, common in winter but only occasional in summer.

Mariners who want to stop at Snug Cove generally tie up at the docks of Snug Cove Marina located behind the ferry dock. Enjoy the walk in the village, through the adjoining Crippen Regional Park and up to the shores of Killarney Lake.

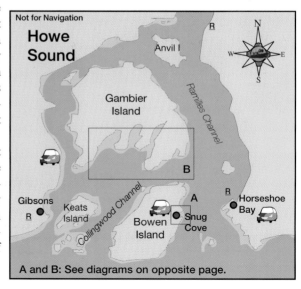

Not for Navigation

Howe Sound

Anvil I

Gambier Island

Ramillies Channel

B

Gibsons

Keats Island

Collingwood Channel

Bowen Island

A

Snug Cove

Horseshoe Bay

A and B: See diagrams on opposite page.

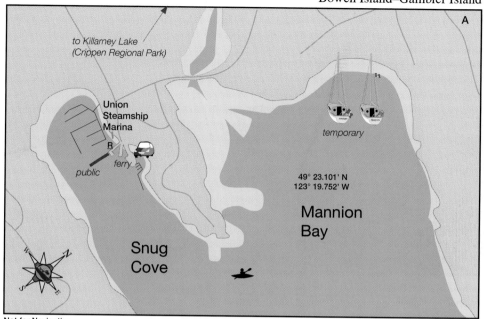

A

to Killarney Lake
(Crippen Regional Park)

Union
Steamship
Marina

R

ferry

public

temporary

49° 23.101' N
123° 19.752' W

**Mannion
Bay**

**Snug
Cove**

Not for Navigation

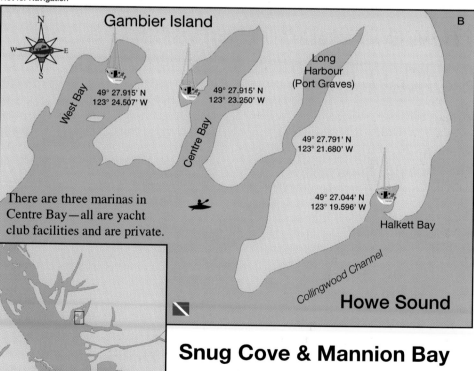

B

Gambier Island

Long
Harbour
(Port Graves)

West Bay

49° 27.915' N
123° 24.507' W

49° 27.915' N
123° 23.250' W

Centre Bay

49° 27.791' N
123° 21.680' W

49° 27.044' N
123° 19.596' W

There are three marinas in
Centre Bay—all are yacht
club facilities and are private.

Halkett Bay

Collingwood Channel

Howe Sound

Snug Cove & Mannion Bay

*There is a large, well established marina in Snug Cove. Do
not anchor in Snug Cove because of the coming and going
of ferries. There is room for anchorage in Mannion Bay but
check wind forecasts as it is open to wind and the wash from
passing vessels.*

Halkett Bay showing the dinghy dock and access to shore. Opposite, bottom: A view up Howe Sound. Halkett Bay is located near the second point up from the bottom, left. Below: West Bay.

Halkett Bay

Charts 3311, 3526, 3512

Access
The bay is located at the southeastern corner of Gambier Island. It opens at Halkett Point off Collingwood Channel.

The Park and Anchorage
Halkett Bay Marine Park has lovely wooded trails, a dinghy float and onshore toilets. There are also information facilities. The park was previously farmland. Anchorage in the bay is semi-protected by a reef in the centre and along the west shoreline. Some disturbance is caused by wind and passing ferries.

Nearby
Vessels entering Howe Sound via Queen Charlotte Channel to the east of Bowen Island will pass Snug Cove en route. This harbour, with its quaint village, is a prime stop for supplies and shopping at a variety of craft and gift shops. Bowen's Killarney Lake (see preceding pages) and surrounding provincial parkland provide peaceful walks amid creeks and farmslands and along the lake shore.

Park facilities
Dinghy dock, mooring buoy, walk-in campsites, toilets, hiking, recommended kayaking, scuba diving nearby.

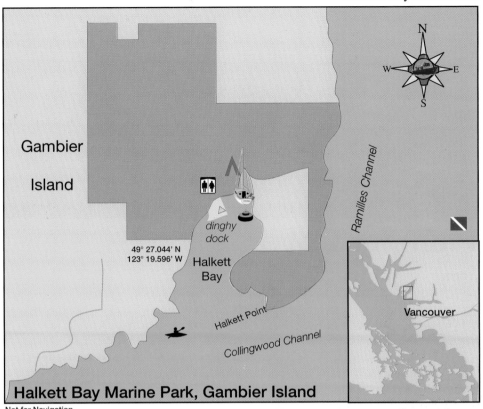

Gambier

Island

dinghy
dock

49° 27.044' N
123° 19.596' W

Halkett
Bay

Halkett Point

Collingwood Channel

Ramilles Channel

Halkett Bay Marine Park, Gambier Island

Vancouver

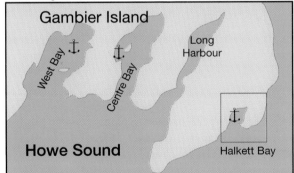

Gambier Island

West Bay

Centre Bay

Long
Harbour

Halkett Bay

Howe Sound

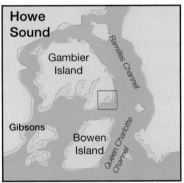

Howe
Sound

Gambier
Island

Ramilles Channel

Gibsons

Bowen
Island

Queen Charlotte Channel

Plumper Cove

Charts 3311, 3534

Access

Keats Island is located at the northwestern side of Howe Sound, opposite Gibsons. Vessels entering the Sound from the Strait of Georgia pass through Shoal Channel past Gower Point on the mainland and Home Island off the southwestern tip of Keats Island. Boats entering Howe Sound from Vancouver may travel around the inside passage between Bowen Island and Gambier Island. Or around the outside of Bowen Island passing Cape Roger Curtis and entering Collingwood Channel. A pleasant cruise is to travel between Worlcombe Island and Pasley Island and then enter Barfleur Passage by passing between Little Popham and Hermit Islands. There is good water on the southwestern side of Hermit Island which is the preferred passage. Across Barfleur Passage cruise around the lower point of Keats Island and adjacent Home Island then up through Shoal Channel and enter Plumper Cove around the north end of Shelter Islets or between Shelter Islets and Keats. But do not leave a wash as there are private moorings along the shore of Keats Island.

The Park and Anchorage

One of the busiest marine parks on the coast, its location relatively near Vancouver ensures a steady flow of visitors in boats of all sizes. Larger vessels anchor out in the cove where there are several mooring buoys, preferably for small to medium sized boats. The dock serving the park will accommodate a fair number of small boats and serves as a dinghy dock for the larger vessels anchored out. The anchorage is sheltered from most winds although some discomfort can be expected when it is blowing directly up Shoal Channel into the anchorage. Above the pebbly beached shoreline is a grassy meadow with adjacent camp sites and picnic tables. The park is encircled by a good walking trail which includes a stop at Observatory Point for a magnificent view into the Sound. A two kilometre trail leads to the park from Keats Landing which is served by passenger ferry out of Langdale.

Nearby

The town of Gibsons across Shoal Channel has shops and all services and facilities. Marinas and fuel docks welcome boating visitors. It is a busy holiday town that sees an influx of visitors with every Sunshine Coast landing of BC Ferries a short way up the Sound at Langdale. There are popular nearby anchorages at West Bay and Centre Bay on Gambier Island, and a small, busy landing at New Brighton on Gambier Island.

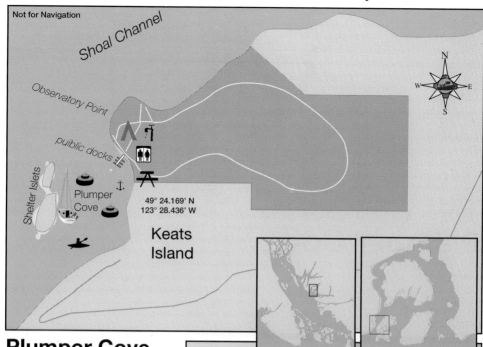

Plumper Cove Marine Park Keats Island

Park facilities
Mooring buoys (8 at last count), boat dock, 20 walk-in campsites, picnic tables, drinking water, toilets, beach hiking, recommended kayaking.

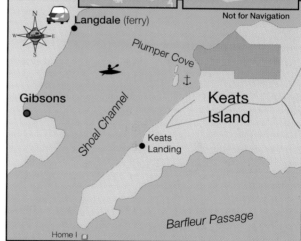

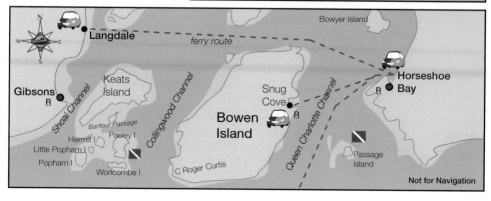

Looking south from the parking lot and launch ramp at Porteau Cove Marine Park. This is also an underwater preserve where scuba diving is popular. Several vessels have been sunk off Porteau as artificial reefs for divers and are clearly marked by buoys just north of the launch ramp.

Porteau Cove

Charts 3311, 3526, 3512

Access

Cruising into the Porteau Cove area one could travel up the east coast of Howe Sound from the direction of Horseshoe Bay towards Britannia Beach. The cove lies beneath the tall Coast Mountains that reach above Howe Sound.

The Park and Anchorage

There is a boat launching ramp which is exposed to open water conditions. An extensive beach is an attraction for campers and day visitors who arrive by vehicle. It has walk-in campsites. There are mooring buoys off the beach and anchoring is possible off the campsite area for short periods provided the wind is not blowing. Temporary anchorage also at Glen Eagle. For scuba divers there are change rooms and an interpretive presentation display with access from the beach to several artificial reefs, comprising a number of sunken vessels. These are marked by buoys just north of the ramp.

Nearby

Across the Sound from Porteau a temporary anchorage may be found in the lee of the **Defence Islands**. Nearby Anvil Island is a picturesque area to circumnavigate, and a visit to Squamish at the head of the Sound could provide a pleasant excursion ashore.

116

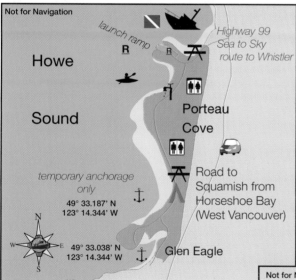

Not for Navigation

Howe

Sound

launch ramp

R   R

Highway 99
Sea to Sky
route to Whistler

Porteau

Cove

temporary anchorage
only
49° 33.187' N
123° 14.344' W

49° 33.038' N
123° 14.344' W

Road to
Squamish from
Horseshoe Bay
(West Vancouver)

Glen Eagle

*View from Porteaux Cove looking
north. Note the scuba divers on the
surface of the water.*

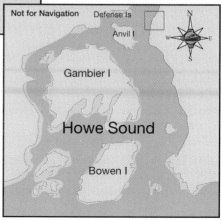

Not for Navigation Defense Is

Anvil I

Gambier I

Howe Sound

Bowen I

Porteau Cove
Howe Sound

Do not confuse
wreck markers for
mooring buoys.

Park facilities

Mooring buoys, walk-in campsites,
picnic tables, drinking water,
toilets, beach, scuba diving.
Launch ramp.

Above: There is a place to anchor temporarily inside the breakwater at Sechelt en route along the long, open and exposed stretch of the Sunshine Coast between Howe Sound and Merry Island. Below: Narrows Inlet off Sechelt Inlet. The waterway includes deep fjords with minimal anchorage. Designated parks along the shores attract kayakers and some mariners to stop and explore.

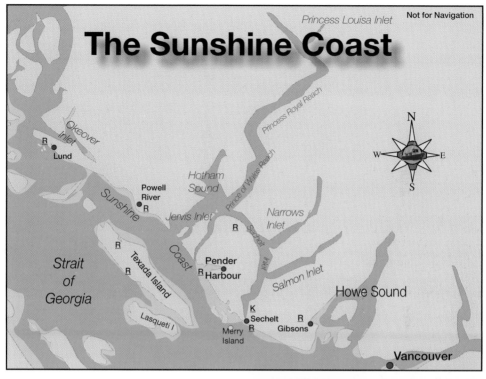

The Sunshine Coast

Princess Louisa Inlet

Not for Navigation

Princess Royal Reach

Prince of Wales Reach

Princess Royal Reach

N W E S

Okeover Inlet

R Lund

Hotham Sound

Sunshine

Powell River R

Jervis Inlet R

Narrows Inlet

R

Sechelt Inlet

Coast

Texada Island R

R

Pender R Harbour

Salmon Inlet

Howe Sound

Strait of Georgia

Lasqueti I

K Sechelt R Gibsons

Merry R Island

Vancouver

Charts 3311, 3312, 3512, 3513, 3514

From Howe Sound travel northwards along the Sunshine Coast towards Thormanby Island or Secret Cove using Merry Island as your landmark. If the seas are rough or building you can take temporary shelter at Sechelt. There is a breakwater (photograph, opposite page) and commercial dock at Selma Park. This First Nations facility is mostly used by private vessels, but there is protection for a few pleasure boats behind the breakwater. Continue up the Sunshine Coast en route to Buccaneer Bay, Smuggler Cove or Secret Cove, by way of Welcome Passage to the east of Merry Island .

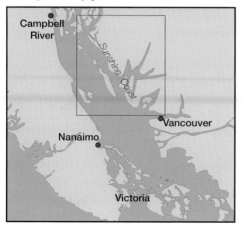

Campbell River

Sunshine Coast

Vancouver

Nanaimo

Victoria

British Columbia became renown for scuba diving after the launching of Diver Magazine *in BC in 1974. The magazine, distributed throughout Canada and the United States and represented at annual trade shows, helped bring large numbers of divers to visit the province. The Sunshine Coast became a major draw when these two divers, sculptor Simon Morris and diving personality Jim Willoughby, helped initiate the sinking of a bronze mermaid at Saltery Bay.*

⌐	Water
Λ	Camping
⚓	Anchoring
⚫	Mooring
🚻	Toilets
🔀	Picnic Tables
◪	Scuba sites
🛶	Kayaking

Buccaneer Bay

Charts 3535, 3311, 3512

Access

Buccaneer Bay is entered from Thormanby Channel at the south end of Malaspina Strait. It lies between North and South Thormanby Islands which are almost one, separated only by a shallow shoal adjacent to a low lying stretch of white sandy beach on the south island that extends to the bottom of the bay at Gill Beach.

The Park (Buccaneer Bay)

This park is known for its adjacent broad, sandy beach that extends to the tip of Sandy Islet on the western side of South Thormanby Island.

Anchorage

Anchor in **Water Bay,** taking extra caution in wind conditions, off the beach at **Grassy Point**. Also in the lee of **Surrey Islands** at the entrance to the bay. Temporary anchorage may be taken also in the small coves on the south eastern side of South Thormanby Island.

Nearby

There is a small community dock at Vaucroft Beach in Buccaneer Bay with access ashore for beachcombing and sunbathing.

Buccaneer Bay

Tattenham Ledge

Welcome Passage

Vaucroft Beach

public dock   temporary

Buccaneer Marine Park

Grassy Point

Surrey Islands

Wolf Point

Water Bay

Sandy Islet

Gill Beach

Not for Navigation

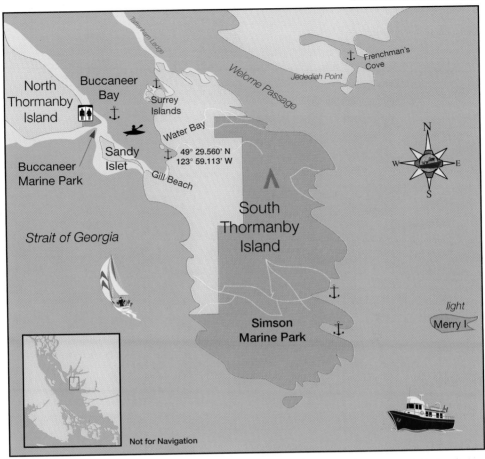

Not for Navigation

Buccaneer Bay and Simson Marine Parks

Anchor out temporarily for excursions to the beach by dinghy. Or anchor lower down in the bay off the beach with overnight stays dependant on weather forecasts. Generally in summer wind conditions allow for comfortable overnight anchoring. Across Welcome Passage lie the havens of Smuggler Cove (Marine Park) and Secret Cove for good anchorage and access to facilities and services.

Park facilities
Toilets, beach.

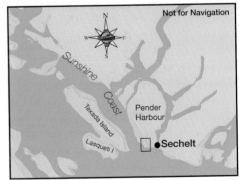

Not for Navigation

Opposite: Looking over Buccaneer Bay in the direction of Sandy Islet. The narrow, sandy isthmus dries at low tide. In summer many boats anchor off the beach in the bay.
Be cautious of northerly blows. The most sheltered anchorage in the Thormanby Islands is in Water Bay. The inset shows Vaucroft Beach extending along North Thormanby Island.

Smuggler Cove

Charts 3535, 3311, 3512

Access

The entrance to Smuggler Cove faces north towards Malaspina Strait and lies just off Welcome Passage south of Secret Cove. When travelling into the entranceway along the southern edge of Isle Capri keep well clear of the reefs that extend into the opposite side of the narrow channel.

The Park and Anchorage

Smuggler Cove is a series of anchorages in tiny bays and an inner bay which can be reached by carefully weaving around France Islet. Rocks, warm shallow water and beaches make swimming and sunbathing popular in the cove. Stern lines can be tied to eyebolts on shore. If you are feeling adventurous, **Frenchman's Cove** in Halfmoon Bay is a difficult anchorage to enter due to rocks and shallows. But it is one of the better protected anchorages in the area. An easy walking trail runs from Frenchman's Cove to a vehicle access road from the highway. It connects the cove with the parking lot. Walking through the forested uplands and around the rocky shore is a favourite pastime of mariners and land-based visitors alike.

Nearby

Secret Cove, with amenities, moorage, fuel and marine services, is a popular stop on the Sunshine Coast. It is also a popular destination. In the opposite direction is South Thormanby Island with its extensive Simson Marine Park area for beach recreation.

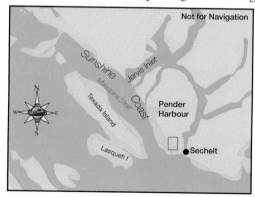

Not for Navigation

122

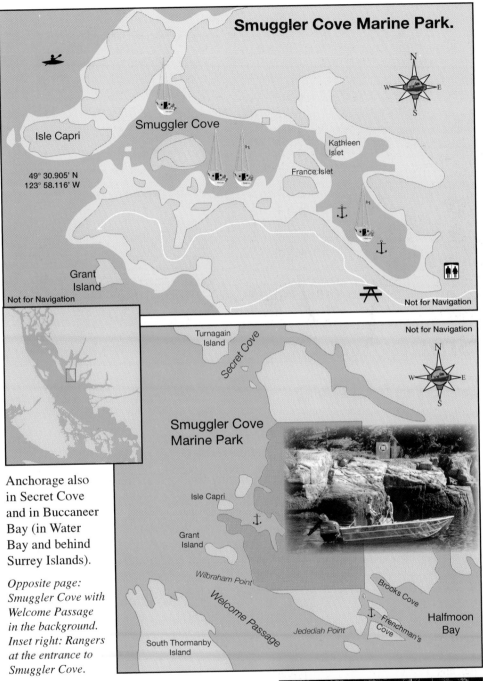

Smuggler Cove Marine Park.

Isle Capri

Smuggler Cove

49° 30.905' N
123° 58.116' W

Kathleen Islet

France Islet

Grant Island

Not for Navigation

Not for Navigation

Not for Navigation

Turnagain Island

Secret Cove

Smuggler Cove Marine Park

Isle Capri

Grant Island

Wilbraham Point

Welcome Passage

South Thormanby Island

Jedediah Point

Frenchman's Cove

Brooks Cove

Halfmoon Bay

Anchorage also in Secret Cove and in Buccaneer Bay (in Water Bay and behind Surrey Islands).

Opposite page: Smuggler Cove with Welcome Passage in the background. Inset right: Rangers at the entrance to Smuggler Cove.

No sewage discharge.

Park facilities

Walk-in campsites, toilets, park host, hiking, fishing.

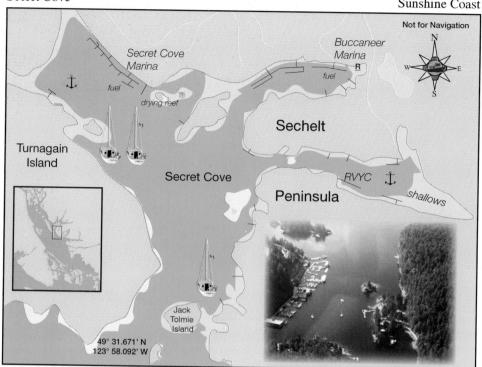

Secret Cove

Charts 3311, 3535, 3512

Access

Enter from Malaspina Strait north of Welcome Passage. Pass the entrance to Smuggler Cove Marine Park when approaching from the south. Go around Turnagain Island when approaching from the north. The water in the cove is shallow but adequate for pleasure craft. A large marina occupies the largest basin in the cove, while yacht club facilities, small marinas and private docks abound along the remaining shorelines. The south arm, occupied by the Royal Vancouver Yacht Club outstation, becomes shallow. Its entrance is narrow. Avoid the rock that protrudes from the port side while entering. Watch also the shoals at the main entrance to the cove adjacent to Jack Tolmie Island and off the island in the centre of the cove.

Anchorage

Anchor in the lee of Turnagain Island opposite the fuel dock and marina or off the Royal Vancouver Yacht Club facility. Approach the former anchorage with caution, minding the reefs east of the fuel dock. Anchor also in the lee of Jack Tolmie Island.

Nearby

Provisions, fuel, moorage, restaurants and hotel facilities are available in Secret Cove. There is a public float which is usually very busy. Good service, fuel and plentiful moorage is available from the large marina in the north arm. Repairs, fuel and yard work are available at the marina in the middle arm.

This is a popular home for fishing enthusiasts, many of whom keep their boats dry stored or in the water and commute to access the adjacent fishing grounds off Thormanby and Merry Island or the shoals up the coast towards Pender Harbour.

Top: Inside Secret Cove a drying reef lies off the marina. Right, top: Anchor opposite the marina after entering. Right, lower: Pass west of Jack Tolmie Island at the entrance to Secret Cove.

Lasqueti Island   Charts 3312, 3536, 3512

Lasqueti Island draws thousand of boats each summer to its sheltered coves and bays. Approaching up the Strait of Georgia from the south, Lasqueti gradually rises out of the horizon as a small ridge to the left of the larger mass that is Texada Island. As you near the islands you begin to identify the smaller islets that lie between the two larger land masses and a short distance off the tip of Lasqueti. These islets afford some immediate shelter from the open waters of the Strait of Georgia but it is not until you have woven your way through them that you find protected overnight moorage.

There are several better known sheltered anchorages on or adjacent to Lasqueti. They include False Bay, Scottie Bay, Skerry Bay, Deep Bay and Boho Bay. Squitty Bay on Lasqueti Island and Deep Bay (all of Jedediah Island) are designated marine parks.

Squitty Bay

Charts 3312, 3512

Access

Enter Squitty Bay off Sabine Channel west of Texada Island. Favour the south shore as you enter, and use a large-scale chart for reference to the reef in the centre of the entrance. The bay is located near the southeastern tip of Lasqueti Island to the north of Young Point and not far from the southern entrance to Sabine Channel.

The Park and Anchorage

Squitty Bay is a very natural setting comprising a narrow passage with a dock attached to the south shore. The bay looks out onto the open waters of the Strait of Georgia from the south end of Lasqueti Island. There is little room to anchor in this tiny cove. Use the dock if space is available.

Nearby

Good gunkholing and some small bays and anchorages. This area has long been known for its good oyster yield. Beware of red tides.

The small size of Squitty Bay can be seen in the photograph above. There is little room for manoeuvring. The dock is usually quite crowded. Be careful of the shallows as you negotiate the entrance. It's best to enter the bay at high tide.

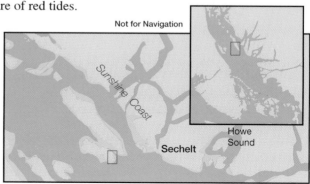

Not for Navigation

Sunshine Coast

Sechelt

Howe
Sound

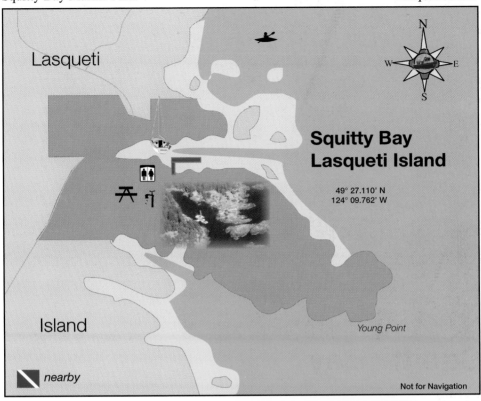

Lasqueti

**Squitty Bay
Lasqueti Island**

49° 27.110' N
124° 09.762' W

Island

Young Point

nearby

Not for Navigation

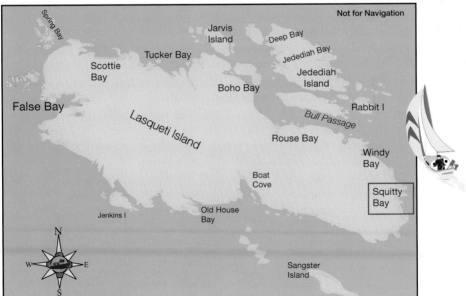

Spring Bay

Jarvis
Island

Deep Bay

Jedediah Bay

Tucker Bay

Scottie
Bay

Jedediah
Island

Boho Bay

False Bay

Rabbit I

Lasqueti Island

Bull Passage

Rouse Bay

Windy
Bay

Boat
Cove

Squitty
Bay

Jenkins I

Old House
Bay

Sangster
Island

Not for Navigation

Park facilities

Boat dock, picnic tables, drinking water, toilets, fishing, recommended scuba diving nearby.

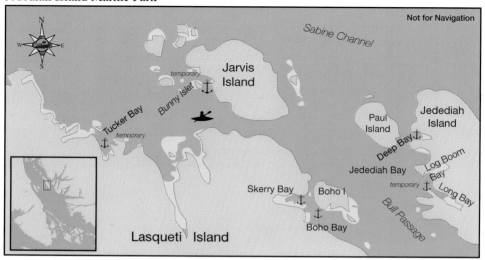

Jedediah Island
Chart 3312

Access

Jedediah Island abuts Sabine Channel opposite the southwest side of Texada Island. **Deep Bay** is located on the northwest side of Jedediah Island opposite Paul Island and is a popular place for those who know it. It is a small cove suitable for two or three boats stern tied to a steep wall. It's the type of anchorage that is yours to enjoy if you are first to arrive. I personally favour leaving it to one or two boats if they are already there rather than trying to squeeze in. Once in place you can poke around in your dinghy, exploring the passages, shoreline and nooks around the adjacent islands. If there is no red tide warning and you have your harvesting licence, look for oysters.

In addition to Deep Bay, on the west side of Jedediah Island, Jedediah Bay has two arms that are suitable for anchorage. They are known as **Log Boom Bay** and **Long Bay**. These two nooks are best as temporary stops only, in their outer waters and during medium to high tides. Mind the drying shallows deeper inside the arms.

Boho Bay
Chart 3312

Boho Bay lies to the south of Boho Island, a short way to the east of Skerry Bay. Anchor in Boho Bay or pass through it to reach the anchorage in Skerry Bay.

A good, protected anchorage can be found south of Boho Island. You may be disturbed at times by the affect of southeast winds. Better protection from such wind can be found in Skerry Bay.

Skerry Bay
Chart 3312

Access is through Boho Bay of which it is an appendage. This anchorage opens off Sabine Channel east of Scottie Bay. It is a sheltered overnight anchorage but it has some shallows to watch for as well as a drying rock at the entrance.

When there are red tide warnings take them seriously. PSP (paralytic shellfish poisoning) is a very serious condition. It has been said that you can make your own test for PSP by tasting the tiniest morsel of shellfish, about the size of a grain of rice, wait about ten minutes and if you experience a slight tingling sensation around the mouth or lips, leave it alone. I suggest you don't even attempt this because if you have any allergy the reaction might be serious.

Above: Looking northwest along Bull Passage with Bull Island to the right. Boho Bay and Skerry Bay can be seen beyond, with boats lying at anchor.
Right: Tied off to shore in Deep Bay, an anchorage best suited for two or three boats only. All of Jedediah Island, including Deep Bay, is a designated Marine Park.

Above: Close view of busy Boho Bay with Skerry Bay beyond looking rather empty of anchored vessels. Some private enterprise works have been known to take up part of the bay as seen by the circular structure between the two bays in this photograph. You can still slide by such an impediment to reach the more protected anchorage in Skerry Bay.
Above, right: Anchored in a sheltered gap among the Finnerty Islands, which lie north of the entrance to False Bay on the west side of Lasqueti Island.

Not for Navigation

Anderson Cove
Texada I
Spring Bay
Scottie Bay
Jarvis I
Jedediah Island
Tucker Bay
Boho Bay
Rabbit I
False Bay
Lasqueti Island
Rouse Bay
Windy Bay
Old House Bay
Squitty Bay
Jenkins I

Scottie Bay

Charts 3312, 3512

Access

Scottie Bay is tucked behind Lindberg Island near the north end of Lasqueti. It is an easy entrance off Sabine Channel, but keep to the left as you enter through the narrow opening into the cove to avoid the reef that protrudes from the southeastern shore of Lindberg Island.

Anchorage

There is room for a good number of boats to anchor in the bay although the presence of private enterprise makes it restrictive at times. Over the years commercial mariculture has encroached increasingly on some favourite anchorages and boating destinations. Scottie Bay is one that has lost some of its appeal as a destination because of fish or oyster farming. If the bay is too busy try False Bay or Boho Bay. A temporary anchorage can be taken outside of Lindbergh Island in the cove protected by the island, marked *60*, that extends into Sabine Channel north of the entrance to Scottie Bay.

Nearby (Other Lasqueti Island anchorages)

Rouse Bay just off Bull Passage is an all weather anchorage for a few boats. The best place is just in the lee of the small islet at the entrance.

Bunny Islet. There is a small cove just off Jervis Island, and Bunny Islet serves as a protective breakwater against most winds for those who choose to drop anchor there.

Tucker Bay has some protection with conditional shelter just off Potter Point, in the lee of Larson Islet or inside the narrow finger to the east of the bay. Explorer carefully as you seek anchorage in Tucker Bay. At the north end of Lasqueti Island, **Finnerty Islands** offer tight but protected anchorage and **Spring Bay** has conditional temporary anchorage.

Old House Bay. If you must stop on the exposed southwest side of Lasqueti Island, this is a protected anchorage from northwest winds.

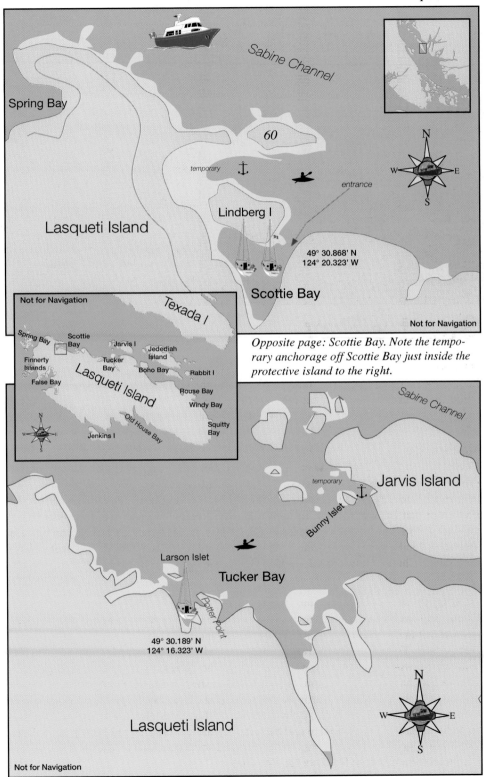

Spring Bay

Sabine Channel

60

temporary

entrance

Lindberg I

49° 30.868' N
124° 20.323' W

Lasqueti Island

Scottie Bay

N
W E
S

Not for Navigation

Not for Navigation
Texada I
Spring Bay
Scottie Bay
Jarvis I
Jedediah Island
Finnerty Islands
Tucker Bay
Boho Bay
Rabbit I
False Bay
Lasqueti Island
Rouse Bay
Windy Bay
Old House Bay
Squitty Bay
Jenkins I
N
W E
S

Opposite page: Scottie Bay. Note the temporary anchorage off Scottie Bay just inside the protective island to the right.

Sabine Channel

Jarvis Island

temporary

Bunny Islet

Larson Islet

Tucker Bay

Potter Point

49° 30.189' N
124° 16.323' W

Lasqueti Island

N
W E
S

Not for Navigation

131

Looking northwards over False Bay.

False Bay

Charts 3536, 3312, 3512

Access

False Bay is a large bay opening on the west side of Lasqueti Island. It is approached across the Strait of Georgia from the direction of Vancouver Island. Many vessels travelling up the Strait from Vancouver and Howe Sound make their way to the bay via Sabine Channel that lies between Lasqueti Island and Texada Island.

Anchorage

Anchoring is favoured in the northern part of the bay to the east of Higgins Island in a fairly well sheltered cove. The favoured spot is in the northernmost cove where there is room for numerous boats to anchor. The *BC Small Craft Guide* says to watch out for the Qualicum winds which blow strong westerly into False Bay. There are rocks off Olsen Island and Higgins Island to be mindful of, so enter False Bay with caution, using the largest scale chart.

From here you can travel across to Pender Harbour or up the coast to Comox and Desolation Sound.

Nearby

The dock in False Bay serves as a landing for people arriving at the island as foot passengers. Just up from the dock is the Lasqueti Island Hotel which offers accommodations and full hotel services. There is no fuel available at the dock.

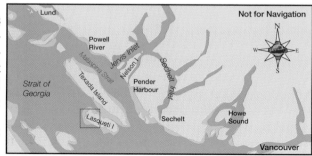

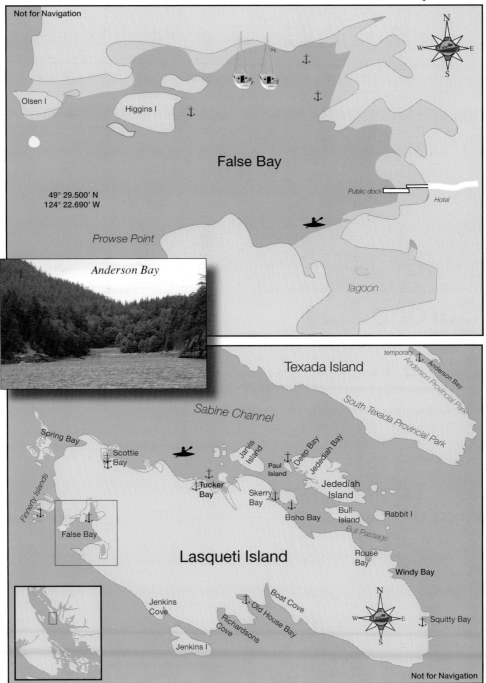

Not for Navigation

N
W · E
S

Olsen I

Higgins I

False Bay

49° 29.500' N
124° 22.690' W

Public dock

Hotel

Prowse Point

lagoon

Anderson Bay

Texada Island

Sabine Channel

temporary · Anderson Bay
Anderson Provincial Park

South Texada Provincial Park

Spring Bay

Scottie
Bay

Jarvis Island

Deep Bay

Jedediah Bay

Paul Island

Jedediah Island

Finnerty Islands

Tucker Bay

Skerry Bay

Boho Bay

Bull Island

Rabbit I

Bull Passage

False Bay

Lasqueti Island

Rouse Bay

Windy Bay

Jenkins Cove

Old House Bay

Boat Cove

Richardsons Cove

Jenkins I

N
W · E
S

Squitty Bay

Not for Navigation

If you are travelling around the south of Texada Island you will find good anchorage in **Anderson Bay** just as you head north up the east side of the island. The late corporal Bob Teather of the RCMP introduced me to this bay. He once told me it was his preferred place of shelter, and going ashore he had encountered good walking trails with breathtaking views. Some reports advise mariners to watch for wind from the southeast.

Garden Bay

Access

This park, which has a shoreline of over 600' (about 200 metres), is located on the north shore of Pender Harbour. Access to the park is by entering Pender Harbour off Malaspina Strait. A dinghy float near Fisherman's Resort provides access to the park.

The Park and Anchorage

The upper reaches of Garden Bay Marine Park include Mount Daniel. The local Sechelt people refer to the mountain as *Kwiss Chiam* which is of great ceremonial and ritual significance. The summit of the mountain and a cemetery on the waterfront are protected archaeological sites.

There are many nooks and crannies in Pender Harbour in which to anchor. The most popular is in Garden Bay. Sheltered anchorage can also be found in the lee of Francis Peninsula and inside Gunboat Bay. Great caution should be exercised in parts of Pender Harbour due to rocks and reefs, shallows and other obstacles. Use a large scale chart such as in the Sunshine Coast chart 3311.

Nearby

Pender Harbour has all services and facilities for mariners, including moorage at a number of marinas. There are restaurants, stores, post office, fuel and launching facilities.

The neighbouring waters are renowned for excellent fishing. Most mariners use dock facilities in Pender Harbour. These include private marinas and the public dock at Madeira Park. Refer to marinas in *Docks and Destinations*.

If you find Pender Harbour a bit on the busy side for your liking and wish for more tranquility, try the anchorage at Green Bay a short distance up Agamemnon Channel. For information on Green Bay turn to page 136.

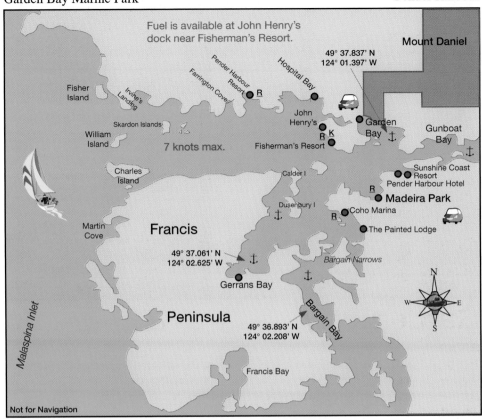

Garden Bay Marine Park, Pender Harbour

Vessels can be anchored in Garden Bay in an open area which is generally protected from wind, although the occasional southerly blow may cause some discomfort. Drop anchor near the shore at the marine park.

Anchor also in **Gerrans Bay** with attention to wind forecasts. Anchor at the head of the bay or off Calder and Dusenbury Islands. In **Gunboat Bay** the recommended spot is near Goat Islet. Mind the depths in this shallow bay. Beware of the rock to port in the narrow entrance. **Bargain Bay** on the south side of Francis Peninsula also offers protected anchorage. **Hospital Bay** is exposed to more wind than other parts of Pender Harbour, but there are good marinas for a comfortable overnight stay. Fuel is available at John Henry's in Hospital Bay. Try Laverne's for light meals, and Garden Bay Hotel and Pub for patio and lounge dining. Good overnight moorage is available at Fisherman's resort.

Park facilities

Open anchorage, dinghy dock, hiking, recommended fishing, scuba diving nearby, viewpoint/point of interest.

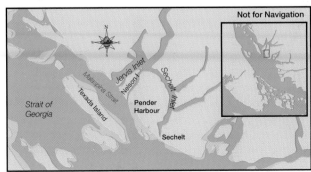

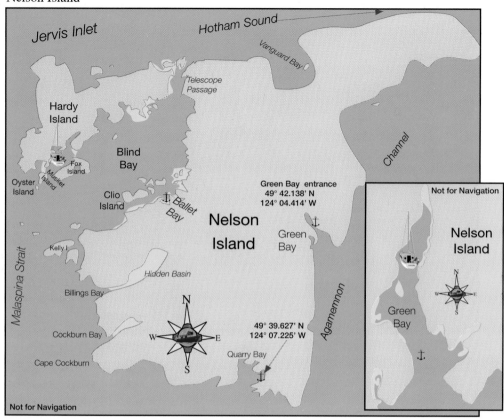

Green Bay

Charts 3312, 3311, 3512, 3514

Access

Out of Pender Harbour turn north up Agamemnon Channel. Green Bay opens to port about midway up the passage.

Anchorage

Green Bay is a quiet, sheltered anchorage but has a large reef in the middle of the arm that opens northwards. It is possible to anchor south of the reef but the most protected place (mostly from passing traffic) to drop the hook is north of the reef. Anchor in 5 fathoms. Beware of rocks near the surface in the centre and the head of the bay.

Nearby

The north end of Agamemnon Channel opens into Hotham Sound. Just to starboard as you leave the channel is the Egmont to Saltery Bay ferry terminal. And beyond that, at the entrance to Sechelt Inlet is the turbulent Sechelt Narrows and the settlement of Egmont. On the northwest side of Nelson Island Blind Bay is a very popular anchorage.

Quarry Bay, a short way out of Pender Harbour, lies at Nelson Island's southern shore. Anchorage here is good in about 6 fathoms. Caution—there is a rock near the shore. Anchor in the bight to starboard after entering the bay.

Cockburn Bay and **Hidden Basin** are both sheltered anchorages but have limited or difficult access. The entrances are narrow and subject to drying, rocks and tides.

Musket Island

Musket Island and adjacent anchorage in the lee of Fox Island.

Access

Musket Island is a small island in Blind Bay. It lies just off the south shore of Hardy Island and is tucked in behind Fox Island. Access from the west of Blind Bay is by entering from Malaspina Strait near the entrance to Jervis Inlet. From Jervis Inlet to the north, Blind Bay may be entered through Telescope Passage.

The Park and Anchorage

Musket Island is undeveloped and the anchorage offshore and in the shadow of Hardy Island makes it a remote and tranquil place to stop. Anchor behind Musket Island or in the adjoining coves north of it.

Nearby

Anchorage in Ballet Bay. This has been one of the anchorages of choice for mariners seeking shelter en route up and down the Sunshine Coast, or as a destination where a beautiful but close and cosy setting is a priority.

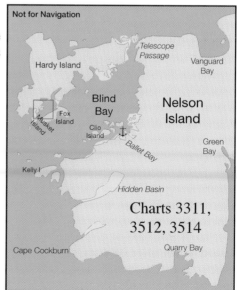

Not for Navigation

Telescope Passage

Hardy Island

Vanguard Bay

Blind Bay

Nelson Island

Fox Island

Musket Island

Clio Island

Ballet Bay

Green Bay

Kelly I

Hidden Basin

Charts 3311, 3512, 3514

Cape Cockburn

Quarry Bay

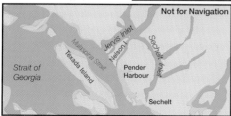

Not for Navigation

Strait of Georgia

Texada Island

Malaspina Strait

Jervis Inlet

Nelson I.

Sechelt Inlet

Pender Harbour

Sechelt

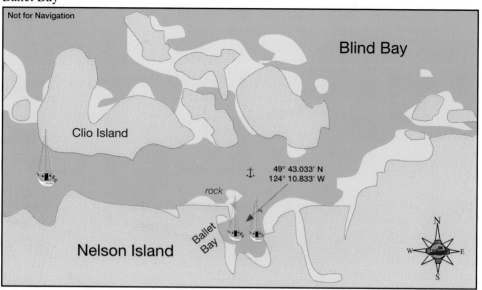

Not for Navigation

Blind Bay

Clio Island

49° 43.033' N
124° 10.833' W

rock

Nelson Island

Ballet Bay

Blind Bay

Charts 3312, 3311, 3512, 3514

This large bay is located at the gateway to Princess Louisa off Jervis Inlet. Many vessels make Blind Bay their rendezvous when heading for that famous destination. **Ballet Bay** and **Musket Island** are the primary anchorages in Blind Bay. Princess Louisa Inlet and its beautiful Chatterbox Falls are among the most famous coastal attractions in British Columbia. See page 144.

Ballet Bay

Access

If you round Cape Cockburn and are looking for shelter, or a place to spend some quality time at anchorage, cruise into the southern portion of Blind Bay and make your way between the northwest shore of Nelson Island and Clio Island.

Anchorage

This is a very popular anchorage. Great care should be taken navigating into it due to rocks and reefs, some dry at high tide. Use a large scale chart. Anchor in the inner or outer coves. The best protection against wind is deep inside the tiny anchorage in Ballet Bay.

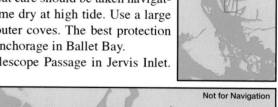

Vanguard Bay. Located beyond Telescope Passage in Jervis Inlet. It is a large open bay with log booms at times and has a rather exposed anchorage. *See diagram page 137.*

Hardy Island. There are several indentations and coves on the Blind Bay side of Hardy Island which offer temporary shelter. But it is best to use Musket Island anchorage.

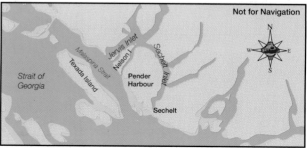

Not for Navigation

Strait of Georgia

Texada Island

Malaspina Strait

Jervis Inlet

Nelson I.

Sechelt Inlet

Pender Harbour

Sechelt

Looking southwest over Blind Bay. Ballet Bay is left of centre. Fox Island and Oyster Island can be seen to the right of the entrance. Hardy Island is in the foreground, seen from Jervis Inlet. Inset: Ballet Bay's entrance in the foreground, opens off Blind Bay. Telescope Passage lies beyond.

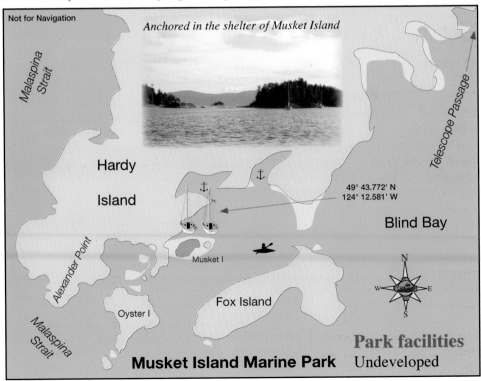

Not for Navigation

Anchored in the shelter of Musket Island

Malaspina Strait

Telescope Passage

Hardy

Island

49° 43.772' N
124° 12.581' W

Blind Bay

Alexander Point

Musket I

Oyster I

Fox Island

Malaspina Strait

N
W E
S

Park facilities
Undeveloped

Musket Island Marine Park

Harmony Islands

Charts 3312, 3514

Access

The Harmony Islands are located on the east side of Hotham Sound to the north of Granville Bay and near the 1,400 feet high cascading Freil Lake waterfall. The sound is reached from Jervis Inlet around Elephant Point and is a good stopover near Princess Wales Reach, the passage to Princess Louisa Inlet.

The Park and Anchorage

This is a quiet and tranquil park area with no facilities or development. The most sheltered anchorage is in the tiny basin created by the natural formation of three islets north of the main island (park). Beware of rocks and reefs in the entrance and anchorage areas. It is possible to anchor between the park and the mainland but use a large scale chart and mind the shallows in the passage. No stern tying or access on private islands. It is best to keep off these, and any other, private islands on the coast.

Nearby

The town of Egmont is a short distance to the south. It has marinas and facilities as well as supplies and amenities for mariners. While at Egmont it is possible to hike in and watch the powerful Skookumchuck Rapids at Sechelt Narrows which run at speeds up to 14 knots. There are other small coves in the vicinity to be discovered, such as Dark Cove in Goliath Bay. Cruise around Hotham Sound and stop in the lee of **Junction Island** in St Vincent Bay for a magnificent view of the mountains and waterfall on the opposite shore. Visit Princess Louisa Inlet–cruise up Princess Wales Reach and through Malibu Rapids.

Park facilities

Fishing, scuba diving.

Top: The Harmony Islands lie beneath towering mountains and nearby waterfalls. Opposite, insets: Cruising up to Princess Louisa Inlet and Skookumchuck Narrows.

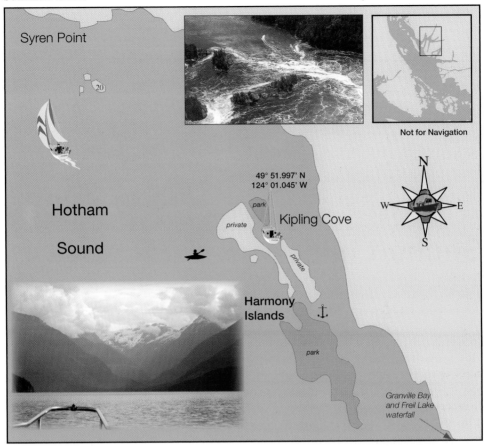

Syren Point

Not for Navigation

49° 51.997' N
124° 01.045' W

park

private

Kipling Cove

Hotham

Sound

private

**Harmony
Islands**

⚓

park

*Granville Bay
and Freil Lake
waterfall*

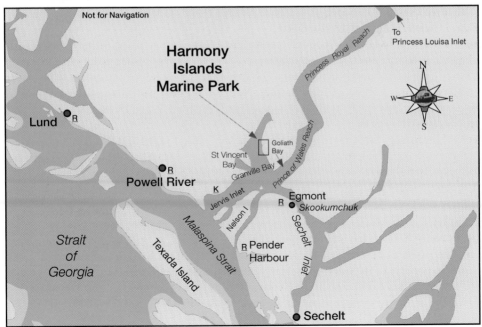

Not for Navigation

**Harmony
Islands
Marine Park**

To
Princess Louisa Inlet

Princess Royal Reach

Lund R

Goliath
Bay

St Vincent
Bay

Granville Bay

Prince of Wales Reach

R
Powell River

K

Jervis Inlet

Nelson I

Egmont

R ●
Skookumchuk

Sechelt Inlet

R Pender
Harbour

**Strait
of
Georgia**

Texada Island

Malaspina Strait

● **Sechelt**

Sechelt Inlet

Charts 3312, 3512, 3514

Access

This is a large sheltered inlet to the east of the Sechelt Peninsula which features eight marine park areas. It is accessed from Jervis Inlet via the tidal Skookumchuck Narrows with its famous Sechelt Rapids, which are known to reach speeds of up to 16 knots. This occurs usually during spring tides when overfalls can reach a stunning 15' (five metres). This is one of the most dangerous waterways on the coast and should not be used without tide and current tables and good charts. Passage should be made only during slack tides, prefereably at high tide. There are several launching ramps inside Sechelt Inlet which can be reached by road from the Sunshine Coast.

The Parks and Anchorages

The cove in **Storm Bay** between Sockeye Point and Cawley Point is a suitable overnight anchorage. Anchor in the lee of the small islet in 2 to 3 fathoms. Or try **Misery Bay**, up Salmon Inlet. Anchor in eight fathoms.

Sechelt Inlet parks are most popular among small boat operators, canoeists and kayakers. They are **Tzoonie Narrows**, on the northern shore of Narrows Inlet, **Kunechin Point** on the north side of salmon Inlet, **Thornhill Creek** at the mouth of the creek of the same name on the south shore of Salmon Inlet, **Nine Mile Point** just south of the entrance of Salmon Inlet, **Tuwanek** on the east side of Sechelt Inlet, **Piper Point, Skaiakos Point** and **Halfway Beach** on the west side.

There is camping, but limited development at the marine parks and little protected overnight anchorage. Exceptions are the tiny coves at either side of Kunechin Point. There is a reef in the small basin on the Salmon Inlet side of the point, so take care when anchoring. Although this cove is generally protected from most winds, some effects of a blow down Salmon Inlet can be felt at times.

Nearby

The town of Sechelt has marinas and launching facilities as well as services and stores for all needs. It is located near Porpoise Bay which lies at the head of Sechelt Inlet. Scuba diving is popular in the inlet, particularly at the site of the *Chaudiere*, a sunken artificial reef off Kunechin Point, and at the Skookumchuck, Tzoonie Narrows and Tuwanek. See *151 Dives* by Betty Pratt-Johnson. It's recommended that you use a dive charter boat for diving the inlet.

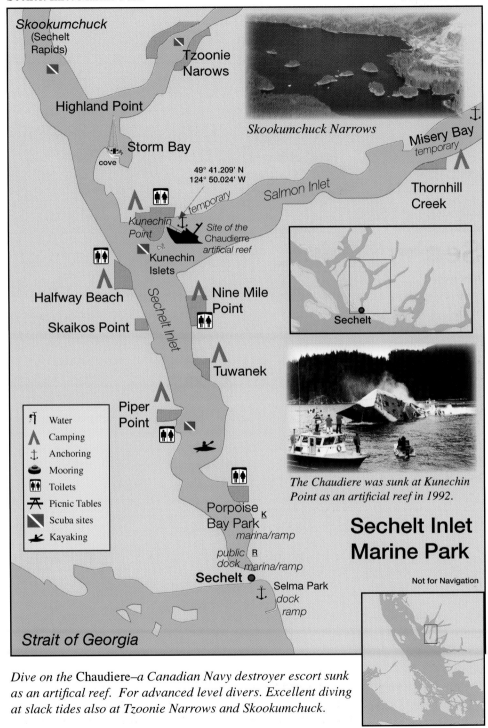

Skookumchuck
(Sechelt
Rapids)

Tzoonie
Narows

Skookumchuck Narrows

Highland Point

Misery Bay
temporary

Storm Bay

cove

49° 41.209' N
124° 50.024' W

temporary

Salmon Inlet

Thornhill
Creek

Kunechin
Point

Site of the
Chaudierre
artificial reef

Kunechin
Islets

Sechelt Inlet

Sechelt

Halfway Beach

Nine Mile
Point

Skaikos Point

Tuwanek

The Chaudiere was sunk at Kunechin
Point as an artificial reef in 1992.

Piper
Point

Legend

- 🚰 Water
- ⛺ Camping
- ⚓ Anchoring
- Mooring
- 🚻 Toilets
- 🛱 Picnic Tables
- Scuba sites
- 🛶 Kayaking

Porpoise
Bay Park K
marina/ramp

public R
dock marina/ramp

Sechelt ●

Selma Park
dock
ramp

Sechelt Inlet
Marine Park

Not for Navigation

Strait of Georgia

*Dive on the Chaudiere–a Canadian Navy destroyer escort sunk
as an artifical reef. For advanced level divers. Excellent diving
at slack tides also at Tzoonie Narrows and Skookumchuck.*

Park facilities

Walk-in campsites, toilets, park host, beach, kayaking, fishing, scuba.

Princess
Louisa
Inlet

Sunshine
Coast

Pender
Harbour

South Coast

Princess Louisa Inlet   Charts 3312, 3514

Access

Take the time to travel up Jervis Inlet to Princess Louisa Inlet. Due to strong tidal flow between tides, passage through Malibu Rapids should be undertaken with caution, using a large scale chart and the tide and current tables. Note: The reference port is Point Atkinson and the secondary port is Malibu Rapids. Monitor wind forecasts.

The Park and Anchorage

Princess Louisa is a major attraction to mariners. Its astounding scenery is legendary. There is a long dock for overnight mooring as well as conditional anchorage off the opposite shore and in the lee of **Macdonald Island**. Mooring buoys were located off the north side of the island.

The park was a gift from James F. Macdonald ("Mac") to the Princess Louisa International Society. In 1953 the land became a provincial marine park.

Nearby

Waterfalls and tall craggy mountains are the features of this deep inlet that cuts into the Coast Range. At the approaches to Jervis Inlet and its outer arm, Princess Royal Reach, the town of Egmont offers services and facilities for overnight mooring and provisions. There is good fishing en route, and at Hardy Island and Nelson Island, scuba diving.

Park facilities

Mooring buoys, boat and dinghy dock, walk-in campsites, toilets, picnic tables, drinking water, hiking, fishing, viewpoint/point of interest. (Mooring buoys at Macdonald Island).

Opposite: The famous Chatterbox Falls seen from the docks at Princess Louisa Inlet.
Above: The dock at the head of the inlet looking south.

144

Not for Navigation

Chatterbox Falls

Princess
Louisa
Inlet

dock

50° 12.271' N
123° 46.155' W

Macdonald Island
50° 11.144' N
23° 47.950' W

Macdonald
Island

No wash
speeds please

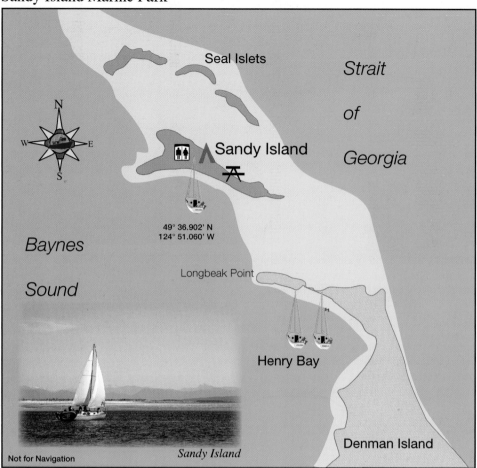

Seal Islets

Strait

of

Georgia

Sandy Island

49° 36.902' N
124° 51.060' W

Baynes

Sound

Longbeak Point

Henry Bay

Not for Navigation

Sandy Island

Denman Island

Sandy Island, adjacent Denman Island

After Nanaimo, or if you cross the Strait of Georgia from Jervis Inlet or the vicinity of Powell River, you can reach Sandy Island Marine Park en route to Comox. Mariners pass the islet on their way to the shelter of Comox from Denman and Hornby Islands or Deep Bay. The harbour at Deep Bay holds a large public marina, has a launch ramp and affords limited anchoring in an open, semi-exposed bay. But if you have time as you cruise up the coast, drop the hook off Sandy Island and venture ashore by dinghy. Walk on the sandy beach and enjoy the spectacular views of the surrounding open waters backed by distant, high mountains.

Princess
Louisa
Inlet

Park facilities

Walk-in campsites, picnic tables, toilets, park host, beach, recommended fishing, kayaking.

Above: Sandy Island. There are few anchorages in the area but lots of protected moorage in Deep Bay and at Comox (inset above). Limited sheltered anchoring space is available at Ford Cove and there is a public dock where moorage is sometimes available. The anchorages at Tribune Bay and Ford Cove should be considered temporary.

Sandy Island

Charts 3527, 3513

Access

The marine park consists of Tree Island and Seal Islets which are grouped off Denman Island in the Strait of Georgia at the north end of Baynes Sound. The park can be reached by boat from Comox to the west or from Denman Island to the southeast.

The Park and Anchorage

Sandy Island is connected to Denman Island by a drying spit at low tide. On the south side of Sandy Island there is a partially sheltered anchorage. The park is known for its white sandy beaches that can be seen across the water from Comox or the Vancouver Island shores adjacent to Baynes Channel. It is a popular 'boating into' picnic site and also has camping facilities with toilets and walking trails.

Best nearby anchorage is in **Deep Bay**. We have stayed at anchor overnight at **Ford Cove** on Hornby Island but it is exposed to wind from the northwest.

Nearby

The town of Comox, which can be entered by careful navigation, has all facilities for mariners, including docks and marinas with launching facilities. Uptown Comox has shops, restaurants and accommodations. Anchor in the protection of **Goose Spit**, being mindful of the shallows that dry at low tide. Use large scale chart 3527

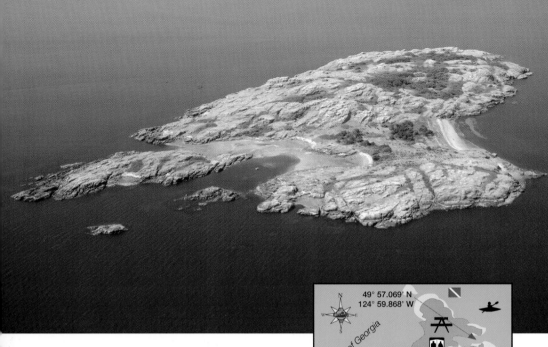

Mitlenatch

Charts 3311, 3538, 3513

Access

The island is located at the northern end of the Strait of Georgia just south of the entrance to Desolation Sound. It can be reached from the west, by going northeast from Comox and Sandy Island or by leaving Campbell River via the south end of Quadra Island (Cape Mudge). From the east travel out of Lund or Powell River. Caution should be exercised when navigating the waters from these two latter departure points due to the rocks and reefs en route to Mitlenatch.

The Park

The island is the nesting place of a variety of species of waterfowl. It is covered with wildflowers in early spring and hosts cactus and other exotic plants. It is used as a research station for botanists and as a preserve for the flora it contains. It is not ideal for overnight anchorage. Anchor off the east side in calm conditions, go ashore and stroll the easy trail or along the beach.

Nearby

Cortes Island lies north of Mitlenatch Island. It has good anchorage and mooring for overnight and extended stays. Gorge Harbour is one of the best anchorages in the area with marina and facilities for mariners and voyagers as well as good fishing, kayaking and scuba diving in the vicinity.

Mitlenatch Island Marine Park

Park facilities

Picnic tables, toilets, park host, beach hiking, fishing, scuba, viewpoint/point of interest.

4

Desolation Sound, to Kingcome Inlet

The Broughton Islands

For expanded information on the waterways, islands and marine facilities in the areas beyond Desolation Sound, from Big Bay to Port Hardy, refer to the author's cruising guide: *North of Desolation Sound*.

Ragged Islands

Charts 3311, 3538, 3513

Access

The town of Lund is a landmark gateway to Desolation Sound. From Lund it is merely a matter of minutes on the northbound voyage before you are in the Ragged Islands (officially called the Copeland Islands). Thulin Passage runs between the mainland shore and the islands to form a sheltered passage for mariners travelling north and south. And the islands themselves offer several protected anchorages for those who wish to stop overnight. One of the most popular anchorages is the one that opens off Thulin Passage on the northernmost of the larger islets in the group.

The Park and Anchorage

This is a beautiful park comprising three larger islands and numerous small islets with rocks, reefs, cliffs, grassy ridges and magnificent views. Anchorage can be found in the basin facing onto Thulin Passage about half way through. Access into the anchorage is safe for pleasure craft, but use a large scale chart and avoid the submerged reef at the south entrance off Thulin Passage. Another cosy anchorage can be found on the west side of the islands but this, like other anchoring spots in the vicinity should be considered temporary. These islands and rocks are excellent for kayakers and canoeists to explore out of Lund. Much of the shoreline is accessible and sparsely forested near the water, leaving good ledges to sit on and admire the views across the approaches to Desolation Sound.

Nearby

The settlements at Lund and its neighbouring islands has a pioneering history. The historic inn at Lund has been developed over recent years to house a variety of stores and boutiques. In Lund there are restaurants and stores including a grocery store, bakery, fresh fish, sports (scuba, kayaking) and others. There are also marine services and fuels. The next available fuel and provisions as you head into Desolation Sound are at Refuge Cove and Squirrel Cove (fuel available on shore, alongside a general store and a pub/res-

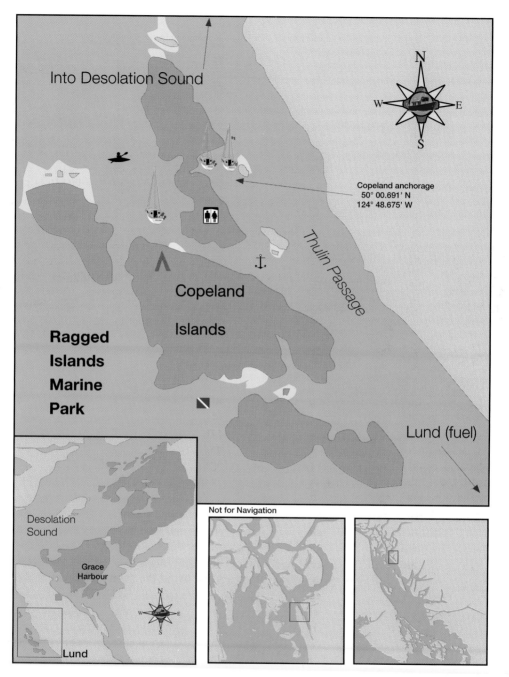

taurant). Approaching the sound, you will pass Bliss Landing at the north end of Thulin Passage and just a short distance beyond is the actual entrance to Desolation Sound.

Park facilities

Walk-in campsites, toilets, fishing, recommended kayaking, scuba.

Desolation Sound Parks

When mariners refer to Desolation Sound they generally include an overall area that encompasses adjacent waterways, islands, mainland inlets and shorelines. For the purposes of this section, the Sound includes the Discovery Islands and takes in the Redonda Islands in the east, Cortes Island to the south, Read Island in the middle and the east side of Quadra Island in the west, with all of the smaller islands and islets nearby as well as sections of Sonora Island thrown in. When we travel north to Stuart Island we ask "is this in the Sound or north of it." No matter, wherever there is a park or place of interest that lies within the above general boundaries, then as far as mariners are concerned it is Desolation Sound.

The marine parks in Desolation Sound proper are clearly shown in the following diagram. Among the best known anchorages in Desolation Sound are Prideaux Haven, Laura Cove, Tenedos Bay and Grace Harbour. Popular access to these harbours is north through

the Strait of Georgia and Malaspina Strait, via the Copeland Islands (Ragged Islands Marine Park) and east, northeast around Sarah Point. Vessels travelling to Grace Harbour travel south of Zephine Head. Mind the drying Stacey Rock off the opposite shore.

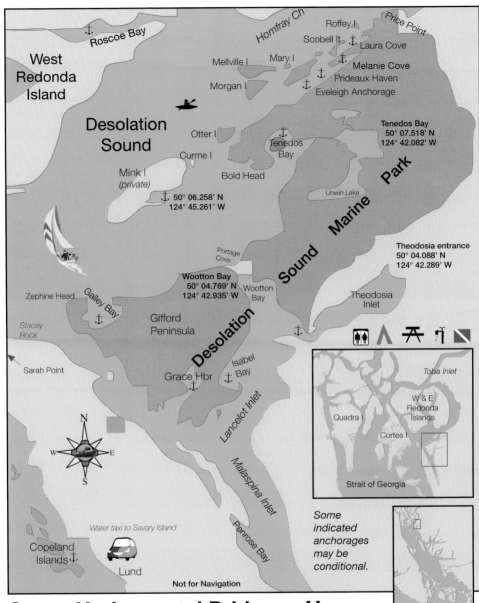

West
Redonda
Island

Roscoe Bay

Homfray Ch

Roffey I.

Scobell It.

Price Point

Laura Cove

Mellville I

Mary I

Melanie Cove

Prideaux Haven

Morgan I

Eveleigh Anchorage

Desolation
Sound

Otter I

Tenedos
Bay

Tenedos Bay
50° 07.518' N
124° 42.082' W

Curme I

Mink I
(private)

Bold Head

Unwin Lake

Sound Marine Park

50° 06.258' N
124° 45.261' W

Theodosia entrance
50° 04.088' N
124° 42.289' W

Portage
Cove

Wootton Bay
50° 04.769' N
124° 42.935' W

Wootton
Bay

Theodosia
Inlet

Zephine Head

Galley Bay

Gifford
Peninsula

Desolation

Stacey
Rock

Sarah Point

Grace Hbr

Isabel
Bay

Toba Inlet

W & E
Redonda
Islands

Quadra I

Lancelot Inlet

Cortes I

N

W   E

S

Strait of Georgia

Water taxi to Savary Island

Malaspina Inlet

Penrose Bay

Some
indicated
anchorages
may be
conditional.

Copeland
Islands

Lund

Not for Navigation

Grace Harbour and Prideaux Haven
Desolation Sound Marine Park

Charts 3312, 3559, 3538, 3541

Opposite: John M. Horton painting of Captain Vancouver exploring Desolation Sound. Bottom: Prideaux Haven, with Melanie Cove in the left foreground.

Park facilities

Anchorages, toilets, trails, good fishing, scuba diving, kayaking, beaches, hiking, fresh water from lakes, waterfalls, scenic viewpoints. (These exist at some of the parks in Desolation Sound).

Grace Harbour

Charts 3559, 3538, 3312

Access

After entering Desolation Sound via the Copeland Islands, there is the choice of continuing to hug the mainland shore and swing around Sarah Point heading for Grace Harbour, or continuing across to Zephine Head, rounding it and voyaging on to Prideaux Haven. Most visitors to Desolation Sound travel to this latter destination for its several large but sheltered coves. And in doing so miss out on the virtues of Grace Harbour. Enter the harbour around Scott Point off Malaspina Inlet.

The Park and Anchorage

If you go farther into Desolation Sound than this beautiful bay you will not find much better. The harbour is made up of a shallow rocky basin at the entrance just off the passage to the main basin as you enter, and a large open bay inside where, in mid summer, it is possible to find boats tied up to one another, anchored in the centre of the cove and stern tied to the shore. Off to the far side of the anchorage is a small stream with a waterfall that has a good flow of cool water, popular for bathing and showering among those searching for a cooling down, or refreshing themselves after several days aboard their boats. The area is a favourite marine park with developed trails for hiking, walking, swimming in the lake, or just sitting and enjoying the views.

Nearby

The nearest facility for provisions and fuel is at Refuge Cove on the southern tip of West Redonda Island. A small one-boat anchorage that I have named **Myrita Cove** can be found just before the entrance to Grace Harbour. It is good for up to one large vessel but not in all weather conditions. Other anchorages and parks in Desolation Sound include those located at adjacent inlets: off Lancelot Inlet, in the lee of the Susan Islets at **Theodosia Inlet**, and at **Isabel Bay** almost opposite the entrance to Theodosia.

There is also anchorage at **Galley Bay** just beyond Zephine Head, or at **Mink Island** a short way off Prideaux Haven. Respect the privacy of home owners in these coves.

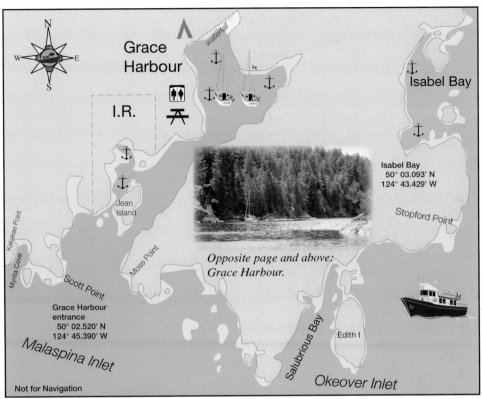

Grace
Harbour

I.R.

Isabel Bay

Isabel Bay
50° 03.093' N
124° 43.429' W

Stopford Point

Jean
Island

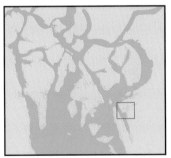

Opposite page and above:
Grace Harbour.

Kakakae Point

Myrtta Cove

Scott Point

Moss Point

Grace Harbour
entrance
50° 02.520' N
124° 45.390' W

Malaspina Inlet

Salubrious Bay

Edith I

Okeover Inlet

Not for Navigation

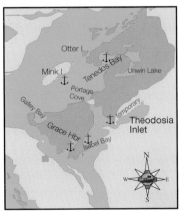

Otter I

Mink I

Tenedos Bay

Unwin Lake

Portage
Cove

Galley Bay

Grace Hbr

temporary

Isabel Bay

Theodosia
Inlet

Below: Mink Island anchorage. Mink Island is private as is
the dock in the cove. Anchor directly facing the entrance. It
is a sheltered, cosy anchorage away from the crowds.

Note: I have named the tiny cove west of the entrance to Grace Harbour after our good friends, Walt and Rita Lee's 54' Monk McQueen motor yacht. It was one of their favoured spots, suitable for one vessel only, in fair weather.

155

Above: The busy anchorages at Melanie Cove (left foreground) and adjacent Prideaux Haven.
Below: Tenedos Bay–part of the Desolation Sound Marine Park area.

Prideaux Haven

Charts 3555, 3312, 3538

Access

Entrance to Prideaux Haven is from Homfray Channel to the east of Eveleigh Island. Keep the reef in the centre of the channel to port as you enter.

The Park and Anchorages

Desolation Sound Marine Park extends from Prideaux Haven in the northeast corner, down to Grace Harbour on the Gifford Peninsula, and includes **Prideaux Haven, Tenedos Bay, Portage Cove, Galley Bay, Isabel Bay** and **Wooton Bay**. Anchorage is popular and best known at **Grace Harbour, Prideaux Haven, Eveleigh Anchorage, Melanie Cove** and **Laura Cove.** There are trails in some park areas and these are marked by signboards ashore at the trail heads. The largest fresh water body in the park is Unwin

Lake located south of Prideaux Haven and east of Tenedos Bay. The shortest hike to the lake is from Tenedos Bay. There is no garbage disposal so plan to leave none. (A garbage scow at Refuge Cove calls at anchorages.)

Nearby

The nearest facility for provisions and fuel is at Refuge Cove on the southern tip of West Redonda Island.

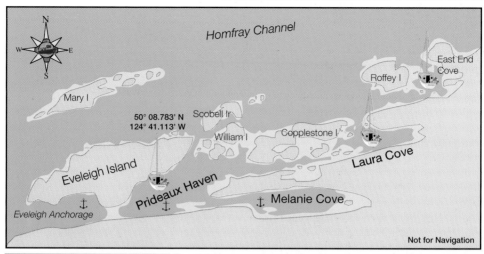

Homfray Channel

East End Cove

Roffey I

Mary I

50° 08.783' N
124° 41.113' W

Scobell Ir

William I

Copplestone I

Laura Cove

Eveleigh Island

Prideaux Haven

Melanie Cove

Eveleigh Anchorage

Not for Navigation

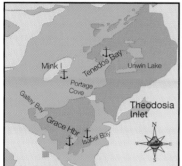

Mink I

Tenedos Bay

Unwin Lake

Portage Cove

Galley Bay

Grace Hbr

Isabel Bay

Theodosia Inlet

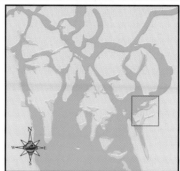

Desolation Sound Marine Park, Prideaux Haven, Melanie Cove and Laura Cove

Another popular, sheltered anchorage is in **Tenedos Bay**. This cosy nook is in the shadow of Bold Head. While the water is deep, there are several suitable spots to drop the hook. Other anchorages and parks nearby include Roscoe Bay on East Redonda Island and at **Pendrell Sound** (page 160) across the channel at East Redonda Island.

Looking towards Prideaux Haven and Melanie Cove from Eveleigh Anchorage.

Roscoe Bay

Charts 3312, 3538

Access

This protected bay is on the east side of West Redonda Island. It is just to the north of Marylebone Point near the junction of Waddington Channel and Homfray Channel in Desolation Sound. The entrance is off Waddington Channel over a drying shoal at the narrows just inside the inlet. Once you are inside, depending on the draft of your boat, you may be there until a later high tide. Plan to stay a while and leave when the shoal is well covered.

The Park and Anchorage

This is one of the most popular anchorages in Desolation Sound. There are toilets and camping facilities ashore and a hiking trail to nearby Black Lake. If you want to sit in your boat for an extended period, this is the place to do it. If you want total peace and quiet, don't expect it during the height of summer, for this is a popular place for families, and children on other vessels may be noisy in their enjoyment of their vacation.

Nearby

Desolation Sound with all of its anchorages and marine park areas. The scenery is outstanding. Refuge Cove at the tip of West Redonda Island is the centre for supplies and services. There is warm water bathing in summer at Pendrell Sound. This lies off Waddington Channel en rout to Walsh Cove.

Park facilities

Picnic tables, camping, drinking water, toilets, beach hiking, fishing.

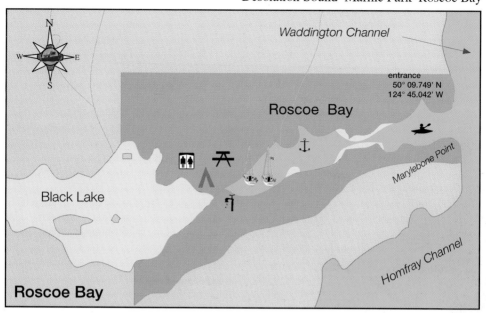

Waddington Channel

entrance
50° 09.749' N
124° 45.042' W

Roscoe Bay

Marylebone Point

Black Lake

Homfray Channel

Roscoe Bay

Not for Navigation

Opposite and right: Looking west into Roscoe Inlet. The narrow entrance is shallow and requires high tide for the passage of all but very small craft. Black Lake looks like an extension of the popular inlet. To the south of the inlet, Homfray Channel can be followed down to Refuge Cove at the tip of West Redonda Island.

Walsh Cove

Charts 3312, 3541

Access

This anchorage with its adjacent marine park is located on the east side of Redonda Island. It is tucked in behind Butler Point, Waddington Channel. Enter the anchorage to the west of Gorges Islands from Waddington Channel, coming in from the south. The anchorage may also be entered or departed north of Gorges Islands, but great care should be taken in this entrance, avoiding the reefs between the islands and the bluff.

The Park and Anchorage

Undeveloped, but some trails may provide a good view of the channel and anchorage. Swimming is popular off the Gorges Islands, but beware of the sharp edged shells and barnacles on the rocks. Deep water. Anchor near shore and stern tie.

Nearby

A dinghy ride around the anchorage is worthwhile. There are pictographs to be found on the almost sheer cliffs at the north end of the cove. A power equipped shore boat can provide pleasant excursions, such as up to the falls in Toba Inlet.

Pendrell Sound

Not for Navigation

See diagram right. Many people make it a regular pilgrimage to go to this warm water destination in summer. The head of the Sound is known for its excellent swimming in surprisingly warm water. The best anchorage is in the lee of the small islet to port, adjacent to a drying inlet as you approach the north end. (Photographs on page 162). Wind conditions in the Sound can be mystifying, usually light or nonexistent while it is blowing, sometimes to extremes elsewhere. Powerboats are urged to travel in Pendrell Sound at no-wake speeds.

Toba Inlet

Walsh Cove

Pendrell Sound

Roscoe Bay

Refuge Cove

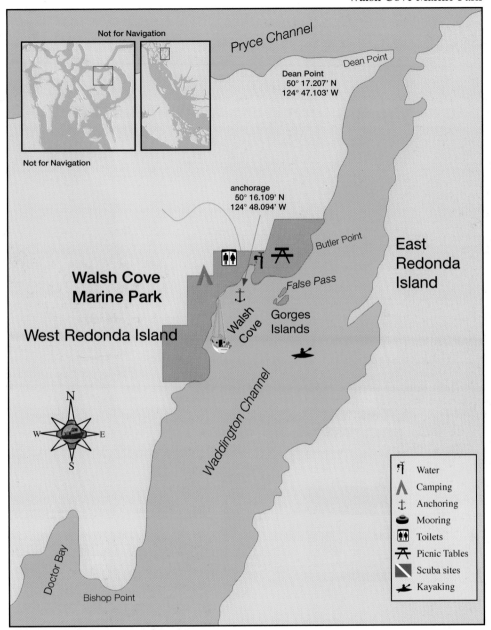

Opposite: Looking down Waddington Channel from the north. Gorges Islands (also inset) can be seen just off Butler Point.

Park facilities

Walsh Cove–boat/dinghy dock, walk-in campsites, picnic tables, drinking water, toilets, park host, beach hiking, fishing, recommended kayaking, swimming, scuba diving, viewpoint/point of interest.

Top and above: Anchorage at Pendrell Sound. The water is warm in summer.
Left: Anchored in Walsh Cove.
Opposite page: Waterfall in Toba Inlet.

Cortes Bay

Charts 3312, 3538

Access

Cortes Bay is located on the east side of Cortes Island, and can be approached directly from the entrance to Desolation Sound at the Copeland Islands, or from the south and west via the south end of Cortes Island.

Anchorage

Boats can anchor anywhere in the bay. But monitor wind forecasts as occasional blows into the bay can cause dragged anchors. If a wind does come up it is wise to post a watch. We have been lucky with calm conditions in Cortes Bay, but many mariners have told us of their windy ordeals. Try to assess the wind forecasts and plan your anchoring in accordance with their direction. Allow lots of scope when anchored in the middle of the bay. Entering and leaving the bay, exercise caution when navigating past the rock marked by a beacon at the entrance. You must favour the south side and keep your speed to a minimum. No-wake speeds in the bay are appreciated by the many local shore-side residents who have boats at their docks.

Nearby

The public dock in Cortes Bay sees a lot of pleasure traffic in summer and usually holds a full compliment of local vessels in winter. It is quite a substantial dock and when anchored out in the bay it can be used readily for going ashore in your dinghy. The yacht clubs that own property in the bay reserve their docks for their own and reciprocal members.

Just to the north of Cortes Bay, Squirrel Cove, a popular but tranquil anchorage, is another of the favoured destinations in Desolation Sound. Yet another nearby sheltered anchorage in the area is Gorge Harbour on the west side of Cortes Island.

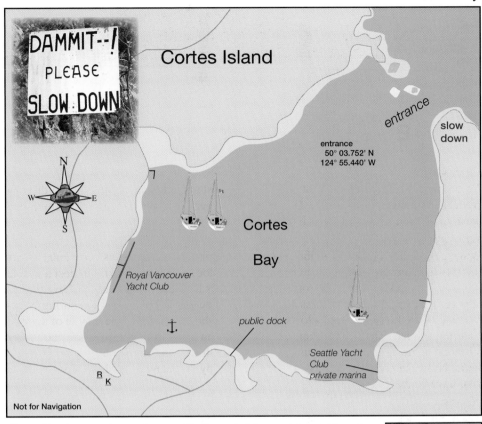

DAMMIT--!
PLEASE
SLOW DOWN

Cortes Island

entrance

slow down

entrance
50° 03.752' N
124° 55.440' W

N
W   E
S

Cortes

Bay

Royal Vancouver
Yacht Club

public dock

Seattle Yacht
Club
private marina

R
K

Not for Navigation

Cortes Bay is a popular anchorage. Monitor wind forecast. Inset: Sign at the entrance to Cortes Bay asks mariners to please be considerate. Proceed in the bay at no wash speeds.

Opposite page: A view of the anchorage and an aerial of the bay looking west. The public dock is seen prominently with favoured anchorage to the north of it. (Kayaking is good in many parts of the area, but be careful of tides, currents and wind.)

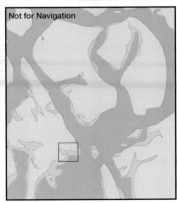

Some mariners tie up at the public dock in Cortes Bay. The landing provides ready access to the road system for long walks on Cortes Island.

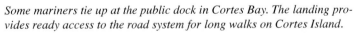

Not for Navigation

Squirrel Cove

Charts 3555, 3312, 3538

Desolation Sound

Access

Travelling north out of Cortes Bay, Squirrel Cove opens into Cortes Island almost directly across from Refuge Cove on West Redondo Island. It is the first major anchorage you find in Desolation Sound when travelling up the coast by way of the Sunshine Coast. Its location is on the west side of Lewis Channel opposite Refuge Cove.

The Park and Anchorage

This cove on the east side of Cortes Island has been one of the most loved and hated anchorages in all the years of pleasure boating on the British Columbia coast. It is a large cove with a convoluted shoreline providing many nooks and corners in which to anchor. Like Cortes Bay to the south, however, it is known to be subject to the occasional strong wind which can cause great discomfort. In summer this is a rare event, but be cautioned, it does happen so make sure your ground tackle is truly secure and that you have lots of room to swing or better yet, that your boat is stern tied to shore. Some logs or snags have been reported on the bottom. Monitor the overnight wind forecast.

A fair amount of the adjacent shoreline is First Nations Reserve land. On the east shore, north of the entrance look for the bakery that provides goods to boats at anchor. For many years someone, like Bill Redel in the '80s and '90s, has run such a service in the cove. More recently it was Marilyn's Salmon restaurant mariners found there. Where on-the-water food services are concerned, at Squirrel Cove and at other waterways, it is a matter of 'expect it to be there if you find it there'.

Nearby

Squirrel Cove General Store at the public dock in the outer cove has groceries and supplies as well as an adjacent restaurant and pub. Go ashore for these items and browse among the available local crafts. Continue up Lewis Channel to Teakerne Arm where another marine park, temporary anchorage, waterfall and warm water lake await. Or travel across Desolation Sound into the popular anchorages at Prideaux Haven, Melanie Cove, Tenedos Bay or Grace Harbour.

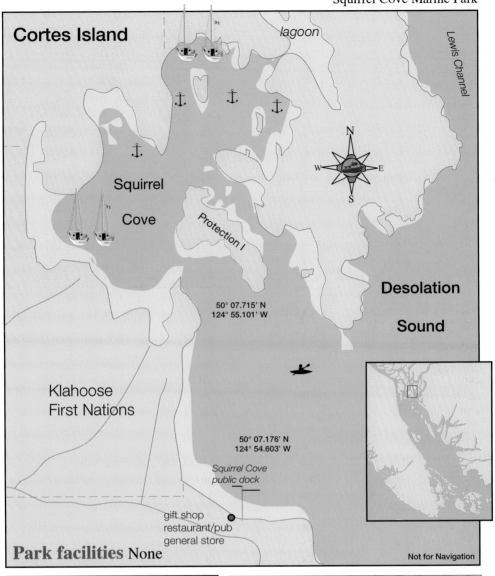

Cortes Island

lagoon

Lewis Channel

N
W E
S

Squirrel

Cove

Protection I

Desolation

Sound

50° 07.715' N
124° 55.101' W

**Klahoose
First Nations**

50° 07.176' N
124° 54.603' W

*Squirrel Cove
public dock*

gift shop
restaurant/pub
general store

Park facilities None

Not for Navigation

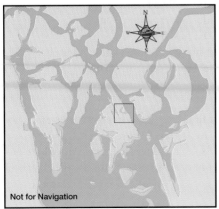

Not for Navigation

*Squirrel Cove anchorage is a popular destination.
There is a store and restaurant near the entrance.*

Teakerne Arm

Charts 3312, 3538

Access

Entrance to this open inlet is from Lewis Channel. Pass Joyce Point and travel the short distance eastwards and across the inlet to the waterfall which tumbles down from Cassel Lake.

The Park and Anchorage

The anchorage is favoured near the fall and best used daytimes only, preferably when there is no northwesterly wind in the forecast.

I recommend against leaving your boat anchored and un-attended. The park is undeveloped, except for the provision and maintence by the Parks Branch of a dinghy float adjacent to the west shore on the approaches to the fall. A single small sized boat could stop at the dock for a short period but because the dock is meant to provide access

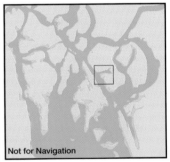

Not for Navigation

for all, leaving a boat tied up at the dock would be inconsiderate of those wanting to land by dinghy.

Anchor just west of the dock, stern tie to shore and row to the dinghy dock. The trail leads up to the lake along the fall.

There is space to anchor in nearby Talbot Cove, but holding is not very good. So if you are planning to spend a night in the area do so only if you are absolutely certain of the wind forecast, otherwise go to the dock at Refuge Cove or anchor in another, more protected place, such as Von Donop Inlet.

Nearby

Walk up beyond the waterfall to the lake where warm water swimming is popular during summer.

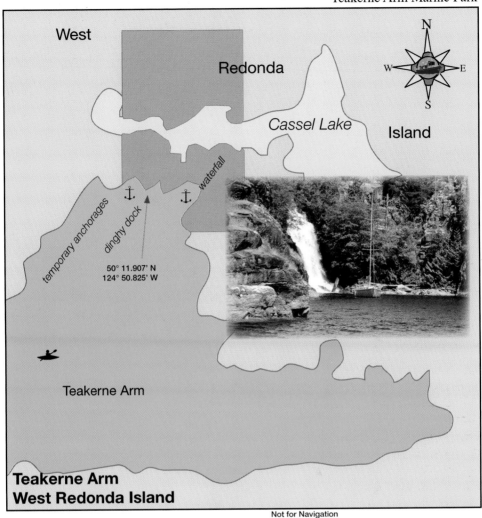

West

Redonda

Cassel Lake

Island

temporary anchorages

dinghy dock

waterfall

50° 11.907' N
124° 50.825' W

Teakerne Arm

**Teakerne Arm
West Redonda Island**

Not for Navigation

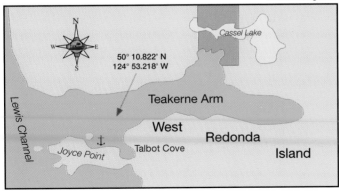

Cassel Lake

50° 10.822' N
124° 53.218' W

Teakerne Arm

West

Lewis Channel

Joyce Point

Talbot Cove

Redonda

Island

Park facilities

Dinghy dock, hiking, fishing, viewpoint/point of interest.

Photo above shows the lagoon, anchorage and dock at Mansons Landing.

Mansons Landing

Charts 3312, 3538

Access

From the southwest, access is via Sutil Channel or from the northwest via Uganda Pass at the north end of Marina Island. Mansons Landing marine park is located at the west side of Cortes Island with its western boundary at Hague Lake.

The Park and Anchorage

The park contains a large lagoon that is an attractive feature of the park, with a white sandy beach, said to be one of the finest in British Columbia. The anchorage in Manson Bay is exposed to some wind conditions, but Cat and Sheep Islets protect from the west. In the park there are picnic tables, toilets and walking trails, but no camping facilites and no water. The park is also accessible by car ferry from Campbell River via Quadra Island.

Nearby

Within the borders of the park there is a public dock, and a short walk away there is a post office, a book store and a co-op store. Another anchorage can be found a short distance to the west, at Gorge Harbour.

Park facilities

Boat dock, picnic tables, toilets, beach, hiking, recommended fishing.

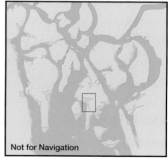

Not for Navigation

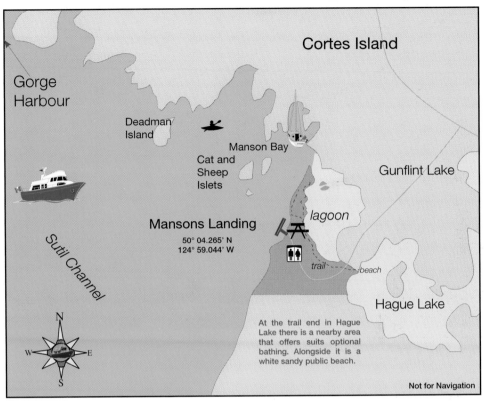

Cortes Island

Gorge Harbour

Deadman Island

Manson Bay

Cat and Sheep Islets

Gunflint Lake

Mansons Landing

50° 04.265' N
124° 59.044' W

lagoon

Sutil Channel

trail　*beach*

Hague Lake

At the trail end in Hague Lake there is a nearby area that offers suits optional bathing. Alongside it is a white sandy public beach.

N
W　E
S

Not for Navigation

Mansons Landing

Cat and Sheep Islets off Mansons Landing. The lagoon lies beyond the beach with the dock.

Gorge Harbour

Access

Entrance is through the narrow gorge from which the harbour has derived its name. Mariners approach from the south and the open waters of the Strait of Georgia, passing Mitlenatch Island, or from the east around the southern tip of Cortes Island. Mind the shallows that extend a long way from the south tip of Cortes. Approach from the west via the narrow Uganda Passage between Marina Island and Cortes with caution.

Anchorage

As you enter through the high rock cliffs at Gorge Harbour look for the ancient rock paintings on the wall. These petroglyphs can be seen to the right of an arrow that points towards them. Most vessels anchoring in Gorge Harbour choose the western portion of the bay although other locations are possible. The most popular anchorage is in the far end beyond the marina. Anchor in 6 to 10 metres (20 to 30 feet). Winds do cause some swinging on the hook but seldom is there a great degree of discomfort. In the harbour there is a small, busy public dock as well as a marina with fuel, services and facilities including a fine restaurant.

Nearby

Whaletown is a fascinating place. It has a public dock and a post office but no services for mariners. There is a roadway around the island that serves to connect Gorge Harbour Marina to Whaletown. The Quadra Island to Cortes Island ferry lands near Whaletown and many RV and camping enthusiasts arrive this way. Walking along the road between the two places provides good exercise. Mansons Landing is another interesting stop nearby. It is located a short distance to the east of the entrance of Gorge Harbour and is a designated marine park. The dock at Mansons provides some access to the park. Anchorage is available on the east side of **Shark Spit** on Marina Island. So instead of just going through Uganda Passage, stop and visit the lovely beach on the spit.

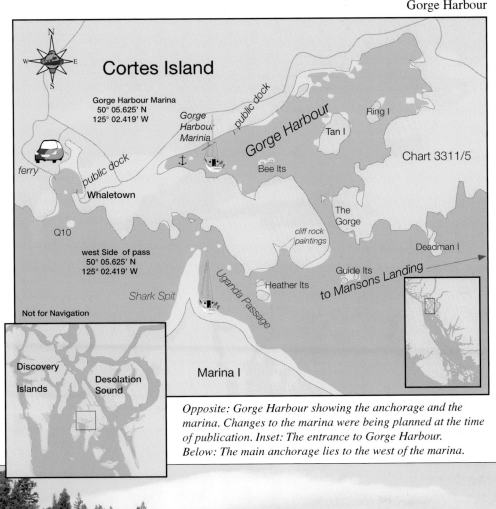

Cortes Island

Gorge Harbour Marina
50° 05.625' N
125° 02.419' W

Gorge
Harbour
Marinia

Gorge Harbour

Chart 3311/5

Ring I

Tan I

Bee Its

public dock

ferry

Whaletown

public dock

Q10

The
Gorge

west Side of pass
50° 05.625' N
125° 02.419' W

cliff rock
paintings

Deadman I

Shark Spit

Uganda Passage

Heather Its

Guide Its

to Mansons Landing

Not for Navigation

Marina I

Discovery
Islands

Desolation
Sound

*Opposite: Gorge Harbour showing the anchorage and the
marina. Changes to the marina were being planned at the time
of publication. Inset: The entrance to Gorge Harbour.
Below: The main anchorage lies to the west of the marina.*

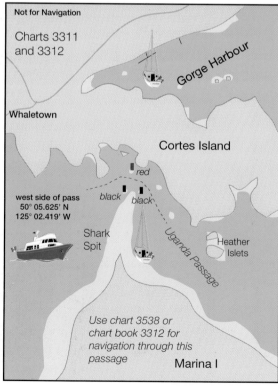

Not for Navigation

Charts 3311
and 3312

Gorge Harbour

Whaletown

Cortes Island

red

west side of pass
50° 05.625' N
125° 02.419' W

black   *black*

Shark
Spit

Uganda Passage

Heather
Islets

Use chart 3538 or
chart book 3312 for
navigation through this
passage

Marina I

Uganda Passage is a short cut from
Read Island and anchorages such as
Evans Bay or those on the west side
of Cortes Island to Gorge Harbour
and Mansons Landing. It obviates the
need to cruise around Marina Island.
The sandy beach along the lee of
Shark Spit appeals to mariners, and
many stop there for a walk or to picnic on the beach. The narrows is well
marked for a safe passage, but keep
close check on the chart and make
sure you follow the rules of the road.

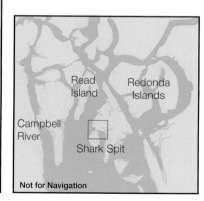

Read
Island

Redonda
Islands

Campbell
River

Shark Spit

Not for Navigation

Evans Bay

Charts 3312, 3538, 3541

Access and anchorage

Evans Bay is prominently located in the Discovery Islands. It opens off Sutil Channel on the east side of Read Island. It has a wide entrance and several possible anchorages at its north end. These are at **Bird Cove** and in nooks along the convoluted shore. Temporary anchorage off Lambert's Beach, which is a regional park, affords an opportunity to go ashore and enjoy a picnic along with the outstanding view. There is a small public dock just south of the beach. This is the Read Island public wharf and is often kept busy with the coming and going of service vessels. Although Evans Bay is open to southerly winds, it offers reasonable shelter in most summer conditions.

Nearby

The best anchorage is at Von Donop Inlet on the opposite side of Sutil Channel. **Carrington Bay, Quartz Bay** and **Coulter Bay**, offer short term anchorage on the Cortes Island side of Sutil Channel, but Von Donop Inlet is by far the most protected anchorage in the area.

Top: Sutil Channel, with Penn Islands in the centre, Read Island to the left.
Right: A view across Sutil Channel, off Coulter Bay.
Bottom: Carrington Bay.

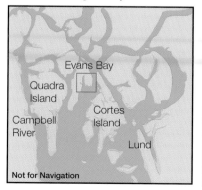

Evans Bay

Quadra
Island

Cortes
Island

Campbell
River

Lund

Not for Navigation

Von Donop Inlet

Charts 3312, 3538

Access

Travelling north up the west side of Cortes Island or across Sutil Channel from Read Island, Von Donop Inlet's opening, facing north, is accessed after passing Whaletown, Coulter Bay, Carrington Bay and Quartz Bay. The Penn Islands lie across Sutil Channel from the entrance. From the north, down Calm Channel, pass the Rendezvous Islands and you will be facing the entrance to Von Donop Inlet, off Sutil Channel.

Park and Anchorage

This large inlet in the west side of Cortes Island is a most beautiful place with nature all around and anchorage that is sheltered and protected against most all conditions. Travel deep inside and anchor near or at the head of the inlet.

Nearby

Almost adjacent to the entrance of Von Donop Inlet is **Quartz Bay**, a suitable overnight anchorage behind the islands in its entrance. Also anchor across Sutil Channel at **Evans**

Bay. Not much farther down Sutil Channel are **Carrington Bay** and **Coulter Bay** where shelter is also possible. Beyond that is **Whaletown** which has a public dock and limited anchorage. Cross Sutil Channel to the anchorage at Rebecca Spit or visit Drew Harbour where **Heriot Bay** has anchorage as well as marina services, hotel, fuel and nearby stores and public dock.

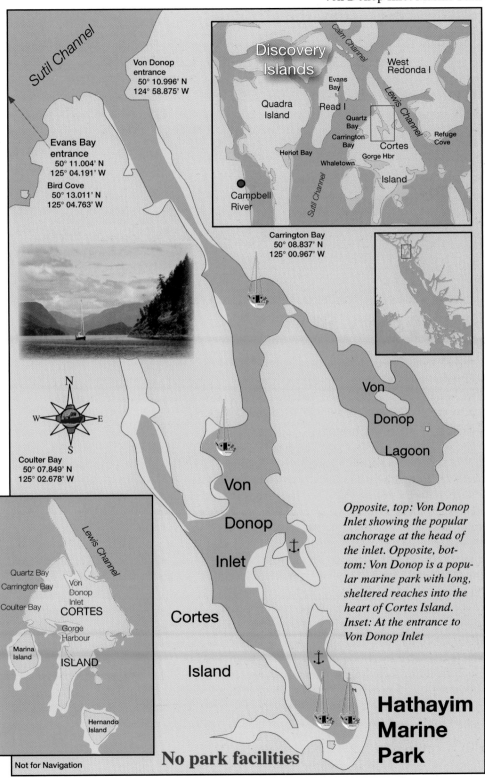

Sutil Channel

Von Donop
entrance
50° 10.996' N
124° 58.875' W

Evans Bay
entrance
50° 11.004' N
125° 04.191' W

Bird Cove
50° 13.011' N
125° 04.763' W

Discovery
Islands

Calm Channel

West
Redonda I

Evans
Bay

Quadra
Island

Read I

Quartz
Bay

Lewis Channel

Refuge
Cove

Carrington
Bay

Cortes

Heriot Bay

Whaletown

Gorge Hbr

Island

Campbell
River

Sutil Channel

Carrington Bay
50° 08.837' N
125° 00.967' W

Von

Donop

Lagoon

Coulter Bay
50° 07.849' N
125° 02.678' W

Von

Donop

Inlet

Cortes

Island

Lewis Channel

Quartz Bay

Von
Donop
Inlet

Carrington Bay

Coulter Bay

CORTES

Gorge
Harbour

Marina
Island

ISLAND

Hernando
Island

*Opposite, top: Von Donop
Inlet showing the popular
anchorage at the head of
the inlet. Opposite, bot-
tom: Von Donop is a popu-
lar marine park with long,
sheltered reaches into the
heart of Cortes Island.
Inset: At the entrance to
Von Donop Inlet*

Hathayim
Marine
Park

No park facilities

Not for Navigation

177

Rebecca Spit

Charts 3312, 3538, 3539

Access

Rebecca Spit is located on the east side of Quadra Island. It is a long narrow strip of land that forms a splendid natural breakwater to Drew Harbour. Drew Harbour is entered from Sutil Channel off Heriot Bay. Vehicle access across Quadra Island is from Vancouver Island via the Campbell River to Quathiaski Cove ferry.

The Park and Anchorage

This large, fairly exposed bay is popular as an anchorage during the summer. The safest anchorage is adjacent to the northwest end of the Spit. Beware of a shallow ledge that protrudes from the beach part way down the shore. It dries at very low tides but is shallow enough at low water for boats to touch bottom at medium low tides. The facilities at Rebecca Spit Marine Park are extensive. It is a picturesque park with white sandy beaches lining both sides of the spit. These are backed by open uplands interspersed with stands of shrubs, grasses and second growth trees. There are many day use facilities including the availability of water, picnic tables and toilets. A boat launch ramp is located near the south end of the park. Taku Marina in Drew Harbour offers overnight moorage.

Nearby

In Heriot Bay there is a public dock as well as a full service marina. The marina is part of the property housing the historic Heriot Bay Inn where accommodations and meals are available. Inside the pub a large poster depicts the old Canadian five dollar bill on which was portrayed a local Heriot Bay fishing boat. Near the Inn are access roads to other island facilities including grocery stores and craft shops. The inter-island ferry serving Whaletown on Cortes Island has a landing at Heriot Bay. Also on Quadra Island, anchor at **Open Bay, Village Bay** or **Moulds Bay,** or farther north in the lee of **Bold Island** but beware of rocks in the narrow passage around it. Stern tie in limited space.

Park facilities

Picnic tables, drinking water, toilets, beach, hiking, fishing, launch ramp.

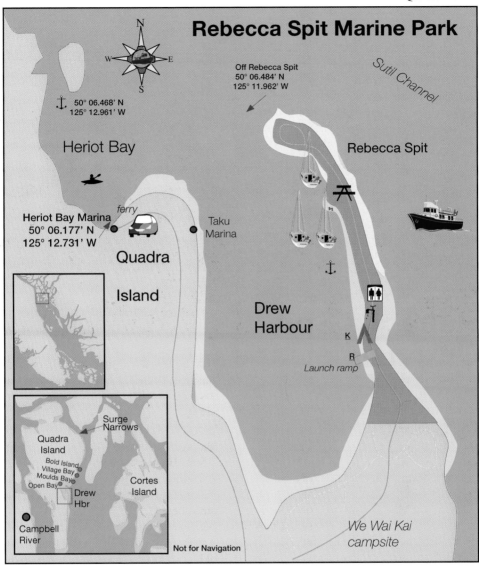

Rebecca Spit Marine Park

Off Rebecca Spit
50° 06.484' N
125° 11.962' W

Sutil Channel

50° 06.468' N
125° 12.961' W

Heriot Bay

Rebecca Spit

Heriot Bay Marina
50° 06.177' N
125° 12.731' W

ferry

Taku
Marina

Quadra

Island

Drew

Harbour

K

R

Launch ramp

Inset map

Surge
Narrows

Quadra
Island

Bold Island
Village Bay
Moulds Bay
Open Bay

Drew
Hbr

Cortes
Island

Campbell
River

We Wai Kai
campsite

Not for Navigation

Opposite, top: Rebecca Spit from the northeast with Drew Harbour beyond. Gowlland Harbour is seen on the west side of Quadra Island. Below: Drew Harbour anchorage from Rebecca Spit.

Octopus Islands

Charts 3312, 3537, 3539

Access

Entrance is from Okisollo Channel at the south end of Hole in the Wall. Access Okisollo Channel from the south via Surge Narrows. From the north, Okisollo Channel opens off Discovery Passage between Sonora and Quadra Islands.

The park is located near the north eastern tip of Quadra Island on the north shore of Waiatt Bay.

The Park and Anchorage

Many islets and coves in Octopus Islands Marine Park make it an ideal place to choose for an extended period at anchor. There are beach areas for sunbathing, swimming or scuba diving. Many visitors go ahore to picnic. The sparsely forested slopes of Quadra Island form a scenic back-drop to a group of small islands and islets near the mouth of the bay. The favoured anchorages are in the two northern coves tucked in behind the islets at the north end of Waiatt Bay.

Nearby

Hole in the Wall is a famed fishing spot. This nearby passage provides access to Stuart Island and Big Bay with its marinas and facilities. Transit through Hole in the

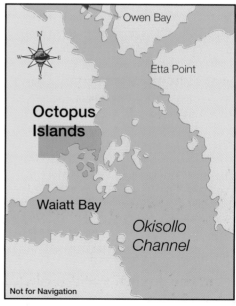

180

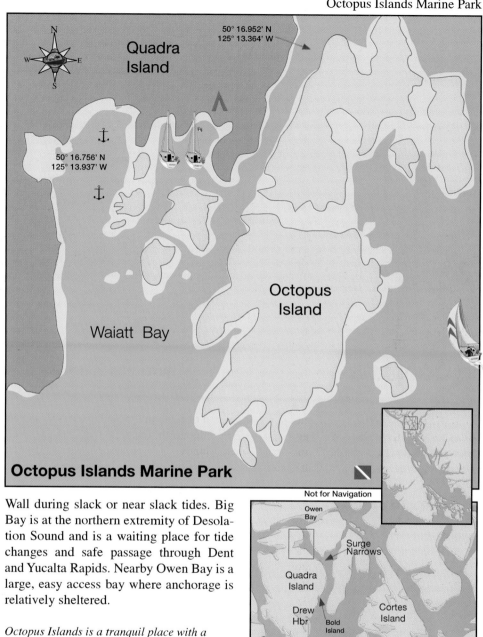

Octopus Islands Marine Park

Not for Navigation

Wall during slack or near slack tides. Big Bay is at the northern extremity of Desolation Sound and is a waiting place for tide changes and safe passage through Dent and Yucalta Rapids. Nearby Owen Bay is a large, easy access bay where anchorage is relatively sheltered.

Octopus Islands is a tranquil place with a narrow passage from Okisollo Channel into its rock-strewn basin, or from the wider open waters of Waiatt Bay. Some anchorage is found in Waiatt Bay but not as protected as in the lee of the islands. A trail leads from Waiatt Bay to Granite Bay on the west side of Quadra Island.

Park facilities

Camping, fishing, recommended kayaking, scuba (strong currents).

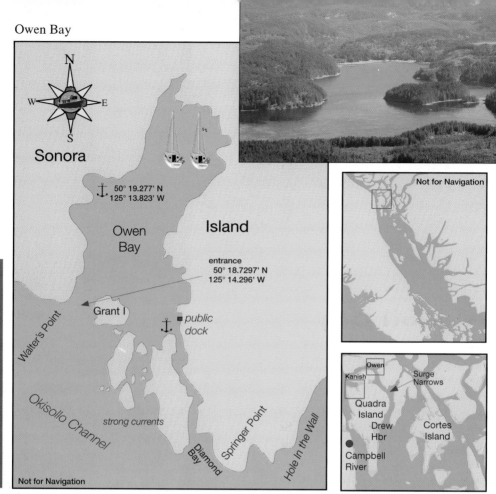

Owen Bay

N
W — E
S

Sonora

⚓ 50° 19.277' N
125° 13.823' W

Owen Bay

Island

entrance
50° 18.7297' N
125° 14.296' W

Grant I

⚓ ■ public dock

Walter's Point

Okisollo Channel

strong currents

Diamond Bay

Springer Point

Hole in the Wall

Not for Navigation

Not for Navigation

Owen
Kanish
Surge Narrows
Quadra Island
Drew Hbr
Cortes Island
Campbell River

Charts 3312, 3537, 3539

Owen Bay

Above: Owen Bay. Note: Okisollo Channel floods 9 knots and Hole in the Wall to 12. Opposite, top: Kanish Bay entrance showing the anchorage adjacent to the island in the lee of Bodega Point.

Access
Owen Bay entrance is just northwest of Hole in the Wall and almost opposite the entrance to Octopus Islands. It opens off Okisollo Channel, which, along with adjacent Hole in the Wall, is a very tide-ripped stretch of water.

Anchorage
A peaceful bay with a choice of places to anchor, most mariners use this bay only for short stops, some overnight. There is space for several boats in the northernmost of two coves halfway up the western shore of Owen Bay. A small public dock on the Sonora Island shore, and tucked behind Grant Island, offers little if any moorage.

Nearby
Octopus Islands Marine Park is a popular anchorage. Hole in the Wall is a good location for fishing. The town of Campbell River is not far by means of Okisollo Channel to Discovery Passage and thence through Seymour Narrows. Surge Narrows at the south end of Okisollo Channel opens through Beazley Pass into Hoskyn Channel, where across the way is the public dock and post office at Surge Narrows (landing).

Kanish Bay

Charts 3312, 3539

Access

Beyond Octopus Islands, Kanish Bay opens off Discovery Passage south of Granite Point, or northwards up Discovery Passage after passing through Seymour Narrows.

Anchorage.

Granite Bay is a popular anchorage and well protected despite the mouth of Kanish Bay which is open to western exposure. **Small Inlet** is a larger anchorage but with a narrow entrance. It is generally well protected from all weather.

Nearby

Otter Cove at Chatham Point. Sheltered anchorage.

Right: A boat sits at anchor in the small cove between Granite Bay and Small Inlet.

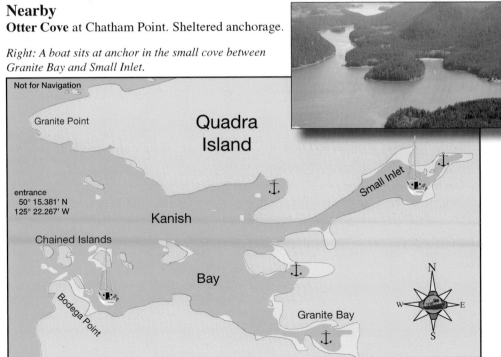

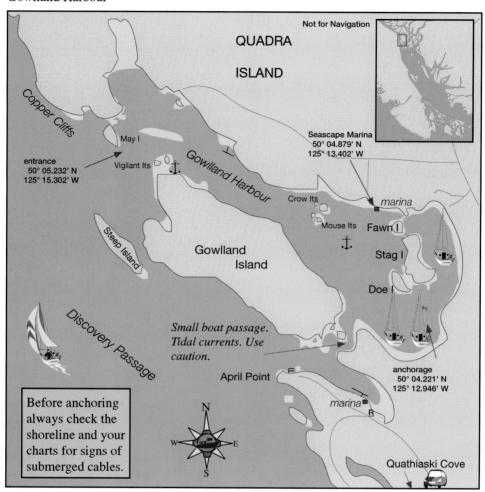

Text in map:

Not for Navigation

QUADRA

ISLAND

Copper Cliffs

May I

Seascape Marina
50° 04.879' N
125° 13.402' W

entrance
50° 05.232' N
125° 15.302' W

Vigilant Its

Gowlland Harbour

Crow Its

marina

Mouse Its Fawn I

Steep Island

Gowlland
Island

Stag I

Doe I

Discovery Passage

Small boat passage.
Tidal currents. Use
caution.

April Point

anchorage
50° 04.221' N
125° 12.946' W

Before anchoring
always check the
shoreline and your
charts for signs of
submerged cables.

N
W   E
S

marina
R

Quathiaski Cove

Gowlland Harbour   Charts 3312, 3540, 3539

Access

Approach Gowlland Harbour from the south or north via Discovery Passage. The easiest and main entrance is north of Gowlland Island. The harbour lies opposite the main downtown waterfront centre of Campbell River. It is a suitable place to lie at anchor in a remote wilderness despite waterfront homes and marinas. It is within a very short distance of populated centres. Another entrance to the harbour for smaller craft, is to the south, between April Point and Gowlland Island. Navigate this passage with much care.

Anchorage

Anchorage is recommended between Crow Islet and Fawn Island or in the lee of Stag Island. Or tucked in the lee of Vigilant Islets. Anchor elsewhere in the open areas of Gowlland Harbour subject to wind forecasts and depths. Seascape Marina in Gowlland Harbour as well as one at April Point, offer overnight moorage.

Nearby

There is a large sport fishing community as well as a busy lumber industry on the Vancouver Island shores, with a great deal of commercial and pleasure craft traffic catered to by

a flourishing marine industry in Campbell River. Down Discovery Passage is Quathiaski Cove, a short distance from Gowlland Harbour, where there are more facilities for mariners, including a cluster of stores a short way up the road from the large public marina. Scuba diving has become somewhat of an industry for the area, and with the sinking in 1996 of the former destroyer escort vessel, HMCS *Columbia*, off Maud Island just south of Seymour Narrows, there has been a noticeable growth of activity in that vicinity.

In the town of Campbell River you will find marinas with moorage and full boating facilities. There are all services, shopping centres, hospital, post office and airport. Charter and scheduled flights, land and sea, fly in and out of Campbell River daily. It is a large town and the hub for many coastal destinations and communities.

*Note: Once decommissioned, a naval vessel loses its HMCS designation.

The photograph above shows Gowlland Harbour from the north. Anchorage is best between Crow Islets and Fawn Island, or tucked in the lee of Vigilant Island. Anchor elsewhere in the open areas of Gowlland Harbour but monitor wind forecasts and check depths.
Below: The sinking of Columbia.
Photo by the author.

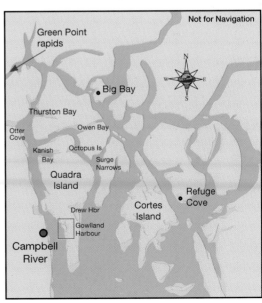

185

Above: A tranquil scene at the narrow, northern entrance to Octopus Islands.
Below: Anchorage in Big Bay area can be found at Mermaid Bay on the south side of Dent Island.

Mermaid
Bay

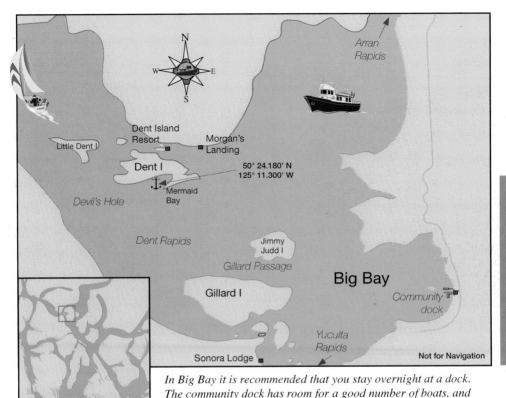

In Big Bay it is recommended that you stay overnight at a dock. The community dock has room for a good number of boats, and nearby marinas offer moorage and other amenities.

Big Bay

Charts 3312, 3541, 3543

Big Bay is at the northern extremity of Desolation Sound and is a waiting place for tide changes enabling safe passage through the tidal waters of Dent and Yucalta Rapids. Travelling south to north or north to south along the BC waterways, Big Bay is a major focal point for all mariners. It is the gateway from Desolation Sound to areas north via Johnstone Strait, and it is on the route south from the busy, narrow passages with their intimidating rapids and whirlpools.

Anchor at **Mermaid's Cove** or sit at the community dock and watch the passage of fishing boats and tugs with their barges under tow, slow moving pleasure craft and a variety of small vessels making their run through the swift tidal waters during periods of slack water.

The larger, commercial and luxury cruise ship lines use Seymour Narrows and travel more directly into Johnstone Strait or Discovery Passage off Campbell River, making that waterway their passage of choice as thoroughfare for their heavy, deep draft vessels. Big Bay is a more tranquil place, though, than Seymour Narrows. As a destination, it attracts a large annual number of visiting sport fishermen who stay at the local lodges, and charter the small fishing boats to go out in quest of the big salmon.

Thurston Bay

Charts 3312, 3543, 3539

Access

The marine park lies along parts of the shoreline of Cameleon Harbour and Thurston Bay. It is located on the northwest side of Sonora Island and should be entered from Nodales Channel which runs into Discovery Passage and the extreme south end of Johnstone Strait. From Stuart Island use Cordero Channel to Nodales Channel.

The Park and Anchorage

A lovely spot to anchor is just off Cameleon Harbour in **Handfield Bay**. A small islet forms a protective breakwater but care should be taken when entering and anchoring, and allow for tide changes and swinging of your boat. The anchorage behind Block Island is the most protected in Thurston Bay. The island is covered in second growth timber for the most part and similar landscape covers the adjacent shore. It is an undeveloped park. **Anchorage Lagoon** should be entered and used with caution due to its shallows as well as rocks near the entrance. A short distance to the north consider Blind Channel as a destina-

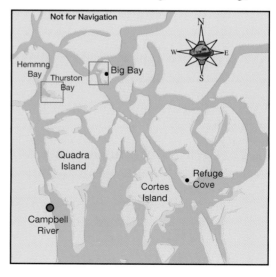

Above: Handfield Bay off Cameleon Harbour. Inset opposite: View over Thurston Bay photographed from above Nodales Channel.

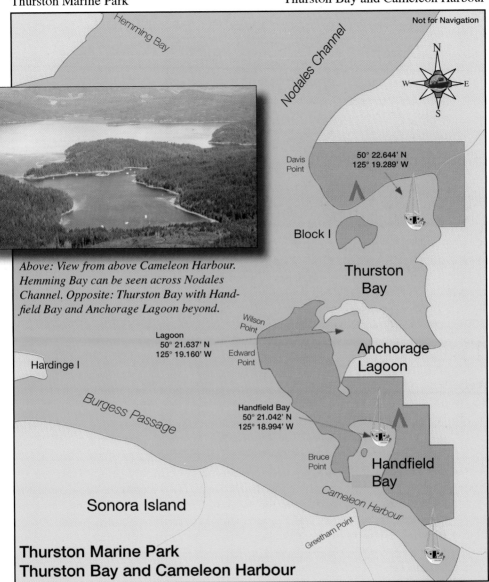

Not for Navigation

Hemming Bay

Nodales Channel

Davis Point

50° 22.644' N
125° 19.289' W

Block I

Thurston Bay

Wilson Point

Lagoon
50° 21.637' N
125° 19.160' W

Edward Point

Anchorage Lagoon

Hardinge I

Burgess Passage

Handfield Bay
50° 21.042' N
125° 18.994' W

Bruce Point

Handfield Bay

Cameleon Harbour

Sonora Island

Greetham Point

*Above: View from above Cameleon Harbour.
Hemming Bay can be seen across Nodales
Channel. Opposite: Thurston Bay with Hand-
field Bay and Anchorage Lagoon beyond.*

**Thurston Marine Park
Thurston Bay and Cameleon Harbour**

tion. There is a marina with grocery and liquor store, post office, restaurant and facilities for mariners. Refer to *Docks and Destinations*
and *North of Desolation Sound* for more on Blind Channel Resort.

Nearby

Across Nodales Channel, **Hemming Bay** is an alternative but less
frequented anchorage. At the north end of Nodales Channel is Cordero Channel leading to Green Point Rapids and Big Bay. To the
south, Discovery Passage leads to Campbell River.

Park facilities

Fishing, recommended kayaking, camping, viewpoint/point of interest.

Cordero Channel.
Tallac Bay to the left
and Erasmus and Mink
Islands on the right.

Blind Channel
(Charles Bay)

Chart 3543

Access and anchorage

From Big Bay on Stuart Island, use Cordero Channel, being mindful of the tidal currents at Dent Island and the timing of the passage to Green Point Rapids, which occur a short way beyond Mayne Passage, but affect a large area of Cordero Channel.

The anchorage at **Charles Bay** is located on the east side of Mayne Channel, opposite the Blind Channel Marina. The marina is one of the best on the coast, and the facilities, such as its fine restaurant, make it difficult to pass up in favour of anchoring. Mayne Channel can be entered from Cordero Channel to the north or from Johnstone Strait to the south. Strong currents run through Mayne Passage but there is shelter from them just north of **Eclipse Islet**. The anchorage is protected also from most prevailing winds.

Nearby

The currents in Cordero Channel and the Green Point Rapids run strongly past Erasmus Island, so care must be taken to find the most suitable anchoring spot, out of the current as much as possible. Drop the hook in **Crawford Anchorage** in the lee of Mink Island.

On the opposite shore, anchorage is also possible in the cove behind the **Cordero Islands**, in the lee of Lorte Island, and at **Tallac Bay**. Conveniently, Cordero Lodge is located nearby. It has some moorage available, and accommodations and a restaurant.

In nearby **Loughborough Inlet**, there is anchorage in **Edith Cove** and elsewhere inside **Beaver Inlet**, which opens off Loughborough to the west. It is a scenic area to explore.

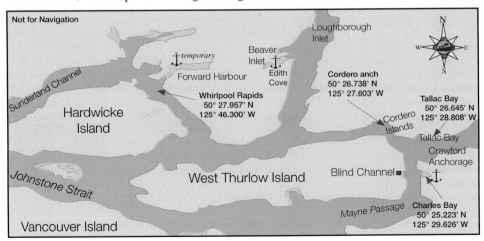

Not for Navigation

Loughborough Inlet

Beaver Inlet

temporary

Forward Harbour

Edith Cove

Cordero anch
50° 26.738' N
125° 27.603' W

Tallac Bay
50° 26.645' N
125° 28.808' W

Sunderland Channel

Whirlpool Rapids
50° 27.957' N
125° 46.300' W

Hardwicke Island

Cordero Islands

Tallac Bay

Crawford Anchorage

Johnstone Strait

West Thurlow Island

Blind Channel ■

Mayne Passage

Charles Bay
50° 25.223' N
125° 29.626' W

Vancouver Island

Above: The anchorage at Charles Bay in the lee of Eclipse Islet. It is a favoured anchorage with protection from most prevailing winds as well as strong tidal currents that run in Mayne Passage. Below: In Forward Harbour. Anchorage is best near the entrance to the harbour, but occasionally windy conditions may require an anchor watch.

Forward Harbour

Located just off Whirlpool Rapids, Forward Harbour is usually an anchorage of choice for boats en route up and down the coast. Mostly because it is located at a distance between other major stops that are convenient for an overnight stop. It is an open harbour with a narrow entrance "guarded" by the sometimes intimidating whirlpools and rushing tides in Wellbore Channel. The wind does blow into the harbour at times and there is a good fetch down the inlet from the northeast. Be ready for the possibility of the occasional disturbance overnight. If you have good ground tackle and have set your hook firmly you should be secure in light to moderate northeasterly blows.

Chart 3544

Port Neville

Charts 3564, 3544, 3545

Access and nearby

After entering Johnstone Strait, you may want to, or need to, find shelter as quickly as possible to escape seas that you were not prepared for. If so, and you have passed Shaw Point at the west end of Sunderland Channel, a recommended destination would be Port Neville. Sometimes the seas in the Strait can be large and uncomfortable and you wish you could find something closer. Tuck into **McLeod Bay** or try to find a sheltered spot, nearby, in **Blenkinsop Bay**.

McLeod Bay is small and mostly very shallow. I once found a log boom in this bay that I tied to while waiting overnight for the wind to die down. If possible, however, it is worth the extra effort to continue to Port Neville.

Anchorage

Port Neville is a large semi-exposed inlet, but just a short distance inside you will find satisfactory anchorage opposite the settlement and its public dock. Use the dock if there is room. Port Neville is an historic place which hopefully can be maintained as such by the present owners and future generations. The old general store building erected in the early 1920s, by the father of the late patriarch Olaf Hansen, still stands as a monument to the pio-

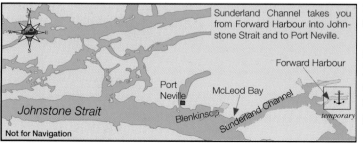

Sunderland Channel takes you from Forward Harbour into Johnstone Strait and to Port Neville.

Forward Harbour

Port Neville

McLeod Bay

Sunderland Channel

Johnstone Strait

Blenkinsop

temporary

Not for Navigation

neering family which settled the land in 1916. Farther inside the port, **Bonesides Bay** is an optional anchorage, but be mindful of the rocky shallows in the bay.

Above: Port Neville showing Milly Island off North Point and the entrance from Johnstone Strait. Inset below: The historic general store building at Port Neville. It has served local settlers, fishermen, mariners and loggers since the early 1900s, and continues to attract many passing vessels. Opposite: Wellbore Channel leading to Forward Harbour (entrance to the harbour is at the upper right of the channel–location of Whirlpool Rapids).

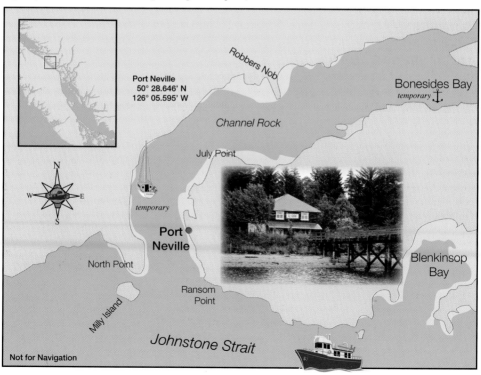

Robbers Nob

Bonesides Bay
temporary

Port Neville
50° 28.646' N
126° 05.595' W

Channel Rock

July Point

temporary

Port Neville

Blenkinsop Bay

North Point

Ransom Point

Milly Island

Johnstone Strait

Not for Navigation

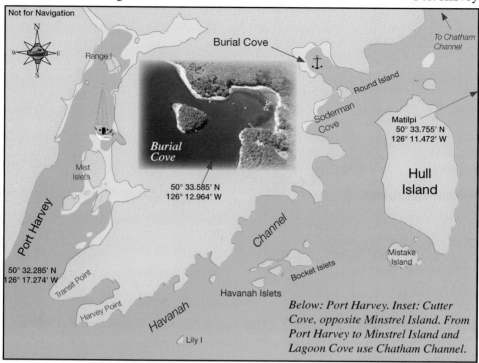

Not for Navigation

N W E S

Range I

Burial Cove

To Chatham Channel

Round Island

Soderman Cove

Matilpi
50° 33.755' N
126° 11.472' W

Burial Cove

50° 33.585' N
126° 12.964' W

Mist Islets

Hull Island

Port Harvey

Channel

50° 32.285' N
126° 17.274' W

Transit Point

Mistake Island

Bocket Islets

Havanah Islets

Harvey Point

Havanah

Lily I

Below: Port Harvey. Inset: Cutter Cove, opposite Minstrel Island. From Port Harvey to Minstrel Island and Lagoon Cove use Chatham Channel.

North of Desolation Sound

Port Harvey

Charts 3564, 3545

Access

Turn off Johnstone Strait at Havannah Channel. This open bay is often passed en route to Knight Inlet. But it is a large anchorage and one of the most highly recommended.

Anchorage and nearby

There is shelter in the lee of the islands lying off the east shore. Range Island near the head of the bay is suitable for almost all conditions. Mist Island provides shelter in south-easterly winds. The anchorages at **Burial Cove** (page 196) and **Matilpi** are cosy, temporary stops en route to Lagoon Cove via Havannah Channel and Chatham Channel.

Kwatsi Bay. This is a very scenic place. Above: The family that owns the marina at Kwatsi Bay. Right: Lagoon Cove.

Lagoon Cove

anchorage
50° 35.736' N
126° 18.858' W

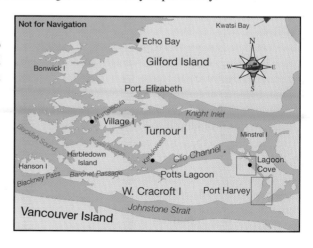

Access

Lagoon Cove is located between East and West Cracroft Islands. It can be accessed from Knight Inlet around the west side of Minstrel Island or through the Blow Hole south of Minstrel Island. Continuing down Clio Channel leads to Potts Lagoon (page 199).

Anchorage and Nearby

There is a popular marina at Lagoon Cove where fuel and some supplies are available. The anchorage is across the cove from the marina. But beware, there is old cable lying at the bottom of the cove and a chance that you will snag your anchor. Sometimes the wind will make the anchorage uncomfortable but usually not for extended periods in summer. This cove almost connects to Cracroft Inlet which runs through via a very narrow, shallow, drying passage to Port Harvey. Explore by small boat. Cutter Cove, opposite Minstrel Island, is used sometimes for anchorage, but is a fairly exposed bay.

Kwatsi Bay

Continue across Knight Inlet to Tribune Channel and proceed to scenic Kwatsi Bay. Here you will find suitable anchorage at the head of the bay north of a small, friendly marina on the west side. Other anchorages in Tribune Channel can be found at Bond Sound (temporary) and Wahkana Bay, but the best is at Kwatsi. Nearby Lacy Falls affords a spectacular vista.

Not for Navigation

Kwatsi Bay

Echo Bay

Gilford Island

Bonwick I

Port Elizabeth

Knight Inlet

Village I

Turnour I

Minstrel I

Harbledown Island

Clio Channel

Lagoon Cove

Hanson I

Baronet Passage

Potts Lagoon

Blackney Pass

Blackfish Sound

W. Cracroft I

Port Harvey

Vancouver Island

Johnstone Strait

Matilpi

50° 33.755' N
126° 11.472' W

Charts 3564, 3545

Access

En route Port Harvey to Minstrel Island and Lagoon Cove, passage is by way of Havannah Channel and Chatham Channel. A short distance before the east end of Chatham Channel is Burial Cove to the west and Matilpi to the east. To reach Matilpi, pass Hull Island, being cautious of Browning Rock at the north end. The narrow passage between Tom Islet and Triangle Island has good water, but beware the reef off Tom Islet, which is clearly marked by kelp in the summer. Some GPS chartmaps show the reef at a slightly different position than it actually is. The Hydrographic Service charts are correct.

Anchorage

The anchorage at Matilpi lies in the lee of Indian Islands. It is the site of a former native village and currently a popular, small anchorage. Beware of the drying rocks in the south end of the anchorage. Enter between the islands or from the north. It is best to anchor off the white shell beach opposite the south end of the northernmost of the two islands.

Left: The north end of Chatham Channel. A cruising power yacht has just passed the location of the Minstrel Island post office. No wake speeds are requested through the entire length of the channel. Below: A sailboat lies at anchor at Matilpi. Note the huge tree afloat off the stern. It had just been cleared after getting tangled in the anchor rode. Bottom: Anchored near the rocks off the southern island at Matilpi. The shallows beyond the boat dry at low tide.

North of Desolation Sound

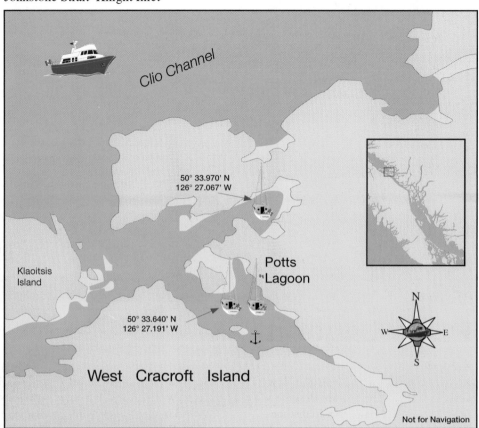

Clio Channel

50° 33.970' N
126° 27.067' W

Potts
Lagoon

Klaoitsis
Island

50° 33.640' N
126° 27.191' W

West Cracroft Island

N
W   E
S

Not for Navigation

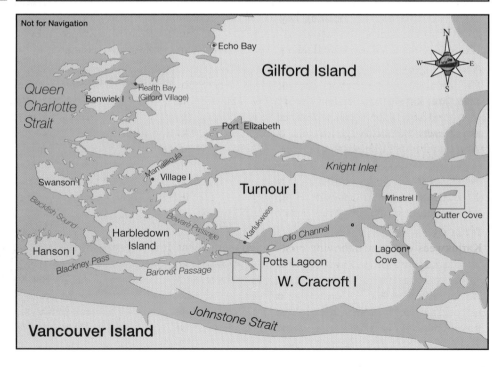

Not for Navigation

Echo Bay

Gilford Island

N
W   E
S

Queen
Charlotte
Strait

Bonwick I

Health Bay
(Gilford Village)

Port Elizabeth

Knight Inlet

Swanson I

Mamalilicula

Village I

Turnour I

Minstrel I

Cutter Cove

Blackfish Sound

Beware Passage

Karlukwees

Clio Channel

Lagoon
Cove

Hanson I

Harbledown
Island

Blackney Pass

Baronet Passage

Potts Lagoon

W. Cracroft I

Johnstone Strait

Vancouver Island

Potts Lagoon

Chart 3545

Access

Potts Lagoon is located near Karlukwees, an abandoned native village that stands at the southeastern end of Beware Passage where it joins up with Baronet Passage. Approach from Telegraph Cove cross Johnstone Strait and enter Baronet Passage through Blackney Passage at the south end of Hanson Island. Travel up Baronet Passage to Clio Channel and enter Potts Lagoon, opening beyond Klaoitsis Island. From Minstrel Island travel down Clio Channel to the lagoon. If you travel to Potts Lagoon from Knight Inlet via Mamililaculla on Village Island take great care going through Beware Passage.

Anchorages

The actual lagoon lies beyond the anchorage and is too shallow for access by anything other than kayaks, canoes and small boats. The anchorage is broken into several main coves and any of these can be entered in relative safety, but mind the reefs to the right as you enter the anchorage from the direction of Karlukwees. Once inside, you can turn to port and tuck into the safety of the north bay, or continue to the right of the island at the entrance, and take sheltered anchorage in its lee. Some swift currents run around the outside of the anchorage and a large reef becomes exposed on the southwestern shore at the entrance. Good shelter from wind, as well as good holding ground in depths of 20 to 30 feet, can be found in various parts of the lagoon.

Nearby

Karlukwees was once a thriving First Nations settlement. It is just opposite the entrance to Potts Lagoon. Old buildings have become ramshackle and have all but disappeared in the encroaching brush. The same is true of the village at Mamaliliculla farther up Beware Passage abutting Native Anchorage off Village Island. These villages are the scene of fascinating history of the coast natives. Their story and that of early European settlers and travellers is told in many books, including *Totem Poles and Tea* (Heritage House) and M. Wylie Blanchet's *The Curve of Time*.

Double Bay

Chart 3546

*Above: Double Bay in the
north side of Hanson Island.*

Access

If you are travelling north up Johnstone Strait and enter Blackney Passage, possibly to retreat from rising wind conditions and mounting seas, you may skirt around the northeast side of Hanson Island in Blackfish Sound and carefully enter Double Bay on the approaches to the Plumper Islands. Or running across Johnstone Strait from Telegraph Cove you can find a passage between the Plumpers and Hanson Island, or around the Plumpers, to Double Bay.

Anchorage

The anchor over the mud flats in the coves that lie beyond the deeper water near the entrance. Or drop the hook in the lee of Spout Islet nearby.

Nearby

Telegraph Cove is a convenient place to stop for gas (no diesel), supplies or to join a whale watching trip.

From Hanson Island you can branch off to many interesting spots in the Knight Inlet vicinity.

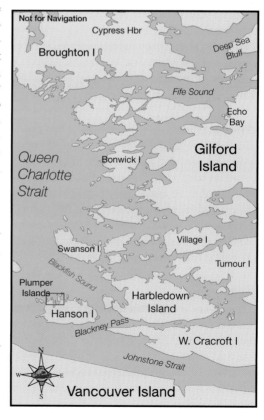

200

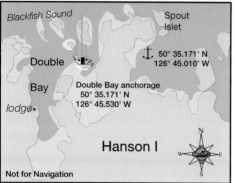

Top: Anchorage in Beware Passage between Turnour Island and Harbledown Island.
Above: Dock at the First Nations village on Gilford Island.

Opposite Telegraph Cove are the **Plumper Islands** with a very tight anchorage protected by a pair of small islands, almost touching at the north end. A strong current rips through between the islets, especially at high tide when there is a lot more water between them. Anchor near the shore of the islet to the right ahead of you as you enter (from the south or from the direction of Telegraph Cove) and then stern tie to the shore. It is not very deep, with about 30 feet under you at a medium tide.

This anchorage will give you shelter from wind and rough seas in northwesterlies in Weynton Passage. It will also provide magnificent sunsets in the right weather conditions, and a view across Johnstone Strait of Telegraph Cove in the distance.

Right: Part of Cormorant Channel Marine Park, the Plumper Islands have limited anchorage between them. Anchor well away from the centre of the passage and stern tie to shore.

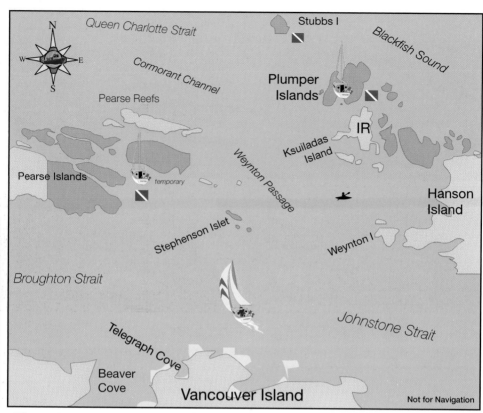

Cormorant Channel

Chart 3546

Access
Access to the park is between Cormorant Channel and Broughton Strait at the junction of Queen Charlotte Strait and Johnstone Strait.

The Park
It includes the eastern portion of the Pearse Islands, **Plumper Islands** and several smaller islands on which there is no development. Temporary anchorage is available in the Plumper Islands and the Pearse Islands.

Nearby
There is moorage at Alert Bay, Sointula or at Telegraph Cove across Johnstone Strait. Scuba diving is available in the vicinity, especially at Stubbs Island. Whales are sighted frequently in this area.

Cormorant Channel
Marine Park
Alert Bay area

Park facilities
There is no development in this park area.
Good kayaking, scuba diving, fishing.

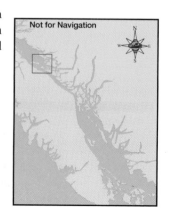

Farewell Harbour, with Whitebeach Pass in the foreground.

Farewell Harbour, Blackfish Sound. Chart 3546

From the Minstrel Island, Knight Inlet vicinity, mariners heading north have the choice of going to Alert Bay and Port Hardy, or up to Echo Bay via the Broughton Archipelago and on to Kingcome Inlet, Sullivan Bay and through Wells Passage back into Queen Charlotte Strait for the passage around Cape Caution. There are achorages and marine parks in the islands of the Broughton Archipelago where one can just sit and while away a lengthy period, or stop overnight en route to a farther destination. The open Queen Charlotte Strait can be rough, but shelter is not far off, with anchorages at places like Farewell Harbour, Double Bay, Waddington Bay, Cullen Harbour or Echo Bay. Supplies are available at Alert Bay, Sointula, Telegraph Cove, Echo Bay, Greenway Sound and Sullivan Bay.

Farewell Harbour opens off Blackfish Sound. Easy entry to the anchorage is through West Passage or Whitebeach Passage either side of Compton Island. It is a large, open bay with a resort located on **Berry Island**. Anchor in the bight to the south of the lodge. There is also protected anchorage on the east side of **Crease Island**.

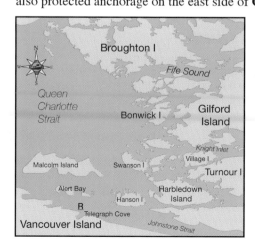

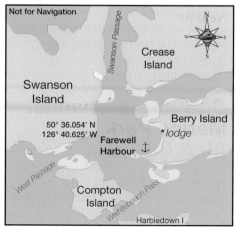

Broughton Archipelago

Charts 3546, 3515, 3547

Access

Located at the southern extremity of Queen
Charlotte Strait, anchorage at Waddington
Bay in the archipelago can be reached by
travelling up Retreat Passage along the
western shore of Gilford Island.

The Park and Anchorage

There is no park development but there are
all weather anchorages at **Joe Cove, Farewell Harbour** and **Waddington Bay**. On
the outskirts of the archipelago, anchorages in the the Echo Bay area include Shawl
Bay, Shoal Harbour and Laura Bay.

Nearby

Echo Bay has facilities for mariners. These
include fuel and groceries, post office and
moorage. A designated marine park area is
located within Echo Bay.

*Top: Spring Passage from Retreat Passage.
Right: Places like Joe Cove are appealing overnight stops. Opposite: View over the Broughton
Archipelago from the west. In the foreground
are passages into Monday Anchorage.*

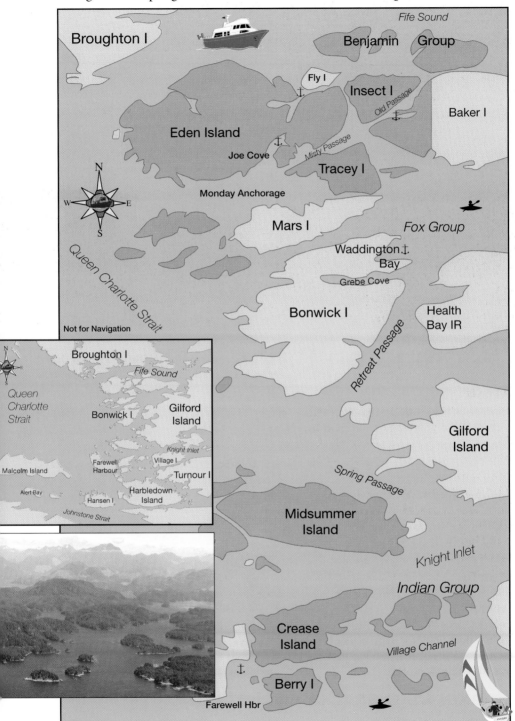

Park facilities

No facilities. Good fishing, kayaking, scuba diving in the vicinity.

Waddington Bay

Charts 3546, 3515

Access

Enter from the northeast, passing south of the Fox Group of islands at the edge of Retreat Passage. Use your large scale chart for the passage into the anchorage.

Anchorage

After winding around and through the many rocks and reefs of this delightful anchorage at the top of Bonwick Island, you will arrive in a cove 20 to 35 feet deep and large enough to swing comfortably at anchor, or find a spot where you can stern tie to the shore. This latter move is always appreciated by others when the anchorage is busy, but here in this archipelago you will most likely find few boats at any given time. Best anchorage is just to the north of the biggest islet in the cove. Small islets are accessible by dinghy and views from atop some of them are stunning, especially at sunset.

Nearby

The marine park at Echo Bay is a short distance north of this pristine anchorage. At Echo Bay you will find limited anchorage plus a floating grocery store and a thriving art community. Original works of fine art can be bought at Echo Bay. Moorage is available there too for those looking for a respite from an extended sojourn away from community living. Also check out the anchorages at Joe Cove and Shoal Harbour.

Booker Lagoon (Cullen Harbour)

Lagoon entrance
50° 46.653' N
126° 44.558' W

Access and Anchorage

At the south side of Broughton Island you will find large, exposed Booker Lagoon with its adjacent Cullen Harbour which offers some protected anchorage (see inset diagram opposite page for location). Watch for westerly winds. Anchor outside the lagoon.

Above: In O'Brien Bay, Simoom Sound. Opposite: Waddington Bay from the east. Below: Booker Lagoon and Cullen Harbour on the south side of Broughton Island.

Fox Group

Bonwick

Island

Waddington Bay

Waddington Bay
50° 42.985' N
126° 37.187' W

N
W E
S

Grebe Cove

Retreat Passage

Gilford
Island

Not for Navigation

Queen
Charlotte
Strait

Cullen Harbour
Fife Sound
Echo
Bay
Waddington
Bay
Bonwick I
Gilford
Island

Malcolm Island
Swanson I
Knight Inlet
Village I
Turnour I

Alert Bay

Above: The entrance to Shoal Harbour is seen clearly at the centre left. On entering, proceed along the narrow channel to where the harbour widens. Turn around the bluff to the right, passing between it and the small island. Continue around the bluff and find anchorage in the bight on the inside. Don't go too far in as it becomes quite shallow at low tides.

Shoal Harbour

Chart 3515

Access

Shoal Harbour lies just south of the entrance to Echo Bay. If you are travelling up through the Broughton Archipelago from places such as Karlukwees or Mamaliliculla you will probably use Retreat Passage and perhaps stop over at Waddington Bay. From there it is quite a short run to Echo Bay. Before reaching Echo Bay you can turn into Shoal Harbour through its narrow entrance on Gilford Island. Keep to the right until you find yourself in a narrow bay which shallows out quickly. This bay reaches westward and is a favoured anchorage.

Anchorage

It is a popular overnight anchorage with several locations in which to drop the hook. A good temporary spot is just behind the small island facing the entrance to the harbour. The favoured safe anchorage is in about 18 feet in the shallow arm angling to the west of the entrance. But don't go in too far as it becomes shallow, and at low tide you may find yourself touching bottom. The wind blows in the area frequently, and some strong breezes funnel into Shoal Harbour. Anchoring in the wider, eastern sections of the harbour, could be uncomfortable and it is best to do so only if you have a large vessel with good holding equipment, or have listened to the wind forecast and determined that calm conditions will prevail.

Nearby

Echo Bay. This is a marine park with marina facilities in the bay as well as a post office and grocery store. Look for works of art by the Bead Lady and other local artists. Singer, song writer Theda Miller entertains and her mother, Yvonne Maximchuk teaches art. Enquire at marinas.

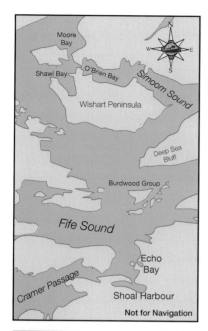

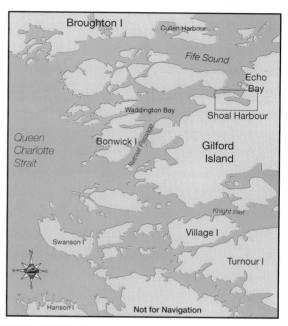

Left: View from the marine park at Echo Bay. A small dock provides access to the park. A floating store and marinas can be seen at the entrance. To the right, not seen in the photo, is a small shop with local artists' work. Below: At anchor off the marine park's sandy beach in Echo Bay.

Maps labels:

Left map: Moore Bay, Shawl Bay, O'Brien Bay, Simoom Sound, Wishart Peninsula, Deep Sea Bluff, Burdwood Group, Fife Sound, Cramer Passage, Echo Bay, Shoal Harbour, Not for Navigation

Right map: Broughton I, Cullen Harbour, Fife Sound, Echo Bay, Shoal Harbour, Waddington Bay, Queen Charlotte Strait, Bonwick I, Retreat Passage, Gilford Island, Knight Inlet, Swanson I, Village I, Turnour I, Hanson I, Not for Navigation

A boat lies at anchor in the centre of Echo Bay. On the right at the entrance is the fuel dock, grocery store and post office. The dock on the left has a craft and art shop.

Echo Bay

Chart 3515

Access

Enter Echo Bay from Cramer Passage or Retreat Passage on the northwest side of Gilford Island.

The Park and Anchorage

There is limited anchorage available in Echo Bay. The favoured location is off the sandy beach at the head of the bay during calm weather and minimal tide change.

A small dock adjacent to the marine park will accommodate one or two small vessels in shallow water. It is often busy during summer and best accessed by dinghy for walking or relaxing in the park. Best bet; If you want to stay over in Echo Bay, is to check in at a marina. There are no facilities in the marine park. However there is a large expanse of lawn surrounded by trees, and a trail leads across the isthmus to the south shore where you can visit Billy Proctor's museum.

Nearby

Echo Bay Resort and Marina at the entrance provides moorage, services and provisions, post office and fuel. Floats at Windsong Sea Village, opposite, have moorage and a craft shop. Just to the south of Echo Bay there is shelter at Shoal Harbour or continue across Fife Sound to the **Burdwood Group** where you can find anchorage off some sandy white beaches *(see diagram on page 209)*.

Not for Navigation

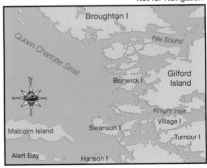

Right: Approaching a good spot to anchor in the Burdwood Group. Opposite: Echo Bay, with Echo Bay Marina to the right and Windsong Sea Village to the left at the entrance. The anchorage is beyond the shallows off the sandy beach. Below: Carol Ellison is the Bead Lady. Above: Theda Miller favours us with a ballad at Echo Bay.

Echo Bay

Cramer Passage

Echo Bay
50° 45.326' N
125° 29.952' W

Shoal Harbour

Billy Proctor's museum

Yvonne Maximchuk, artist

Not for Navigation

Fuel, marinas, groceries, art, moorage

Gilford

Echo Bay

public dock

sandy beach

Island

Echo Bay
Gilford Island

Not for Navigation

Park facilities

Boat dock, walk-in campsites, drinking water, toilets, adjacent marina facilities. See **Docks and Destinations** for more information.

View over Sunday Harbour and Monday Anchorage with Fife Sound and Kingcome Inlet in the distance.

Kingcome anchorages

Access
Not far north of Echo Bay lies the entrance to Kingcome Inlet. But the entire area I like to refer to as Kingcome incorporates the north side of the Broughton Islands and places such as Shawl Bay, Laura Bay, Sullivan Bay, Greenway Sound and Wells Passage to Queen Charlotte Strait. The area is entered from about Minstrel Island in Knight Inlet, or from Alert Bay, travelling via the Plumper Islets and Blackfish Sound, or across Queen Charlotte Strait into Wells Passage.

Anchorages
The popular anchorages in the area include **Waddington Bay, Shoal Harbour, Shawl Bay, Echo Bay, Laura Bay, Tracey Harbour** and **Dickson Island**. There are many more nooks and crannies where anchorage is possible. It just takes a careful scrutiny of your charts to determine what the possibilities are. Not all apparent anchorages are suitable for all weather, so look for the physical surroundings and ensure you are protected against prevailing winds.

Nearby
Alert Bay, Port McNeil and Port Hardy are major centres of differing sizes where many to all services are available for mariners. Marinas around the periphery of the area at Telegraph Cove, Minstrel Island, Lagoon Cove, Echo Bay, Greenway Sound and Sullivan Bay cater to recreational vessels. The accompanying diagrams show where protected and conditional anchorages can be found. Local artist Yvonne Maximchuk and Billy Proctor collaborated on a book, *Full Moon Flood Tide*, which gives a good acount of the area.

Viner Sound   Charts 3515, 3547

Just a short distance up island from Echo Bay, this long, narrow sound tapers to a drying shallows that has a First Nations Reserve adjacent to the beach. Limited anchorage.

Simoom Sound   Charts 3515, 3547

Depart Echo Bay northward via Raleigh Passage. Enter between Deep Sea Bluff and

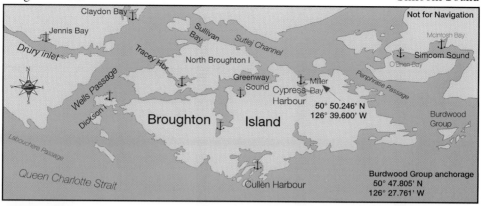

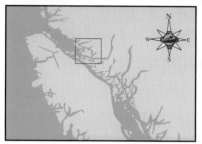

Pollard Point on the Wishart Peninsula. This is a large inlet not to be confused with the settlement of Simoom Sound (also spelled Simoon Sound) one cove north of Echo Bay. Anchorages in this large leg of water include **O'Brien Bay** and **McIntosh Bay** beyond Hannant Point. You have to make your way past this latter point to find reasonable anchorage which offers shelter, especially in O'Brien Bay, from most winds except easterlies.

Cypress Harbour   Charts 3515, 3547

Cypress Harbour is located northeast on Broughton Island. We anchored in Cypress Harbour one year in a heavy rainstorm and watched the coming and going of loggers and trolling fishermen nearby. Anchorage is best at **Miller Bay**, just inside the entrance. It is a good place to stop before an excursion up Kingcome Inlet.

Laura Cove

Laura Bay

Charts 3547, 3515

Access

Laura Cove, in Laura Bay, lies opposite the entrance to Simoom Sound. The bay is off Penphrase Passage just north of Hayle Bay on Broughton Island. After leaving Echo Bay it is not far to Raleigh Passage and beyond to the Pearse Peninsula.

Anchorage

The cove is formed by the shelter of adjacent Trivett Island which connects to Broughton by a sunken sandbar at high tide. This bay is fairly well protected from wind. Some current runs through so anchor securely, using a shore line as well. Favoured position is in about 30 feet directly between the rock in the cove and the north shore (to the right of the rock in the photograph above).

Larger vessels tend to choose the more spacious area where the shoreline is deeper indented in the narrow peninsula (location of top boat shown in the photograph). The shallows seen in the lower part of the photograph connect through a narrow, shallow, small craft passage into Penphrase Passage and it is this connection that causes all the current during tidal changes.

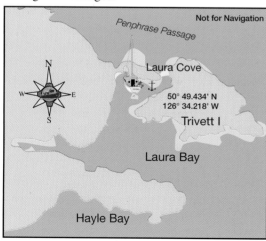
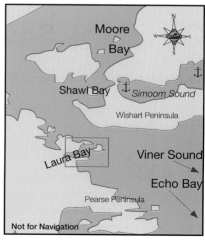

Shawl Bay with Gregory Island, and Moore Bay beyond.

Shawl Bay

Charts 3547, 3515

Access

This bay almost connects with the head of Simoom Sound. It is entered at the confluence of Penphrase Passage and Kingcome Inlet.

Anchorage

There are several sheltered spots to anchor in **Moore Bay**. Pass Gregory Island through the narrow passage that connects the two bays, but only in a small boat, at high tide. Or go around the island to reach the anchorage. Shawl Bay Marina has served the boating community for decades and is a worthwhile stop instead of anchoring. **Moore Bay** lies at the entrance to Kingcome Inlet and is a suitable staging area for trips up that long, deep fjord. Visits to Kingcome village have become restricted, so enquire about the status, at Shawl Bay Marina. There are mooring buoys and a dinghy dock in Moore Bay as well as several spots to anchor along the northern shore, or in the lee of the small island to the south. Caution: watch for Thief Rock in the middle of the bay.

Greenway Sound

Charts 3547, 3515

This is a large inlet formed by the waterway between Broughton Island and North Broughton Island. For many years, the marina, located a short way into the Sound, has provided moorage for visiting vessels. Some choose to anchor opposite the marina, or behind **Lion Islets** near Broughton Lagoon or in the lee of Broughton Point at the entrance to Carter Passage. Near the site of the marina, a small dock provides access to the **Broughton Lakes Marine Park**. This park has no facilities, but a good trail lead to the lake.

Claydon Bay

Charts 3547, 3515

Off Grappler Sound, with careful navigation there is good shelter in this enclosed bay. Choose the lee anchorages depending on wind direction. This and nearby **Turnbull Cove** are more of a destination than a stop along the way. See *North of Desolation Sound*.

Jennis Bay

Above: Anchorage in Jennis Bay. Inset: Marina owner, Tom Allo and daughter Charlie Marie.

Located in Drury Inlet, Jennis Bay affords good anchorage in a slightly out of the way place for those anxious to leave Wells Passage for northern destinations. But it makes a suitable stop while waiting for good weather to proceed north. Or for those who are looking for an extended stay in a quiet anchorage after returning from north of Cape Caution.

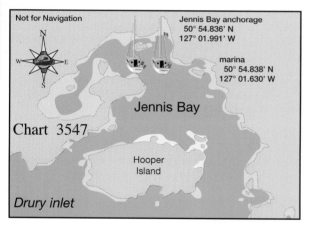

The bay was once a busy logging site but now has a welcoming marina with guest moorage and facilities. Best location to drop the hook is in the lee of the peninsula and the island in the middle of the bay.

Nearby. Dickson Island has good anchorage in a small bay, located close to the entrance of Wells Passage.

In Grappler Sound, anchorage is best in **Claydon Bay** or **Turnbull Cove.**

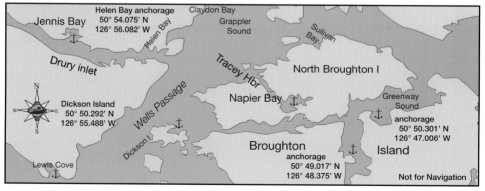

216

Napier Bay (Tracey Harbour)   Chart 3547

For those who want to spend some time close to where Wells Passage opens into Labouchere Passage and Queen Charlotte Strait, Tracey Harbour is a good choice. Anchor in Napier Bay at the head of Tracey Harbour. For even more peace and tranquility try Jennis Bay or **Helen Bay** in Drury Inlet. In Napier Bay a submerged pipeline runs across the shallows. Be sure to anchor clear of it. Also watch for the low profiled logs off Carter Point that apparently serve as a breakwater. Grappler Sound opens off Patrick Passage opposite Sullivan Bay.

Top: Tracey Harbour runs deep into North Broughton Island and ends in sheltered Napier Bay. Above: Turnbull Cove, Grappler Sound.

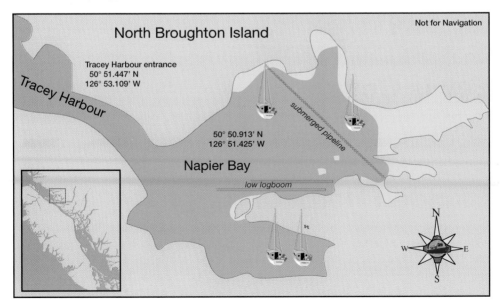

Not for Navigation

North Broughton Island

Tracey Harbour entrance
50° 51.447' N
126° 53.109' W

Tracey Harbour

submerged pipeline

50° 50.913' N
126° 51.425' W

Napier Bay

low logboom

N
W   E
S

Dickson Island

Chart 3547

Dickson Island is a lot closer to the entrance of Wells Passage than Napier Bay or Jennis Bay. It can be reached just outside the western entrance to Carter Passage that divides Broughton Island from North Broughton Island.

This is anchorage for those who have just entered the shelter of Wells Passage after a long trip up or down Queen Charlotte Strait and are in need of a rest, or for those who want an early morning or weather start into the Strait en route to Cape Caution.

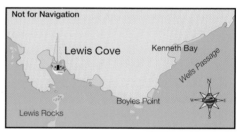

Use Lewis Cove as an anchorage only when wind conditions are from the north northwest. Southerlies blow into the cove. Passage around Lewis Rocks in adverse wind condition.

Lewis Cove

Chart 3547

Opening just outside of Wells Passage into Queen Charlotte Strait, this small cove is suitable for anchoring when winds are favourable. Beware of Lewis Rocks on the approach. Some mariners find this a useful stop when waiting for suitable sea conditions in order to proceed northwards to Cape Caution.

Blunden Harbour

Chart 3548

As you travel up the east side of Queen Charlotte Strait towards Cape Caution you may want to stop at one of the two better-known anchorages along the way. Blunden Harbour and Allison Harbour are not only transitional stops but also popular destinations. Property in Blunden Harbour belongs to people of the First Nations. When we first visited the harbour in the 1980s, there were remains of a longhouse and burial boxes in the trees

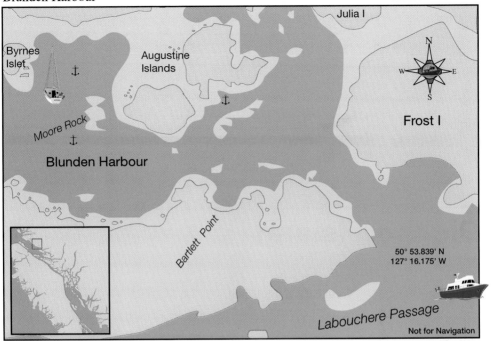

Opposite, top: Dickson Island in Wells Passage that opens into Queen Charlotte Strait. Opposite centre: A view over North Channel and Lewis Cove from the opening of Wells Passage onto Queen Charlotte Strait. Lewis Rocks lie in front of the cove.

on Burial Islet. There was a time not long ago when you could walk along the beach in Blunden Harbour and pick up trading beads left with the village people by Captain Vancouver and other early explorers and traders. I dare say if you look hard and long enough you may still find the odd one buried in the sand.

Access
Blunden Harbour can be reached off Queen Charlotte Strait when travelling north out of Wells Passage. Pass the Raynor Group and navigate cautiously to avoid reefs off the harbour. Coming from the north down Richards Channel you round Browning Island and make your way carefully into Blunden Harbour.

Anchorage
Look for the white sandy beaches in Blunden Harbour. There is shallow anchorage in all parts of the harbour. Find a suitable spot and go ashore by dinghy to enjoy the ambience of this quiet historic place. Periodic windy conditions occur in the anchorage.

Allison Harbour   Charts 3921, 3550

Access. Allison Harbour is a transitional stop as well as a popular destination. Approach carefully being mindful of the rocks and reefs off the entrance.

Anchorage. As you travel up the harbour the favoured anchorage is in the two coves on the east shore just beyond the rock awash. Anchor also in the cove at the old settlement site or in the shallows at the head of the inlet. The anchorage is good in most weather conditions. *See diagram page 220.*

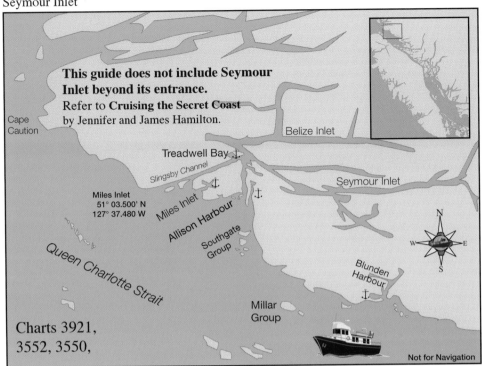

This guide does not include Seymour Inlet beyond its entrance.

Refer to **Cruising the Secret Coast** by Jennifer and James Hamilton.

Cape Caution

Belize Inlet

Treadwell Bay

Slingsby Channel

Miles Inlet
51° 03.500' N
127° 37.480 W

Miles Inlet

Allison Harbour

Southgate Group

Seymour Inlet

Queen Charlotte Strait

Blunden Harbour

Millar Group

Charts 3921, 3552, 3550,

Not for Navigation

North of Desolation Sound

Seymour Inlet

When travelling northward from Allison Harbour, find anchorage en route in the entrance to Seymour Inlet, at Miles Inlet on Bramham Island and at Treadwell Bay.

Miles Inlet faces into Queen Charlotte Strait and is an excellent shelter. Enter between Bramham Point and McEwan Point, and anchor in one of the branches at the head of the inlet.

Treadwell Bay is in Seymour Inlet between Quiet Point and Anchor Islands. It can be reached from Allison Harbour up Schooner Channel (with extreme caution navigating this waterway–chart 3921) or via Slingsby Channel. Anchor well up in the north end of the bay, minding a drying reef at the south side of the anchorage.

Opposite page: Totems in the village of Fort Rupert. Beaver Harbour and its launch ramp and an old church building at the village.

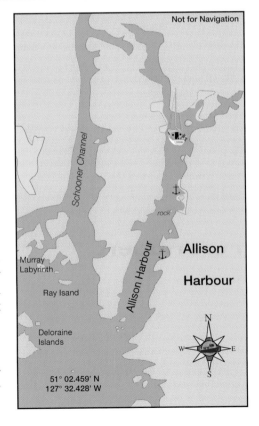

Not for Navigation

Schooner Channel

Murray Labyrinth

Ray Isand

Deloraine Islands

rock

Allison Harbour

Allison

Harbour

51° 02.459' N
127° 32.428' W

Beaver Harbour

This tranquil harbour lies just south of the mouth of Port Hardy. It opens to Queen Charlotte Strait and affords possible anchorage in the lee of the Cattle Islands.

Fort Rupert

Lying at Beaver Harbour, on the banks of north Vancouver Island, this historic native village is a notable one where Captain Vancouver stopped while exploring the coast. It became a post of the Hudson's Bay Company and existed as such for many years. Today, native artists and carvers have put the village on the map, as a producer of fine carvings and works of art.

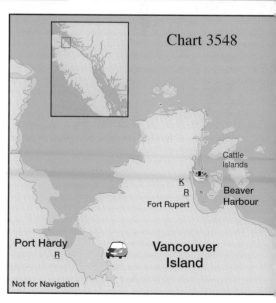

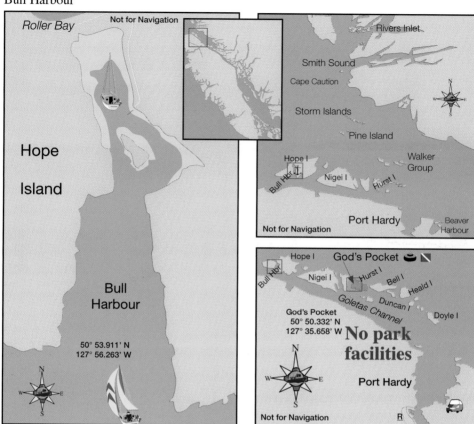

North of Desolation Sound

God's Pocket

Hurst Island
Marine Park

Charts 3549, 3605

Access

A short distance out of Port Hardy, en route Goletas Channel to Bull Harbour, is God's Pocket. It is located on Hurst Island off Christie Passage and is a haven for boats crossing Queen Charlotte Strait from Cape Caution when the winds and waves come up. God's Pocket can be reached from the Strait via Christie Passage between Hurst and Balaklava Islands. It is also a stop for vessels travelling northbound, when weather dictates they hole up until calmer conditions prevail. Rough conditions can occur frequently in this region.

The Park and Anchorage

The park, comprising Hurst and Bell Islands, is a popular destination for scuba divers who use God's Pocket facilities as a resort. Hurst Island was designated a marine park in 1996. The park has no public facilities but the resort at God's Pocket caters to vacationers booked into their cabins as well as passing vessels when space permits. There are two mooring buoys near the docks and limited anchorage can be taken in the cove.

Nearby

Port Hardy is the nearest urban area where marinas and docks cater to overnight moorage for transient and resident vessels. It is a large town with all amenities. In summertime Alaska-bound ferries and those serving the Discovery Coast, between Cape Caution and Bella Bella, leave from Port Hardy.

Above: Bull Harbour on a misty morning. Below: God's Pocket on Hurst Island. This island is a marine park which has no park amenities. God's Pocket Resort caters to guests of the resort. Locals use the cove as an anchorage while awaiting calm conditions in Queen Charlotte Strait.

Bull Harbour

Charts 3549, 3598, 3605

Access

Travel from Port Hardy up Goletas Channel towards the northern tip of Vancouver Island. Enter the harbour at the south side of Hope Island. Just outside the harbour is the Nahwhitti Bar. This is a shallow bar that extends across the top of Goletas Channel off the Nahwhitti River and must be crossed when travelling beyond Bull Harbour and past the southwest of Hope Island. At maximum flood or ebb and in windy conditions this crossing can be uncomfortable. Time your passage across the bar to coincide with slack tides.

Anchorage

Bull Harbour can be a major stop for mariners on a trip around Vancouver Island.

Often, in the Port Hardy area, fog encroaches on the coast, and Bull Harbour is a good place if you have to make a forced temporary stop. Or stop there anyway. The harbour is a sheltered anchorage. Just across the isthmus at top of the island you can stroll along the beach at Roller Bay and look far northwards in the direction of Calvert Island across Queen Charlotte Sound. We once watched gray whales swimming in the surf right up alongside the beach.

5

Cape Caution
to Prince Rupert

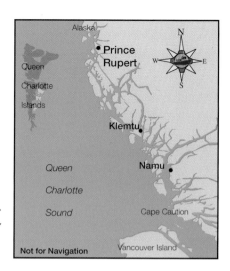

Travelling north

Many mariners cruising north to Alaska prefer to continue on to their destination once past Cape Caution. But if time permits, stop and enjoy some of the anchorages and parks between Rivers Inlet and Prince Rupert.

For expanded information on the islands and waterways beyond the scope of this book, refer to *Cruising The Secret Coast* by Jennifer and James Hamilton.

The BC coast north of Cape Caution is remote and tranquil. Former canneries, such as the one below at Goose Bay, may be found with some buildings partially restored to serve as a fishing lodge. Left: Tides are extreme on the north coast, leaving some marine life exposed at low water. Above: Waterfall in Lowe Inlet.

Sunset in Smith Sound.
Photo by Sharon Allman.

Beyond Cape Caution
Charts 3550, 3605

Make your way up the east coast of Queen Charlotte Strait after leaving the sanctuary of Blunden Harbour or Allison Harbour. As you approach Cape Caution you will notice increasing swells from the open ocean. I usually stay about five miles off Cape Caution to avoid the shallows and their accompanying shorter, steeper waves. Long, slow swells slowly lift your craft and drop you into the following trough. And as long as these swells remain gentle, the passage is comfortable. When the wind is up and tides are adverse, the comfort of the passage can be diminished substantially. Choose weather that will permit a safe and comfortable passage. But if the wind picks up, and you want to escape deteriorating conditions, consider the options of continuing to Rivers Inlet or another destination you have planned, or turning into a sheltered cove along the way, such as the anchorage in Treadwell Bay, at the entrance to Seymour Inlet.

Beyond Cape Caution there are several attractive options. In Smith Sound you may stop at **Jones Cove** just east of Egg Island or proceed along the shore to **Takush Harbour** or **McBride Bay** using chart 3934. Anchor in **Anchor Bight** in the lee of Indian Island. On the north shore of the sound, **Millbrook Cove** is the anchorage of choice. This is the site of an old cannery. It has numerous rocks and reefs, but careful navigation using a large scale chart will help you find a spot to drop anchor either in the 22 feet (7.3 metre) head of the cove or in the 10 foot (3 metre) opening to the west.

Egg Island–Jones Cove
Charts 3934, 3605

If the sea becomes too uncomfortable and you are in the vicinity of Egg Island it is possible to find temporary shelter in the lee of the island. One year while we were cruising south, heavy fog and worsening conditions late in the day dictated that we either turn back on a lengthy detour from our passage or take shelter in Jones Cove or the lee of Egg Island. The forecast was such that an overnight stay at Egg Island looked possible. And so we spent the night in a gently rolling swell and continued around Cape Caution in easier conditions next day. Jones Cove lies just about two-and-a-half miles east of Egg Island. Cross Alexandra Passage and enter the cove around Macnicol Point. It is a small anchorage with good holding in shallow water.

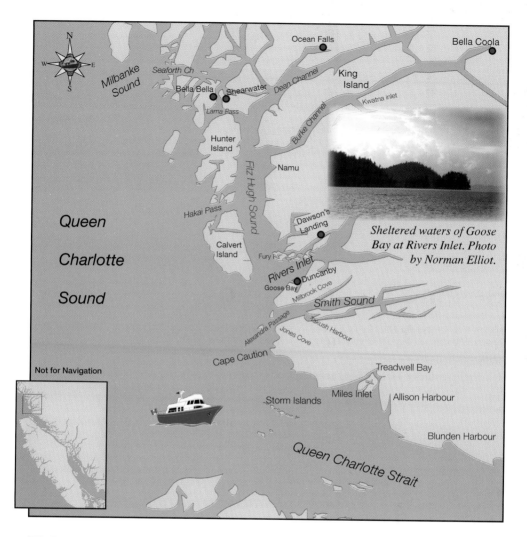

Sheltered waters of Goose Bay at Rivers Inlet. Photo by Norman Elliot.

Takush Harbour
Charts 3931, 3934, 3605

If your destination is Smith Sound then you may be looking for an anchorage such as Takush Harbour. It is a quiet, scenic anchorage with several nooks and basins. Anchorage can be found in Anchor Bight, the west arm of Takush Harbour, which is entered through a narrow passage between Gnarled Islets and Anchor Islets. Keep north of the shoal extending from east Anchor Islet. Best anchorage location is between Ship Rock and Abrupt Point. The south arm of Takush Harbour, **Fly Basin**, is also a good shelter, protected by reefs and submerged rocks. Enter with caution. Farther up Smith Sound is **McBride Bay**, another fairly sheltered anchorage.

Millbrook Cove
Charts 3931, 3934

On the north shore of Smith Sound, Millbrook Cove is a more popular and larger anchorage than Takush Harbour. Entrance is from the sound just east of Shield Island. Enter west of Millbrook Rocks. Anchor deep inside Millbrook Cove after entering, being wary of the rocks and reefs at the entrance.

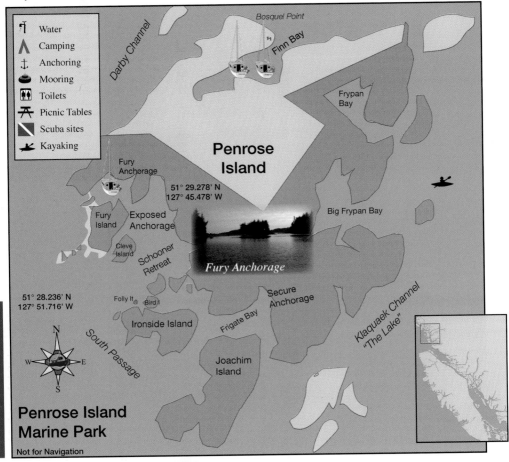

Legend:
- Water
- Camping
- Anchoring
- Mooring
- Toilets
- Picnic Tables
- Scuba sites
- Kayaking

Bosquel Point

Darby Channel

Finn Bay

Frypan Bay

Penrose Island

Fury Anchorage

51° 29.278' N
127° 45.478' W

Fury Island

Exposed Anchorage

Cleve Island

Schooner Retreat

Fury Anchorage

Big Frypan Bay

51° 28.236' N
127° 51.716' W

Folly It

Bird I

Secure Anchorage

Ironside Island

Frigate Bay

Klaquaek Channel "The Lake"

South Passage

Joachim Island

N
W — E
S

Penrose Island Marine Park

Not for Navigation

Penrose Island and Fury Anchorage

Chart 3934

Access

The island lies between Fitz Hugh Sound and Rivers Inlet off Klaquaek Channel. Fury Anchorage can be reached through Schooner Retreat and Exposed Anchorage, from South Passage at the southern end of Fitz Hugh Sound. Navigate south and east around Cleve Island to enter the anchorage, using a large scale chart and taking care to avoid reefs and rocks off Folly Islet and Bird Island.

The Park and Anchorages

While there are some sheltered anchorages on the east side of the island, the most popular and sheltered anchorage can be found in the lee of **Fury Island** in Schooner Retreat on the south west side of Penrose Island. Enter Schooner Retreat with great care. *Exploring the North Coast of British Columbia* by Don Douglass covers the approaches very well. This is an anchorage that will draw you back again. Anchor anywhere in the cove in suitable depths. Other secure anchorages in the coves of this sheltered retreat include **Exposed Anchorage, Frigate Bay** and **Secure Anchorage**. The *Sailing Directions* states that moorage in **Schooner Retreat** is secure in strong gales provided good ground tackle is used. Along the southwest shore you will find sandy shell beaches to explore. The park

Fury Anchorage, adjacent to Exposed Anchorage and Penrose Island Marine Park.

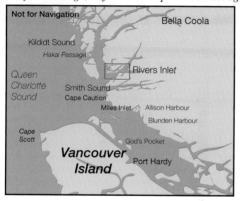

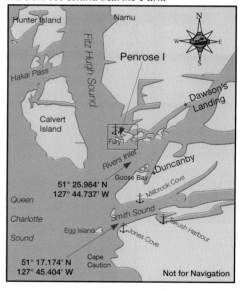

Park facilities

Beach hiking, recommended kayaking, scuba diving, fishing.

is not developed and can be appreciated for its tranquil surroundings. Fishing, kayaking and scuba diving are popular activities in the vicinity.

Nearby

Channels and narrow passages to explore by kayak, dinghy or powered shoreboat make this an exciting adventureland while your boat lies at anchor. Klaquaek Channel, the calm waterway inside the shelter of Penrose Island, is known locally as The Lake. There are several fishing lodges in this area of Rivers Inlet as well as a dock and store with fuel and supplies at Dawson's Landing. **Finn Bay** at the north of Penrose Island is a large, open anchorage which provides good shelter. **Goose Bay** at the south side of Rivers Inlet offers shelter for those wanting to explore that side of the inlet. Anchor off the island near the mud flats at the head of Goose Bay for the best available shelter. The marina at Duncanby Landing nearby carries a variety of necessities for mariners.

At Fougner Bay in Burke Channel near Namu.

Green Island Anchorage

Charts 3921, 3935

A preferred stop by many is in the shelter of Green Island at the entrance to Illahie Inlet, just north of Addenbroke Island. Enter from Fairmile Passage just north of Corvette Islands. Stop here en route north and you may stay longer than intended. Anchor over a soft bottom in about 25 feet.

Fish Egg Inlet

Charts 3921, 3935

This large inlet opens into the mainland just north of Rivers Inlet. It comprises four arms: **Joe's Bay, Waterfall Inlet, Oyster Bay** and **Mantrap Inlet**. Cruising yachtsmen we have met who have explored the inlet say it is well worthwhile venturing into. But do so with great caution. It was charted only in recent years and there may be some rocks and shallows yet to be discovered. There are reports of good anchorages inside.

Fifer Bay (see chart 3921), which is located south of Adenbroke Island, has anchorage for small boats. It can be a tricky entrance due to rocks and reefs on the approaches.

Kwakume Inlet

Chart 3935

Kwakume Inlet is entered about midway between Kwakume Point and Whidbey Point off Fitz Hugh Sound. Its narrow fairway, which opens between rocky shorelines, includes one rock that is awash lying just a short distance west of the entrance.

Koeye River Chart 3935

About five miles north of Kwakume Inlet is Koeye River. It opens north of Koeye Point. Mind the rock at the entrance. Fishermen favour the shallow bay in the lee of the point as a suitable anchorage for small boats.

Warrior Cove

Three and a half miles north of Koeye River, up Fitz Hugh Sound, you will find Warrior Cove to the south of Ontario Point. The entrance is partially obstructed by a small islet. Just beyond Ontario Point is Kiwash Cove (temporary stop only). Its entrance is obstructed by a rock. Anchor deep inside the cove.

Namu Charts 3936, 3727

Beyond Warrior Cove is Namu, a popular stop for mariners en route up the inside passage. Namu has offered many marine services over the years including first aid, accommodations, fuel, water and supplies. On early occasions when we stopped there we found a restaurant, grocery store, chandlery and fuel available. You may not necessarily find these conveniences, therefore plan your travels so that you can enjoy them if they are available and get by if not. There is a passage leading into Rock Inlet beyond Namu.

Anchorage is said to be not suitable in Rock Inlet or in Harlequin Bay. (I have marked it on my chart as acceptable, but there are snags on the bottom.)

Anchor in **Fougner Bay** in Burke Channel. This is a tranquil anchorage and well worth the stop.

Fuel is available at Dawsons Landing, Duncanby, Bella Bella, Shearwater, Bella Coola and Klemtu.

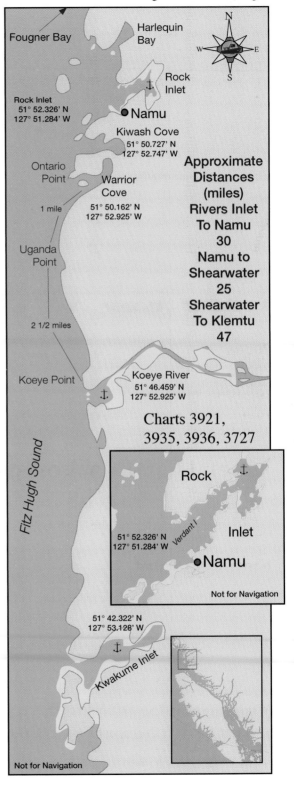

Fougner Bay

Harlequin Bay

Rock Inlet

Rock Inlet
51° 52.326' N
127° 51.284' W

Namu

Kiwash Cove
51° 50.727' N
127° 52.747' W

Ontario Point

Warrior Cove
51° 50.162' N
127° 52.925' W

1 mile

Uganda Point

2 1/2 miles

Koeye Point

Koeye River
51° 46.459' N
127° 52.925' W

Approximate Distances (miles)

Rivers Inlet To Namu
30

Namu to Shearwater
25

Shearwater To Klemtu
47

Charts 3921, 3935, 3936, 3727

Rock

Verdant I.

Inlet

51° 52.326' N
127° 51.284' W

Namu

Not for Navigation

Fitz Hugh Sound

51° 42.322' N
127° 53.128' W

Kwakume Inlet

Not for Navigation

231

Hakai Pass
Chart 3935

Access

Travelling northward up Fitz Hugh Sound, Hakai Pass opens to the west between Calvert Island and Hunter Island. The park area is comprised of an island archipelago which includes Goose Island, Hecate Island, the north end of Calvert Island and the south end of Hunter along with myriad other small islands and islets. Coming from the north, access is by way of Fisher Channel and Fitz Hugh Sound.

The Park and Anchorage

This is one of the largest parks on the coast. Anchorages are located in and off **Pruth Bay** at the head of Kwakshua Channel. There are spectacular white sandy beaches, cosy coves and inlets, especially facing the open Pacific. The pounding surf is a typical west coast phenomenon.

Nearby

The settlement at Namu across Fitz Hugh Sound is one of several former coastal communities on the north coast. It has some facilities for mariners. Hakai Beach Resort at the head of Pruth Bay is a busy, working sports fishing lodge. You will find excellent fishing, scuba diving, kayaking, beachcombing and hiking in the vicinity of Hakai Pass, and at its western entrance in particular. On the north edge of Hakai Pass and the south end of Hunter Island are challenging and interesting waterways as well as ideal anchorages such as **Adams Harbour, Goldstream Harbour, Lewall Inlet** and **Sea Otter Inlet**. At this latter anchorage, just south of the entrance, there is little room to swing, so a stern line is recommended. See pages 234 and 235. *Note: Safety Cove on Calvert Island is used by many but is not necessarily a good anchorage. It shelves very steeply, leaving little suitable holding ground.* Visit **Kildidt Sound** out of Hakai Pass—see page 234.

Park facilities (Pruth Bay)

Beach hiking, recommended kayaking, scuba diving, fishing.

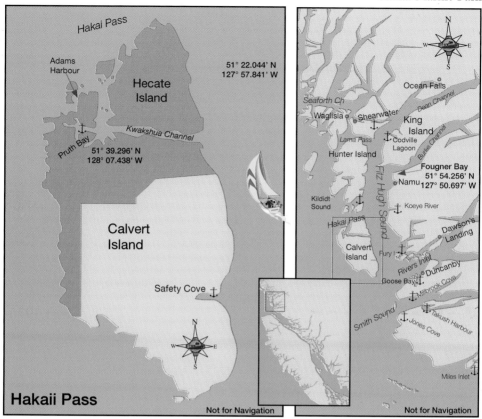

Hakaii Pass

Hakai Pass

Adams
Harbour

Hecate
Island

Kwakshua Channel

Pruth Bay

51° 22.044' N
127° 57.841' W

51° 39.296' N
128° 07.438' W

Calvert
Island

Safety Cove

Not for Navigation

Ocean Falls

Seaforth Ch

Waglisia   Shearwater   King
Island

Lama Pass   Codville
Lagoon

Hunter Island

Dean Channel

Burke Channel

Fougner Bay
51° 54.256' N
127° 50.697' W

Namu

Kildidt
Sound

Koeye River

Hakai Pass

Fitz Hugh Sound

Dawson's
Landing

Calvert
Island

Fury I

Rivers Inlet   Duncanby

Goose Bay   Millbrook Cove

Smith Sound   Takush Harbour

Jones Cove

Miles Inlet

Not for Navigation

Opposite: Beach facing the open Pacific at Hakai Pass, a short walk from Pruth Bay. Inset: At anchor in Pruth Bay. Below: Pulled up on a beach in the Serpent Group of the Hakai Pass area.

Sharon Allman photo

Goldstream Harbour Charts 3935, 3936

Access and Anchorage

This protected anchorage lies at the northern tip of Hecate Island and is reached by a passage around the south end of Hat Island off Fitz Hugh Sound.

Two preferred spots to drop the hook are immediately in the lee of a small peninsula that projects northwards from Hecate Island or all the way around the bottom of Hat Island as you approach the rocks and reefs forming a barrier from Hakai Pass.

Lewall Inlett Charts 3935, 3936

Access and Anchorage

Off the south end of Nalau Passage, runnning deep into Sterling Island is Lewall Inlet, a shallow, narrow passage that affords tranquil anchoring.

There is a shallow spot just off to the right at the end of the entrance passage, so make sure your swing does not take you over that spot. Use a large scale chart for navigating the rocks and islets outside and around this anchorage.

Sea Otter Inlet Charts 3935, 3936, 3937

Access and Anchorage

Sea Otter Inlet opens into the east side of Hunter Island. Pass south of Hanna Islet as you approach from Fitz Hugh Sound. Use a large scale chart for navigating.

Use the south arm for all weather anchorage. The other arms of this three-armed inlet also offer fair protection. The north arm, Crab Cove is slightly exposed to the south.

Long Point Cove Charts 3939, 3729

Access and Anchorage

Long Point Cove lies at the north east corner of Hunter Island. Enter off Fisher Channel opposite Lagoon Bay (Codville Lagoon). Find shelter in about 6 fathoms near the head of the cove.

Lizzie Cove Charts 3939, 3937

Access and Anchorage

Enter off Cooper Inlet from Lama Passage after turning out of Fisher Channel. The *Sailing Directions* recommends local knowledge for avoiding rocks at the entrance.

There are numerous rocks in Cooper Inlet. Lizzie Inlet has suitable anchorage for small vessels in about 8 fathoms in the middle of the cove. **Jane Cove** is another nearby anchorage. Watch for a rock at the entrance, between Strom Point and Gibson Point.

Evans Inlet Charts 3939, 3729

Access and Anchorage

This large inlet lies just north of Codville Lagoon (see page 240). Use Luke Passage or Matthew Passage. Enter between Brend Point and Bold Point. Anchor at the head of the inlet in the lee of Boot Island in about 16 fathoms.

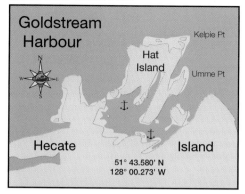

Goldstream
Harbour

Kelpie Pt

Hat
Island

Umme Pt

Hecate

Island

51° 43.580' N
128° 00.273' W

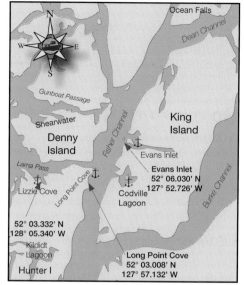

Ocean Falls

Dean Channel

Gunboat Passage

Shearwater

King
Island

Denny
Island

Fisher Channel

Lama Pass

Evans Inlet

Long Point Cove

Evans Inlet
52° 06.030' N
127° 52.726' W

Lizzie Cove

Codville
Lagoon

Burke Channel

52° 03.332' N
128° 05.340' W

Kildidt
Lagoon

Hunter I

Long Point Cove
52° 03.008' N
127° 57.132' W

Hecate Island

Hat Island

above

Hakai Pass

Goldstream Harbour

Rattenbury
Island

Hecate
Island

Adams
Harbour

Pruth Bay

Kwakshua Inlet

51° 39.296' N
128° 07.438' W

Calvert Island

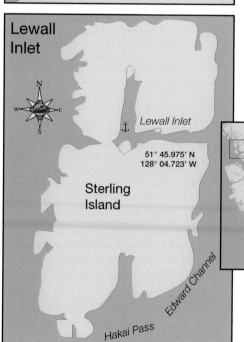

Lewall
Inlet

Lewall Inlet

51° 45.975' N
128° 04.723' W

Sterling
Island

Hakai Pass

Edward Channel

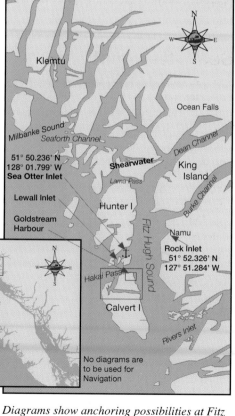

Not for Navigation

Klemtu

Ocean Falls

Milbanke Sound

Seaforth Channel

Dean Channel

Shearwater

King
Island

51° 50.236' N
128° 01.799' W
Sea Otter Inlet

Lama Pass

Lewall Inlet

Hunter I

Goldstream
Harbour

Fitz Hugh Sound

Namu

Rock Inlet
51° 52.326' N
127° 51.284' W

Hakai Pass

Calvert I

Rivers Inlet

No diagrams are
to be used for
Navigation

Diagrams show anchoring possibilities at Fitz Hugh Sound areas. Follow the sequence of anchorages in the text, opposite, with reference on the diagrams from south to north.

Above: Dryad Point light on the north end of Campbell Island Marine Park at the entrance to Seaforth Channel.

Shearwater and Kakushdish Harbour

Chart 3939, 3938
3935, 3937

Access

Shearwater lies east of Bella Bella and Waglisla (New Bella Bella). It is located on the north side of Denny Island in Kliktsoatli Harbour.

Cruising north via Lama Passage you will travel up the east side of Denny Island, round Bella Bella Island and enter Kliksoatli Harbour from the north using chart 3939 of the harbour. Shearwater lies on the west side of the harbour protected to some extent by Shearwater Island. Bella Bella, a station for the Coast Guard and Fisheries, is on the northwest shore of Denny Island almost directly opposite Waglisla on Campbell Island.

East of Shearwater and Kliktsoatli Harbour is Kakushdish Harbour. Enter via the passage south of Cypress Island.

Anchorages

Kakushdish offers anchorage for small craft in relatively good shelter. Enter over a shoal, with caution, using a large scale chart. Anchor at the head of the harbour.

It is possible also to anchor off Shearwater. This bay is open and quite exposed to the possibility of wind. There are mooring buoys on the eastern shore of the harbour, but are mostly private. Most mariners passing through this area take overnight moorage at Shearwater Marina. This area is a major junction for vessels en route north and south. In the harbours at Shearwater and Waglisla you will find supplies, restaurant, boat repairs, charter and scheduled flights, post office and other facilities. BC Ferries calls at Waglisla.

Nearby

There are anchorages in Gunboat Passage en route to Ocean Falls and Bella Coola, or in Seaforth Passage and the Milbanke Sound area en route to Prince Rupert and Alaska.

Kildidt Sound and its numerous islands of the Breadner Group should not be missed if time permits. The islands and islets of the group lie off the south west side of Hunter Island. Popular anchorages in and adjacent to the group lie around **Spider Anchorage**, with the most popular being **Hurricane Anchorage** on Hurricane Island. **Brydon Anchorage**, also on Hurricane island, **Kittyhawk Anchorage** in the Kittyhawk Group and two anchorages in Spitfire Channel (North and West anchorages) also provide shelter. Names given to the anchorages and islands are derived from WWII patrols over the area.

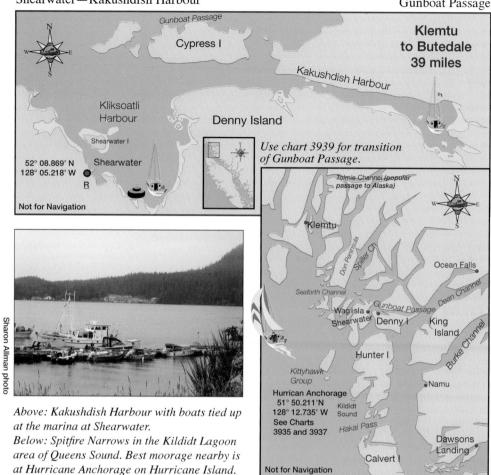

Gunboat Passage

Cypress I

Kakushdish Harbour

**Klemtu
to Butedale
39 miles**

Kliksoatli
Harbour

Denny Island

Shearwater I

52° 08.869' N
128° 05.218' W

Shearwater

R

*Use chart 3939 for transition
of Gunboat Passage.*

Not for Navigation

Toimie Channel *(popular
passage to Alaska)*

Klemtu

Don Peninsula

Spiller Ch

Ocean Falls

Seaforth Channel

Dean Channel

Waglisla

Gunboat Passage

Shearwater Denny I

King
Island

Burke Channel

Hunter I

Namu

Kittyhawk
Group

Hurrican Anchorage
51° 50.211'N
128° 12.735' W
See Charts
3935 and 3937

Kildidt
Sound

Hakai Pass

Dawsons
Landing

Calvert I

Not for Navigation

Sharon Allman photo

*Above: Kakushdish Harbour with boats tied up
at the marina at Shearwater.*
*Below: Spitfire Narrows in the Kildidt Lagoon
area of Queens Sound. Best moorage nearby is
at Hurricane Anchorage on Hurricane Island.*

Sharon Allman photo

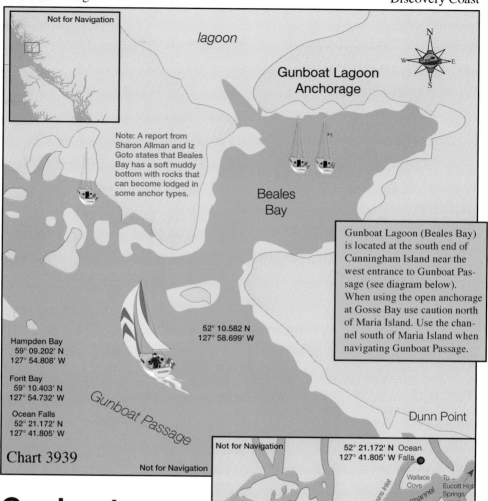

Not for Navigation

lagoon

Gunboat Lagoon
Anchorage

Note: A report from
Sharon Allman and Iz
Goto states that Beales
Bay has a soft muddy
bottom with rocks that
can become lodged in
some anchor types.

Beales
Bay

Gunboat Lagoon (Beales Bay)
is located at the south end of
Cunningham Island near the
west entrance to Gunboat Passage (see diagram below).
When using the open anchorage
at Gosse Bay use caution north
of Maria Island. Use the channel south of Maria Island when
navigating Gunboat Passage.

52° 10.582 N
127° 58.699' W

Hampden Bay
59° 09.202' N
127° 54.808' W

Forit Bay
59° 10.403' N
127° 54.732' W

Ocean Falls
52° 21.172' N
127° 41.805' W

Gunboat Passage

Dunn Point

Chart 3939

Not for Navigation

Gunboat Lagoon Anchorage

Access and Anchorage

The lagoon opens off the west side of
Gunboat Passage immediately west
of Dunn Point. From Shearwater pass
Manson Point and cross the passage
travelling west. Enter Beales Bay or
the small craft anchorage west of the
entrance with caution minding the
shallows and reefs. Good anchoring
in most weather conditions.

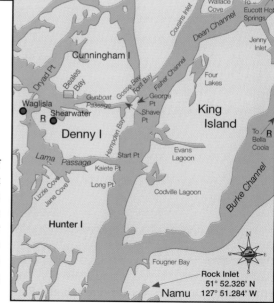

Not for Navigation

52° 21.172' N Ocean
127° 41.805' W Falls

Wallace
Cove

To
Eucott Hot
Springs

Cousins Inlet

Dean Channel

Jenny
Inlet

Cunningham I

Dryad Pt

Beales
Bay

Gosse Bay

Forit Bay

Fisher Channel

Four
Lakes

Waglisla

Gunboat
Passage

George
Pt
Shave
Pt

R

Shearwater

King
Island

To
Bella
Coola

R

Denny I

Hampden Bay

Evans
Lagoon

Lama Passage

Start Pt

Kaiete Pt

Long Pt

Codville Lagoon

Burke Channel

Lizzie Cove
Jane Cove

Hunter I

Fougner Bay

Rock Inlet
51° 52.326' N
127° 51.284' W

Namu

Sunset approaches at Gunboat Lagoon. Inset: Ocean Falls at the head of Cousins Inlet.

Gosse Bay
Chart 3939

Access and Anchorage
Northwest of Maria Island near Denny Point at the east end of Gunboat Passage. Good in about 40 to 50 feet. Used mostly by larger vessels.

Hampden Bay
Charts 3939, 3729

Access and Anchorage
Via Hampden Point which lies a short distance southwest of Shave Point at the extreme south eastern tip of Cunningham Island. Pass between Maria Island and Denny Point approaching from the west. Good anchorage in all conditions.

Forit Bay
Chart 3939

Access and Anchorage
Off Gunboat Passage at Fisher Channel. Enter through a narrow passage with a drying rock and a rock awash just north of Flirt Island. Good anchorage in about 16 to 30 feet.

Ocean Falls
Charts 3939, 3729

Access
Cruise up Fisher Channel to Dean Channel from Gunboat Passage, crossing Johnson Channel and rounding the tip of Florence Peninsula. Enter Cousins Inlet and travel to its head where picturesque, historic Ocean Falls is located.

Anchorage
Anchorage is at the head of the inlet but there is little point anchoring at Ocean Falls. There is an ample dock which is adequately protected in the wind conditions that prevail during summer. There is power and water available at the dock.

Wallace Bay lies on the east side of Cousins Inlet. Pass Benn Point and find the anchorage just over a mile before Barba Point. It is not a deep cove, but rather one more popularly used by larger vessels arriving at night. Prefer Ocean Falls docks.

Codville Lagoon

Charts 3939, 3936, 3729

Access

Codville Lagoon is located inside Lagoon Bay on the west side of King Island off Fisher Channel. Enter the Bay across Fisher Channel from Pointer Island and Lama Passage. The Lagoon is entered through a narrow passage in which a rock with less than six feet of water over it at low tide lies just north of mid channel.

The Park and Anchorage

The Lagoon is a fine all-weather anchorage with Codville Island occupying a large area of the lagoon. You can lie at anchor in the lagoon and just enjoy the excellent scenery. Mind the drying rocks in the north part of the lagoon. Consult chart 3729.

It is also not far to the extensive waters of Sagar Lake. In summer, a 20 minute hike to the lake along a rustic trail, that begins in the easternmost corner of the lagoon, will be rewarded with a red sandy beach and warm water swimming.

Codville Lagoon is in the general area of the increasingly popular Discovery Coast. Marine parks and anchorages in the area offer a variety of experiences ranging from tranquil tree-surrounded bays to open ocean and sandy surf-pounded beaches.

Nearby

Shearwater, Waglisla, Namu, Ocean Falls, Bella Coola and Klemtu offer mariners a range of facilities that include moorage, groceries, supplies and other services.

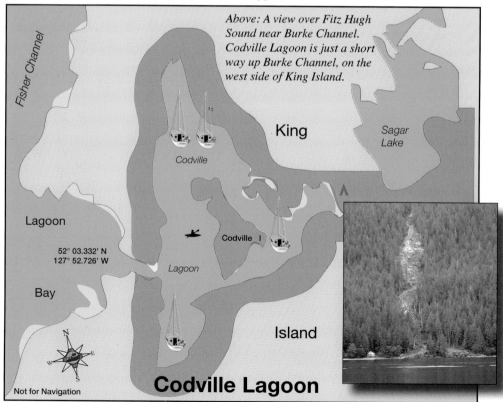

Fisher Channel

Above: A view over Fitz Hugh Sound near Burke Channel. Codville Lagoon is just a short way up Burke Channel, on the west side of King Island.

King

Sagar Lake

Codville

Lagoon

52° 03.332' N
127° 52.726' W

Codville I

Lagoon

Bay

Island

Codville Lagoon

Not for Navigation

Sir Alexander Mackenzie Cairn   Charts 3939, 3729

Sir Alexander Mackenzie Provincial Park is a designated historic site on the north shore of Dean Channel. If you are travelling up the channel to **Eucott** or **Nascall Hot Springs**, a cairn commemorating Mackenzie's historic overland journey can be seen, 43 feet above the shoreline, on a bank adjacent to Elcho Point at the entrance to Elcho Harbour. Here, Sir Alexander Mackenzie inscribed a rock commemorating his arrival at the coast in July, 1793. He was the first European to cross continental North America. The park is not developed. A plaque commemorating his historic voyage was placed at the site, later removed to the museum at Bella Coola and then reestablished at the original site.

Top: The Sir Alexander Mackenzie cairn in Dean Channel. Opposite: Slide on the mountainside in Codville Lagoon. Photo Sharon Allman.

Codville Lagoon
Park facilities
Anchorage, beach, hiking, fishing, viewpoint.

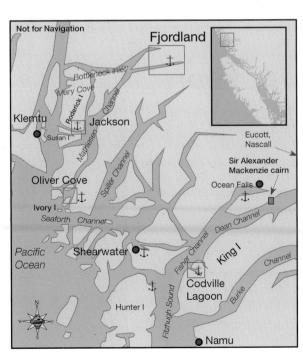

241

Oliver Cove

Charts 3710, 3938, 3728

Access

This is in the general area of the popular Discovery Coast. You will probably use Reid Passage, as an alternative to the open waters of Milbanke Sound, when travelling from Shearwater and Waglisla via Seaforth Channel northbound in the direction of Klemtu. Turn between Watch Island and Ivory Island into the marked passage to Perrin Anchorage and Powell Anchorage, and enter Reid Passage going north. Oliver Cove is on the east side of Port Blackney at the north end of Reid Passage. The general location is at the south end of the Don Peninsula, near the junction of Milbanke Sound and Mathieson Channel. It may be entered from Reid Passage about one nautical mile north of Carne Rock light where Reid Passage narrows considerably. The entrance to Oliver Cove is a little tricky and care should be taken to avoid the rock and ledge beneath the surface.

Also be mindful of the drying ledges extending from the shores to north and south of the anchorage entrance. There is a small islet with an adjacent slightly submerged rock extending from it just off Diver Point.

The Park and Anchorage

This cove provides good anchorage for small boats. Mind the rocky ledge in the middle of the entrance. It is covered by at least six feet of water at low tide. Anchoring on top of it will not provide a secure hold. Go directly towards the east shore and anchor in 30 to 40 feet (use chart 3710). Oliver Cove Marine Park is not developed.

Nearby

Boat Inlet and **Passage Cove**, both opening off Reid Passage just south of Oliver Cove, offer conditional anchorage. Boat Inlet is a particularly appealing place to anchor but has a very shallow entrance. Low water could keep you out or inside until the tide rises. Shearwater, Waglisla, Namu, Ocean Falls, Bella Coola and Klemtu offer mariners a range of facilities that include moorage, groceries, supplies and other services.

Jackson Narrows

Use this passage between Susan and Roderick Islands preferably only at high water slack. There is a possible temporary anchorage in the cove to the west of the narrows. The best overnight anchorage is in Rescue Bay east of the narrows. The centre of the bay is about 50 feet deep. Mind the drying rock and the reef extending from the east shore.

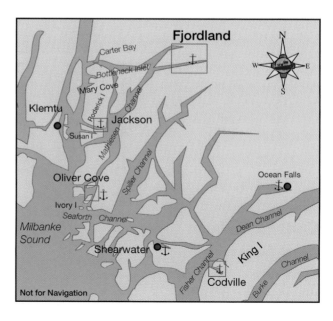

Not for Navigation

242

Above: Wreck of Ohio *at Carter Bay.*
Kayaking in these areas is most pleasurable but extreme caution should be exercised when dealing with narrow, tidal passages, open wind-swept waters and fast moving larger vessels.

Nearby Jackson

If you follow Finlayson Channel up the west side of Susan Island you will find coves and inlets along the way. These include **Nowish Cove** on Susan Island and **Mary Cove** on Roderick Island, either of which will provide reasonably good temporary anchorage. Overnight in these is subject to a tide and current or weather watch. **Bottleneck Inlet** a short way beyond Mary Cove is a better anchorage.

Jackson Narrows Charts 3734, 3711

Park facilities

Anchorage, viewpoint, kayaking.

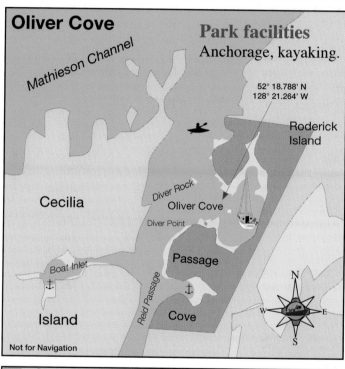

Oliver Cove

Park facilities
Anchorage, kayaking.

Mathieson Channel

52° 18.788' N
128° 21.264' W

Roderick Island

Cecilia

Diver Rock
Oliver Cove
Diver Point

Boat Inlet

Passage

Island

Reid Passage

Cove

Not for Navigation

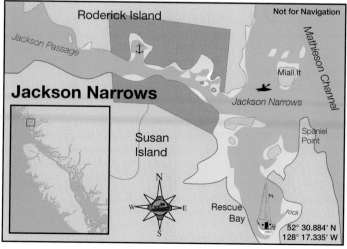

Roderick Island

Not for Navigation

Jackson Passage

Mathieson Channel

Miall It

Jackson Narrows

Jackson Narrows

Spaniel Point

Susan Island

Rescue Bay

rock

52° 30.884' N
128° 17.335' W

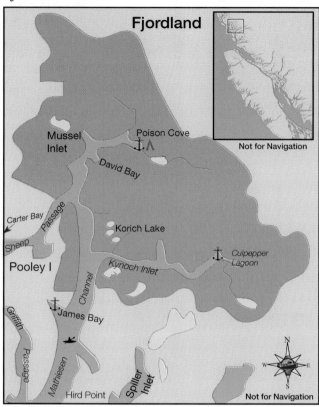

Right: In a sheltered anchorage off Grenville Channel, typical of the nature of the terrain in the area—towering mountains and deep fjords.

Nearby you will find James Bay with anchorage for boats up to about 200 feet in 16 fathoms on a mud and shell bottom.

There is a conspicuous waterfall in Kynoch Inlet–anchor at the head of the inlet.

Fjordland

Charts 3962, 3734, 3738, 3902

Access

This park covers a wide area. It includes Kynoch Inlet, Mussel Inlet, part of Pooley Island and the northern portion of Mathieson Channel. Entrance to the waterway is via Mathieson Channel or Sheep Passage.

Anchorage

Several anchorages provide good shelter including the tidal **Culpepper Lagoon** at the head of Kynoch Inlet. Use your chart and check the depths. Also monitor wind and changes in direction of the wind after arrival. Other anchorages en route into Fjordland include **Rescue Bay** and **James Bay**. Rescue Bay is suitable for small boats. Look for a depth of about nine fathoms near the head of the bay (previous pages). James Bay, about seven miles north of Hird Point offers comfortable shelter to craft of up to about 200 feet in length. A temporary stop may be made at **Carter Bay** at the entrance to Sheep Passage.

The Park

This is an undeveloped recreational area that covers a glacially gouged fjord which is one of the finest examples of its kind on the BC coast. Impressive scenery includes sheer granite cliffs rising thousands of feet, the soaring Coast Mountains peaks and imposing waterfalls such as the conspicuous one about one-and-a-half miles from Garvey Point on the north shore of Kynoch Inlet. This, with the lush river estuaries and heavily forested uplands, makes Fjordland one of the most desirable boating destinations on the coast of British Columbia.

Park facilities

Viewpoint, tranquil anchorages, recommended fishing.

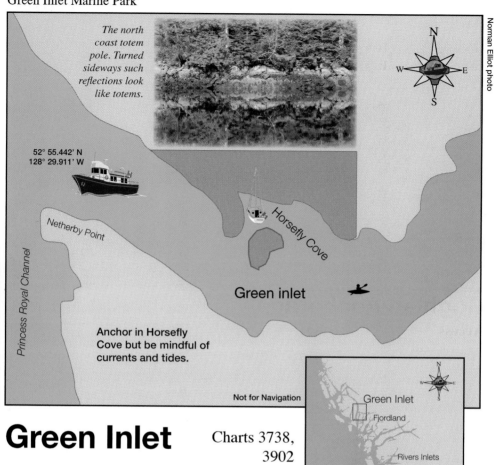

The north coast totem pole. Turned sideways such reflections look like totems.

Norman Elliot photo

52° 55.442' N
128° 29.911' W

Netherby Point

Princess Royal Channel

North of Cape Caution

Horsefly Cove

Green inlet

Anchor in Horsefly Cove but be mindful of currents and tides.

Not for Navigation

Green Inlet

Fjordland

Rivers Inlets

Kingcome

Green Inlet

Charts 3738, 3902

Park facilities
Undeveloped. No facilities.

Access
Entrance to this park is opposite Princess Royal Island off Princess Royal Channel just north of Tolmie Channel (not far north of Klemtu). Enter around Netherby Point.

The Park and Anchorage
The park is part of a scenic fjord which is considered one of the more spectacular in the region. The features include a tidal lagoon with reversing rapids and estuary. The anchorage is sheltered over a sandy and rocky bottom. It is subject to currents and while the best anchorage is in **Horsefly Cove**, it may not be the best holding anchorage in the area. The park is not developed.

Nearby
The native village of Klemtu. This important coastal community provides fuel and supplies as a probable last replenishment stop heading north, before Prince Rupert or Kitimat. Hartley Bay, 60 miles up the coast from Klemtu, has some provisions and fuel. Nearby anchoring is possible at **Nowish Cove** or **Mary Cove**, both opening off Finlayson Channel across from Klemtu. Or at **Khutze Inlet** farther north in Princess Royal Channel.

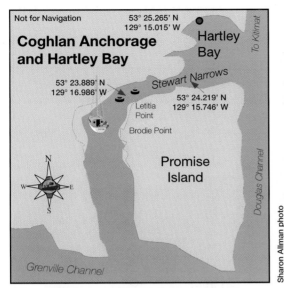

Not for Navigation

53° 25.265' N
129° 15.015' W

Coghlan Anchorage and Hartley Bay

Hartley Bay

To Kitimat

53° 23.889' N
129° 16.986' W

Stewart Narrows

53° 24.219' N
129° 15.746' W

Letitia Point

Brodie Point

Promise Island

Douglas Channel

N
W E
S

Grenville Channel

Sharon Allman photo

Coghlan Anchorage

Charts 3742, 3745, 3711, 3944

Access

Coghlan Anchorage is in the lee of Promise Island in Stewart Narrows. It is about two-and-a-half miles from Hartley Bay. Several mooring buoys are placed just off Letitia Point on Promise Island.

Anchorage

It is a suitable place for temporary stops while waiting for tide or overnight en route up Grenville Channel. There are also spacious docks, and fuel, at Hartley Bay, as well as a store in the village.

Nearby

A short distance north of Green Inlet is **Khutze Inlet**. Small boats and those easy to handle in tight spaces, will find anchorage near the shallow head of this inlet.

Bishop Bay, and its famed hot springs, is located not far up Ursula Channel off Princess Royal Channel.

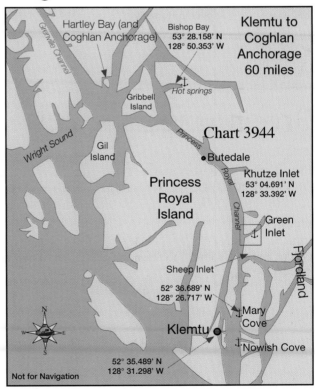

Grenville Channel

Hartley Bay (and Coghlan Anchorage)

Bishop Bay
53° 28.158' N
128° 50.353' W

Klemtu to Coghlan Anchorage 60 miles

Hot springs

Gribbell Island

Wright Sound

Gil Island

Princess

Chart 3944

Butedale

Princess Royal Island

Royal Channel

Khutze Inlet
53° 04.691' N
128° 33.392' W

Green Inlet

Sheep Inlet

52° 36.689' N
128° 26.717' W

Fjordland

Mary Cove

Klemtu

Nowish Cove

52° 35.489' N
128° 31.298' W

Not for Navigation

N
W E
S

Waterways of the north coast route include several temporary and more sheltered anchorages where weather dictates the length and comfort of your stay.
Photograph by Sharon Allman, above, shows a boat at anchor beneath the falls at Khutze Inlet.

The distance from Grenville Channel to the anchorage in Lowe Inlet makes this a preferred overnight stop. Klewnuggit, Baker and Kumealon Inlets are deeper into the mainland and therefore farther distances have to be travelled to find anchorage in those harbours.

Lowe Inlet

Charts 3772, 3902

Access

I saw a sailboat struggling against the tide as we entered Lowe Inlet to anchor overnight. It must have been an hour later when the boat turned up in the anchorage. It had made practically no progress beyond the entrance from Grenville Channel and eventually gave up and came in for the night. The inlet opens off the main channel for Prince Rupert, about 16 miles north of Wright Sound at the south end of Pitt Island.

The Park and Anchorage

The area from Union Passage to Klewnuggit Inlet is designated marine park. Inside Lowe Inlet there are shallows in the vicinity of Verney Falls in Nettle Basin, which slope gently into the deeper reaches of the bay. Some vessels anchor right in the stream of the river water flow. Additional anchorage is a short way off this current. A large sweep of the bay to the southeast of the falls becomes shallow and dries at low tide, so anchor in a good

Entering Lowe Inlet.

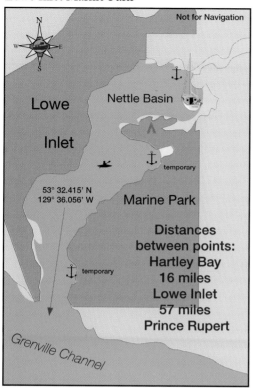

Not for Navigation

Lowe

Inlet

Nettle Basin

temporary

53° 32.415' N
129° 36.056' W

Marine Park

temporary

**Distances
between points:
Hartley Bay
16 miles
Lowe Inlet
57 miles
Prince Rupert**

Grenville Channel

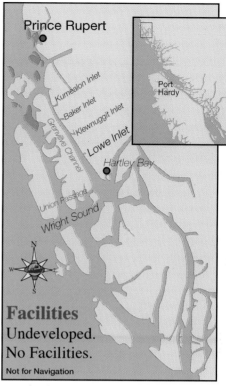

Prince Rupert

Kumealon Inlet

Baker Inlet

Grenville Channel

Klewnuggit Inlet

Lowe Inlet

Hartley Bay

Union Passage

Wright Sound

Port Hardy

Facilities
Undeveloped.
No Facilities.

Not for Navigation

depth allowing for the large tidal change. Anchorage is also suitable at times in the outer section of the inlet for mariners wanting to make a quick return to Grenville Channel.

Nearby

The native village of Hartley Bay lies just off Wright Sound. The public docks in this bay are quite substantial, and fuel and provisions can be purchased in the village. The community was applauded for their help when the ferry *Queen of the North* sank in 2006.

Anchored in Lowe Inlet

A tranquil scene in Grenville Channel by marine artist John M. Horton (www.johnhorton.ca). Inset, opposite: Waterfall in Grenville Channel near Klewnuggit Inlet.

Klewnuggit Inlet

Charts 3772, 3902

Access

The entrance off Grenville Channel is between Rogers Point and Silas Point. It is about midway between the south end and the north end of Grenville Channel.

The Park and Anchorage

There are no facilities in this undeveloped park area. The anchorage in the inlet is poor due to too great a depth for comfort. Anchor in 9 fathoms in Inner Basin at the head of East Inlet. Temporary stop in Narbannah Bay.

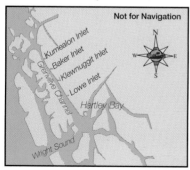

Not for Navigation

Kumealon Inlet
Baker Inlet
Klewnuggit Inlet
Grenville Channel
Lowe Inlet
Hartley Bay
Wright Sound

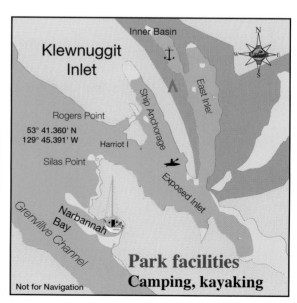

Inner Basin

Klewnuggit Inlet

Rogers Point
53° 41.360' N
129° 45.391' W

Harriot I

Silas Point

Ship Anchorage

East Inlet

Exposed Inlet

Narbannah Bay

Grenville Channel

Park facilities
Camping, kayaking

Not for Navigation

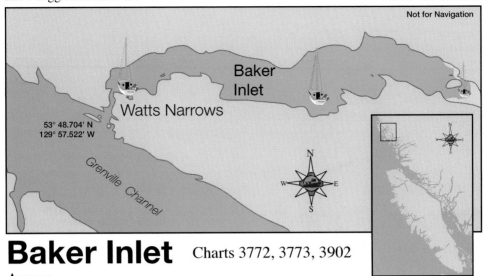

53° 48.704' N
129° 57.522' W

Baker Inlet   Charts 3772, 3773, 3902

Access
The inlet is a little beyond half way along Grenville Channel. It has a very narrow entrance with strong tidal currents. Use Prince Rupert tide tables and enter or leave at slack.

Anchorage
The anchorage lies just inside the inlet, through Watts Narrows. Turn to starboard through the narrows and anchor in 3 to 10 fathoms or in 11 fathoms at the head of the bay.

Kumealon Inlet   Charts 3773, 3902

Access
Kumealon Inlet opens off Grenville Channel a short way north of Baker Inlet.

Anchorage
Anchor in about 6 fathoms at the head of Kumealon Inlet or in the cove behind Kumealon Island at the entrance to the inlet. While we did not anchor here ourselves, Robert Hale reports in *Waggoner* cruising guide that there are two uncharted rocks in the southeast corner near the shore in the inner basin. The entrance to the adjacent lagoon is encumbered with rocks and tidal rapids at the north end. Best anchorage is found in the eastern corner of the inlet behind foul ground and the small island covered with shrub.

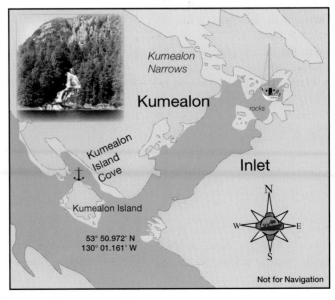

53° 50.972' N
130° 01.161' W

Prince Rupert

Chart 3957

Above: Sailing under power past Metlakatla just out of Prince Rupert en route to Chatham Sound and Alaska.
Opposite: Moored at Goose Bay.

We found little good anchorage in the immediate vicinity of Prince Rupert. The recommended spot is at a cove on the Tsimpsean Peninsula opposite Cow Bay. But here we were disturbed by wind and eventually took moorage at the Prince Rupert Yacht Club. Stop at Prince Rupert for all your needs as you continue your voyage up or down the coast. If you are headed for Alaska you will find two good anchorages en route, at Dundas Island and in Foggy Bay (Alaskan waters). See ***Docks and Destinations***.

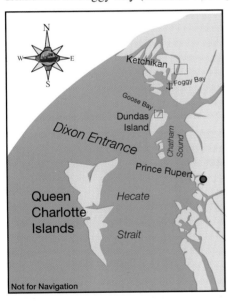

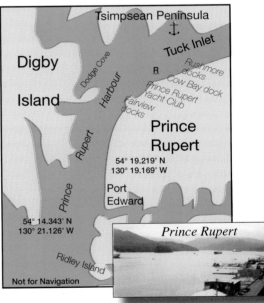

Prince Rupert

Goose Bay (Prince Rupert to Ketchikan)

En route to Ketchikan an easy place to stop, is at Goose Bay on Dundas Island, or the adjacent, larger, **Brundige Inlet**, where you can sit and wait for the seas to be calm for a safe passage across Dixon Entrance. Leave Prince Rupert early to avoid rising winds across Chatham Sound and make your way up to the north end of Dundas Island. Chances

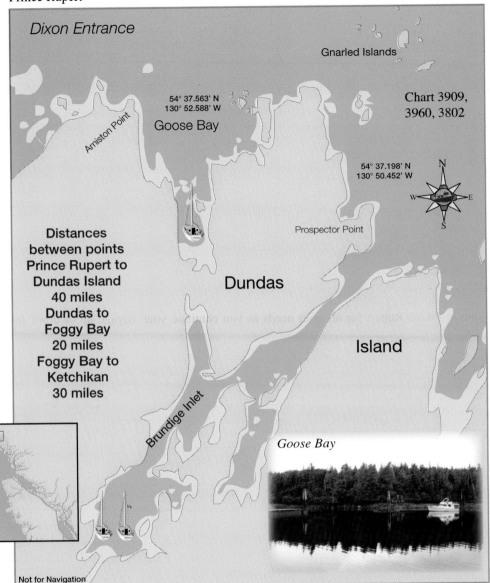

Dixon Entrance

Gnarled Islands

54° 37.563' N
130° 52.588' W
Goose Bay

Arniston Point

Chart 3909,
3960, 3802

54° 37.198' N
130° 50.452' W

N
W E
S

Prospector Point

**Distances
between points
Prince Rupert to
Dundas Island
40 miles
Dundas to
Foggy Bay
20 miles
Foggy Bay to
Ketchikan
30 miles**

Dundas

Island

Brundige Inlet

Goose Bay

Not for Navigation

are the wind and seas will be up by the time you reach Dixon Entrance. Or, if you are planning a two day voyage from Prince Rupert to Ketchikan, stop in at the anchorage of your choice. Brundige is a deep inlet which requires a bit of time to reach the best anchoring spot. Which means it takes extra time to reach the open water for crossing Dixon Entrance. Goose Bay is a smaller inlet and closer to the open crossing, but with a tricky entrance. Use large scale chart 3909 and navigate carefully to the inner cove. A float is often available for tying up. Or anchor nearby in the shallows taking care to allow for the dropping tide. Cross Dixon Entrance when the tide and wind are favourable. If you are powering across, often an early start will see you clear of the open water before the wind comes up. If you cross late in the day and need a place to spend the night stop in at **Foggy Bay**. Sailing yachtsmen, of course, usually take the wind in their stride.

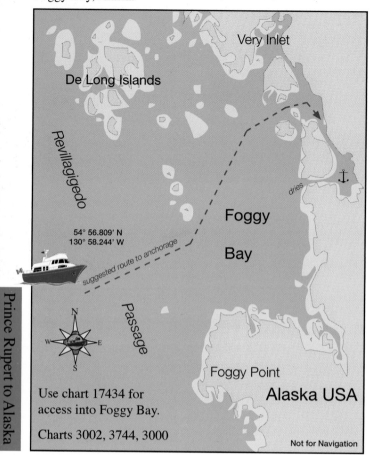

Very Inlet

De Long Islands

Revillagigedo

54° 56.809' N
130° 58.244' W

suggested route to anchorage

Passage

Foggy

Bay

dries

Foggy Point

Alaska USA

Use chart 17434 for
access into Foggy Bay.

Charts 3002, 3744, 3000

Not for Navigation

Dundas Island

Queen
Charlotte
Islands

Not for Navigation

**Foggy
Bay**

Prince Rupert to Alaska

En Route to Ketchikan

With great care, cross Dixon Entrance via Chatham Sound from Prince Rupert. As you travel between Dundas Island and Cape Fox on the Alaska southern shore you have the open Pacific off to port and Hecate Strait adjacent. Dixon Entrance and Hecate Strait conjure up all sorts of terror to the uninitiated. But with careful weather monitoring, a safe passage across Dixon Entrance is possible. Take shelter in Foggy Bay if you need to, on the other side. However, observe customs formalities.

Clearing Customs

If you decide to stop at Foggy Bay be sure you have precleared customs by calling ahead from Prince Rupert. Or if you find you need to stop en route before reaching and clearing at Ketchikan, call from your boat and ask permission to stop at Foggy Bay, promising to contact Customs again immediately on arrival in Ketchikan. Note: Customs officers are not obliged to grant you permission. Then even after clearing at Ketchikan, it is necessary to clear customs again at other harbours in Alaska.

If you decide to go to the Queen Charlottes, cross Hecate Strait from Prince Rupert or Dixon Entrance from Dundas Island, with due caution–or if you are travelling from the south, cross Queen Charlotte Sound over the top of Vancouver Island. All of these access routes to the Queen Charlotte Islands are through open Pacific waters and extreme attention should be paid to weather, tide and currents and wind forecasts. The marine park-

Photo above: Sunset at Goose Bay on Dundas Island. Waiting for the morning and an early crossing of Dixon Entrance to Ketchikan, USA.

lands of the Queen Charlottes offer multitudes of scenic views and panoramas along with wild and convoluted coastal bays and coves. The use of charts and marine guides in the Queen Charlotte Islands is essential.

Gwaii Haanas National Park, Moresby Island
Naikoon Park, Graham Island

Charts 3802, 3854, 3894, 3890, 3895

The inclusion in this guide of the Queen Charlottes is simply as reference to the fact that Gwaii Haanas is a national park and Naikoon Park is a provincial park, both included in the Parks Branch list of coastal parks. If you do venture across the open waters to the Queen Charlottes there is an incredible diversity of scenic wonders to view, from lost native villages to marine and bird life in abundance. In addition to being a major tourist attraction as a wildlife sanctuary, the islands are a popular destination for visiting mariners, kayakers and scuba divers.

The trip across Hecate Strait is close from Prince Rupert. However the waters are shallow and tide and wind can make it a very nasty stretch. Plan any crossing to coincide with calm sea conditions. For more information on facilities and anchorages in the Queen Charlottes you should contact the **Parks Board at 250-847-7320**. Also check the website at *www.env.gov.bc.ca/bcparks*

6

West Coast of Vancouver Island

West Coast

For expanded information on the waterways and marine facilities beyond the scope of this book, refer to: *Docks and Destinations* and *Voyages to Windward*.

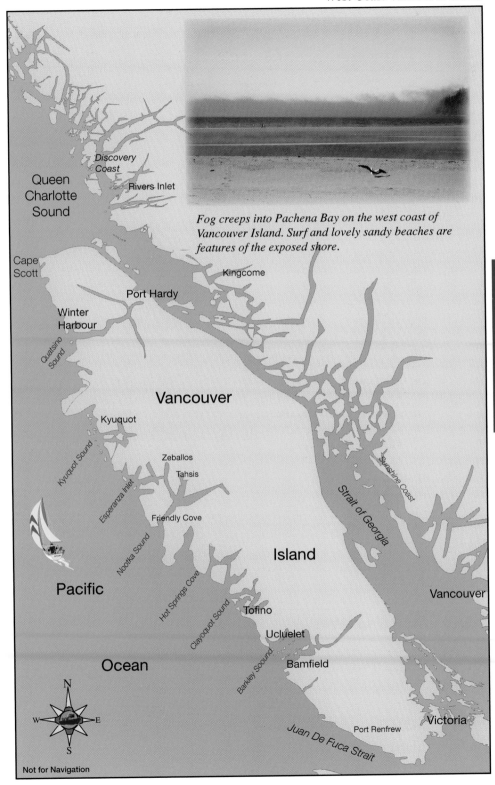

Queen
Charlotte
Sound

Discovery
Coast

Rivers Inlet

*Fog creeps into Pachena Bay on the west coast of
Vancouver Island. Surf and lovely sandy beaches are
features of the exposed shore.*

Cape
Scott

Kingcome

Port Hardy

Winter
Harbour

Quatsino
Sound

Vancouver

Kyuquot

Kyuquot Sound

Zeballos

Tahsis

Esperanza Inlet

Friendly Cove

Nootka Sound

Island

Strait of Georgia

Sunshine Coast

Pacific

Hot Springs Cove

Clayoquot Sound

Tofino

Ucluelet

Barkley Sound

Bamfield

Vancouver

Ocean

N
W   E
S

Juan De Fuca Strait

Port Renfrew

Victoria

Not for Navigation

Cape Scott, Sea Otter Cove

Charts 3624, 3625, 3598, 3744

Access

Reach Raft Cove or Cape Scott's San Josef Bay from Bull Harbour or from Port Hardy, over the north end of Vancouver Island. Travelling north, approach Cape Scott from Winter Harbour.

The Park

Cape Scott is a rugged coastal area where one-time development has succumbed to the forest. It is a popular destination for hikers and those who love the wilderness. Paths lead in from the distant roadhead.

Sea Otter Cove is a sheltered anchorage. Mooring buoys were installed for the commercial fishing fleet, well inside the cove. But don't count on these, because many buoys are being removed for lack of maintenance. To the south, **Raft Cove** is a temporary stop while out fishing along the northern, exposed coast.

Nearby

Nearest facilities are at Winter Harbour. There you will find marinas and anchorage as well as a well-stocked grocery store.

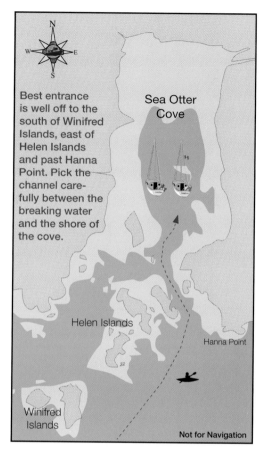

Best entrance is well off to the south of Winifred Islands, east of Helen Islands and past Hanna Point. Pick the channel carefully between the breaking water and the shore of the cove.

Sea Otter Cove

Helen Islands

Hanna Point

Winifred Islands

Not for Navigation

Cape Scott

Park facilities

Beach hiking, fishing and kayaking recommended.

Sea Otter Cove

Park facilities

Anchorage, beach hiking, kayaking, fishing.

Raft Cove

Park facilities

Beach hiking, fishing.

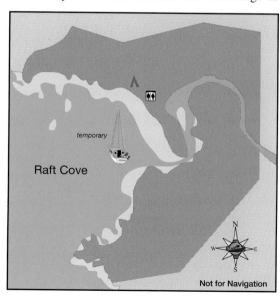

temporary

Raft Cove

Not for Navigation

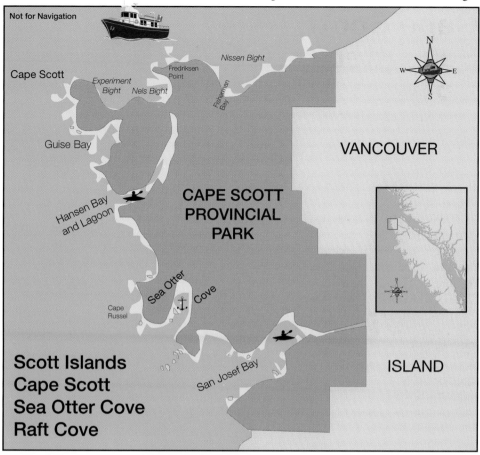

Not for Navigation

Cape Scott

Experiment Bight · Nels Bight

Nissen Bight

Fredriksen Point

Fisherman Bay

Guise Bay

VANCOUVER

Hansen Bay and Lagoon

CAPE SCOTT PROVINCIAL PARK

Sea Otter Cove

Cape Russel

Scott Islands
Cape Scott
Sea Otter Cove
Raft Cove

San Josef Bay

ISLAND

Settlement

Danish settlers attempted to colonize Cape Scott in 1898, but broken government promises of a road and other assistance, eventually drove them away, leaving a ghost settlement to succumb to nature. Hansen Bay was named for the first settler, and Experiment Bight and Guise Bay for the vessel and captain of one of the earliest vessels to visit the cape.

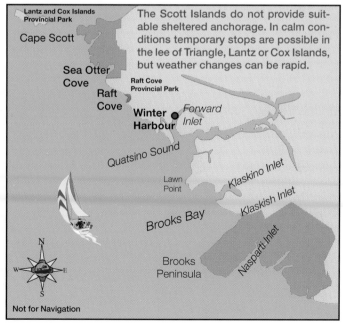

Lantz and Cox Islands Provincial Park

Cape Scott

Sea Otter Cove

Raft Cove Provincial Park

Raft Cove

Winter Harbour · Forward Inlet

Quatsino Sound

The Scott Islands do not provide suitable sheltered anchorage. In calm conditions temporary stops are possible in the lee of Triangle, Lantz or Cox Islands, but weather changes can be rapid.

Lawn Point

Klaskino Inlet

Klaskish Inlet

Brooks Bay

Nasparti Inlet

Brooks Peninsula

Not for Navigation

West Coast Vancouver I

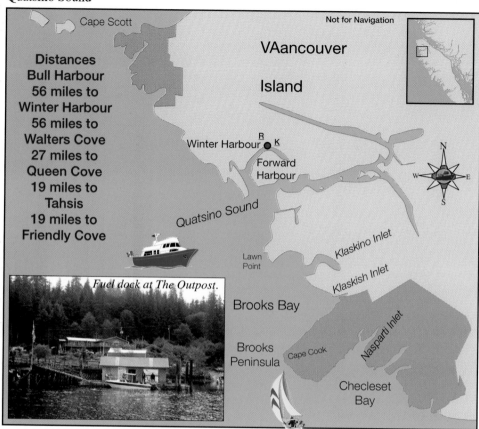

Distances
Bull Harbour
56 miles to
Winter Harbour
56 miles to
Walters Cove
27 miles to
Queen Cove
19 miles to
Tahsis
19 miles to
Friendly Cove

Fuel dock at The Outpost.

Quatsino Sound

Charts 3679, 3624, 3605, 3681, 3690

Access

The cruise south down the coast from Cape Scott can be exhilarating. If the wind picks up it will either drive you along at a quickened pace as you slide down some increasing swells or smack you in the face as you run into them. My trips along this stretch have all had the seas or wind from the north. Timing is important to avoid severe conditions. Enter Quatsino Sound and Forward Inlet around Kains Island. Pass either side of Hunt Islets and Matthews Island to port lining up with the entrance to Winter Harbour.

Anchorages

Anchor in the lee of Matthews Island in **North Harbour**, Forward Inlet, or in the expansive waters of **Winter Harbour**. The inlet shallows out as you get closer to the north shore. Most mariners will spend time at the Winter Harbour docks visiting the settlement, where a wooden walkway lines the waterfront. Groceries, fuel and other supplies are available at The Outpost.

Continue up Quatsino Sound to **Koprino Harbour** where you can stop for a while, but this is not a recommended sheltered spot, so look beyond by venturing on up to Drake Island. In the north side of Drake Island is **Pamphlet Cove**, a small protected bay for good overnight anchorage in 15 to 30 feet. Opposite the island on the south shore of Quatsino Sound is **Julian Cove**, entered through a narrow passage immediately adjacent to **Smith Cove**

Below: The boardwalk connects the waterfront community in Winter Harbour. Left: The boardwalk at Winter Harbour in the 1970s. Above: Anchored at North Harbour in Forward Inlet.

Above: The waterfront in Winter Harbour. Left and below: Anchorage and private moorings in Pamphlet Cove on Drake Island, Quatsino Sound, and entering Varney Inlet.

Pamphlet Cove

Varney Inlet

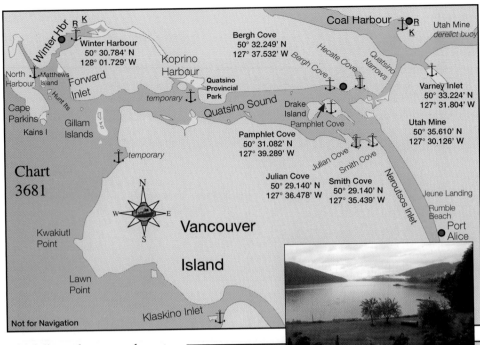

Coal Harbour R
Utah Mine
derelict buoy

Bergh Cove
50° 32.249' N
127° 37.532' W

Hecate Cove

Quatsino Narrows

Winter Hbr R K

Winter Harbour
50° 30.784' N
128° 01.729' W

Koprino Harbour

Bergh Cove

North Harbour Matthews Island
Forward Inlet

Quatsino Provincial Park

temporary

Varney Inlet
50° 33.224' N
127° 31.804' W

Cape Parkins Hunt Its

Quatsino Sound

Drake Island

Gillam Islands

Kains I

Pamphlet Cove

Utah Mine
50° 35.610' N
127° 30.126' W

temporary

Pamphlet Cove
50° 31.082' N
127° 39.289' W

Julian Cove

Smith Cove

Neroutsos Inlet

Chart
3681

N
W   E
S

Julian Cove
50° 29.140' N
127° 36.478' W

Smith Cove
50° 29.140' N
127° 35.439' W

Jeune Landing

Rumble Beach

Port Alice

Vancouver

Island

Kwakiutl Point

Lawn Point

Klaskino Inlet

Not for Navigation

which lies a short way closer to the entrance to Neroutsos Inlet. Either of these coves provides a sheltered anchorage, but Julian is preferred. **Hecate Cove** is on the opposite shore just beyond **Bergh Cove**–identified as you approach it by the public landing, on its eastern shore, for Quatsino Village. This was once a thriving Scandinavian settlement. Visit the local museum. Anchorage at Bergh Cove is good but subject to traffic wash. The more spacious Hecate Cove appears exposed but provides fair to good

Not for Navigation

Museum at Bergh Cove Hecate
Cove

Bergh Cove

Quatsino

Eagle Manor Resort

Leeson Rk

View over Quatsino Sound looking west from Eagle Manor Resort at Quatsino.

IR

Ohlsen Point

Quatsino Sound

anchoring. Anchor in Varney Inlet beyond Quatsino Narrows or at Coal Harbour. Take temporary anchorage at Utah Mine, but do not use the derelict buoy. Visit Rumble Beach near Port Alice where the Port Alice Yacht Club may provide dock space for brief transient visits. Rumble Beach village is adjacent to the marina and has all services and facilities. Dock space is also possible at Jeune Landing a short way north of the yacht club.

Nearby

Explore Quatsino Sound at your leisure taking in some of the anchorages mentioned above, or continue down the coast visiting anchorages in Brooks Bay, described in this chapter. Farther up Quatsino Sound you can travel to Coal Harbour, Holberg or Port Alice, all of which offer limited moorage or casual, relatively exposed anchorage.

Above: The lighthouse on Kains Island at the entrance to Quatsino Sound.

Two Major Sheltered Anchorages
Between Winter Cove and Brooks Peninsula

If the weather is favourable there is an inclination just to scoot down the coast from the shelter of Winter Harbour to the haven of Kyuquot Sound. Or vise versa. Going south, or north, rounding Brooks Peninsula can be rough, and so in smooth weather the tendency is to just simply go. But in doing so you would be missing out on the possibility of stopping at two of the most tranquil anchorages on the coast.

Klaskino Inlet cuts deep into the island about midway between Lawn Point and Brooks Peninsula. It is the northernmost of two favoured anchorages in Brooks Bay, and is often the one of choice for mariners wanting a brief temporary stop en route between the major points. Use a large scale chart for Kwakiutl Point and Lawn Point (provincial park) when travelling south, that will take you around a shallow area and then closer in to the shore before angling towards the anchorage. Enter south of Anchorage Island where, once inside, you will find calm water and, possibly, one or two mooring buoys.

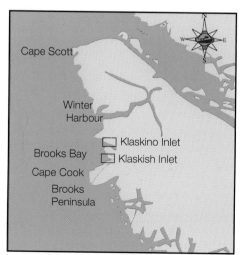

Klaskish Inlet, farther south, is tucked in deep east at the north end of the Brooks Peninsula. Easiest entrance is around the north end of McDougal Island.

If you have lots of time to spend exploring Brooks Bay, then you may want to stop in this anchorage, where you can find a suitable spot off McDougal Island or in **Klaskish Basin** for a comfortable overnight stay. The entrance to the basin is narrow. Anchor in sufficient depth as it shallows out substantially towards the head of the basin.

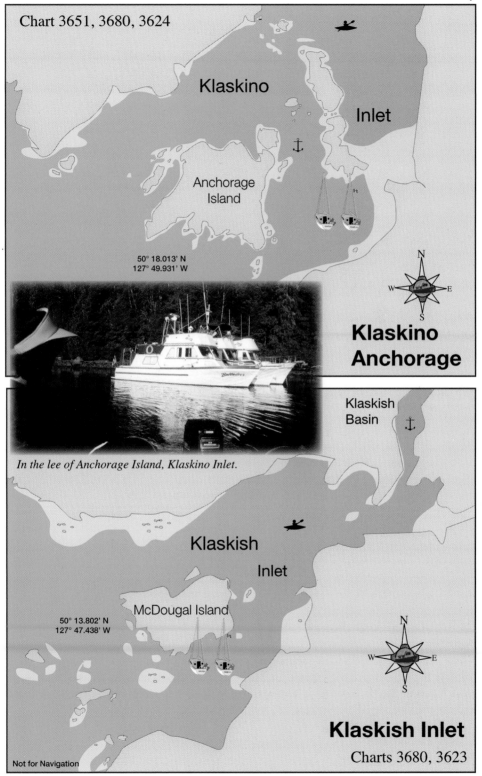

Chart 3651, 3680, 3624

Klaskino

Inlet

Anchorage
Island

50° 18.013' N
127° 49.931' W

N
W   E
S

**Klaskino
Anchorage**

Klaskish
Basin

In the lee of Anchorage Island, Klaskino Inlet.

Klaskish

Inlet

McDougal Island

50° 13.802' N
127° 47.438' W

N
W   E
S

Klaskish Inlet

Charts 3680, 3623

Not for Navigation

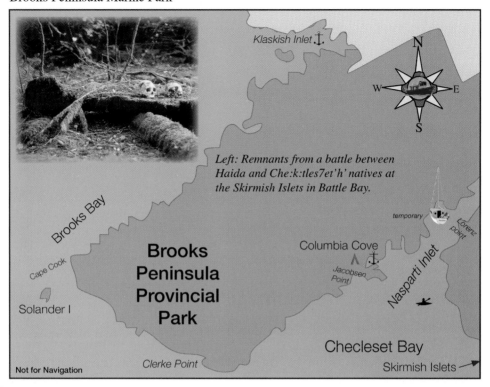

Left: Remnants from a battle between Haida and Che:k:tles7et'h' natives at the Skirmish Islets in Battle Bay.

Brooks Peninsula

Charts 3680, 3683, 3623, 3624, 3604

Access

Travelling south from Quatsino Sound and the anchorages at Klaskino and Klaskish you will have to round this major cape on the west coast of Vancouver Island. Fog or rough seas fanned by strong winds can often be the order of the day. Pick a good weather forecast and travel around the cape from Brooks Bay to Nasparti Inlet.

The Park and Anchorage

The best haven of safe anchorage at the mouth of Nasparti Inlet is in **Columbia Cove** just beyond Jacobsen Point. The cove was named for Captain Robert Gray's trading ship. The anchorage is sheltered from the incoming swells. Farther eastward, temporary anchorage can be taken in indentations into the northern shore of the inlet. Kayakers paddling along many sections of the Brooks Peninsula's convoluted and jagged shoreline will find natural beaches and sites for pitching tents and staying overnight. Temporary anchorages along the way allow for larger boats to stop and launch gunkholing expeditions by dinghy.

Nearby

Farther south there is sheltered anchorage at the **Bunsby Islands** or beyond at Kyuquot. Explore the ragged groups of islands in the vicinity of Checleset Bay, including the **Skirmish Islets** at **Battle Bay** where you will find suitable temporary anchorage to stop and explore the historic islets. Acous Peninsula is the site of an ancient native village.

Park facilities

All weather anchorages, beach, fishing, recommended kayaking.

Bunsby Islands Marine Park   Chart 3683

They are fascinating and historical. The coves in the waterways among the eastern group of islands provides shallow anchorage and protection from most weather conditions. It is not uncommon to view whales passing through Gay Passage.

Battle Bay

Above: Passing Solander Island in calm seas.

Visit the Skirmish Islands in this bay, but treat them with respect. They reveal remains of war canoes and tribal members lost in a war between the Kwakiutl and the Clayoquots.

Barter Cove

Entrance to this (exposed) anchorage is opposite Walters Cove. It is an historic area where a major and final battle was waged between warring aborignal tribes.

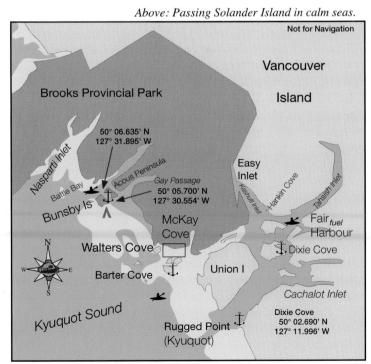

Not for Navigation

Brooks Provincial Park

Vancouver

Island

50° 06.635' N
127° 31.895' W

Naspardi Inlet

Acous Peninsula

Gay Passage
50° 05.700' N
127° 30.554' W

Battle Bay

Bunsby Is

Easy
Inlet

Kashutl Inlet

Hankin Cove

Tahsish Inlet

McKay
Cove

Fair fuel
Harbour

Dixie Cove

Walters Cove

N
W   E
S

Barter Cove

Union I

Cachalot Inlet

Kyuquot Sound

Rugged Point
(Kyuquot)

Dixie Cove
50° 02.690' N
127° 11.996' W

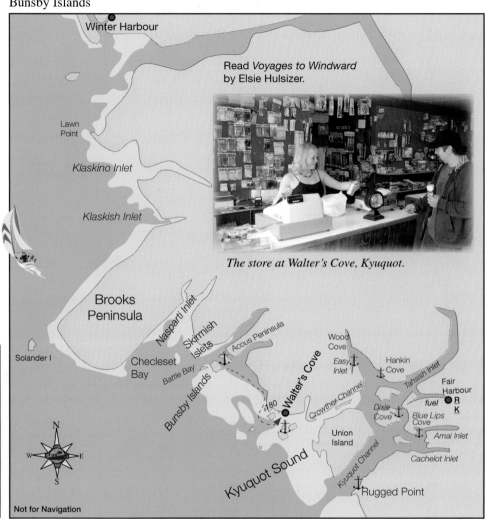

Winter Harbour

Read *Voyages to Windward*
by Elsie Hulsizer.

Lawn
Point

Klaskino Inlet

Klaskish Inlet

The store at Walter's Cove, Kyuquot.

Brooks
Peninsula

Nasparti Inlet

Skirmish
Islets

Acous Peninsula

Checleset
Bay

Battle Bay

Bunsby Islands

Solander I

180'

Walter's Cove

Crowther Channel

Wood
Cove

Easy
Inlet

Hankin
Cove

Tahsish Inlet

Fair
Harbour

fuel   R
        K

Dixie
Cove

Blue Lips
Cove

Amai Inlet

Union
Island

Kyuquot Channel

Cachelot Inlet

Kyuquot Sound

Rugged Point

N
W   E
S

Not for Navigation

Kyuquot Sound

Charts 3651, 3683, 3604

Access

Visit the islands of Battle Bay and stop in at the Bunsby Islands as you travel south from Brooks Peninsula, passing behind the Barrier Islets along the Vancouver Island shore. The Bunsby Islets are a favourite among mariners, including paddlers, because of their strategic location, beautiful waterway, and the calm, shallow anchorages indented into them. The one to the east of Gay Passage has a canal-like, tree-lined inlet with low grassy banks that winds deep into it. When heading for Walters Cove, navigate towards the island marked 180' on your chart. Round it to the west and follow the passage into the cove. If travelling west to east from the open ocean, Rugged Point is passed when entering Kyuquot Sound. The islets and rocky Barrier Reef that run along the coast at this point are interesting and a sheltered option for navigating north or south.

Anchored in the Bunsby Islands.
Inset: Fuel dock at Fair Harbour.

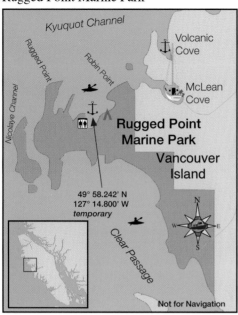

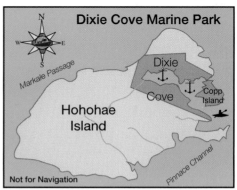

Rugged Point
Dixie Cove
Kuyuqot Sound

Charts 3682, 3623, 3604

From the north on the inside of the Barrier Islands, Rugged Point will be passed if continuing along Clear Passage. Use the Barrier Islands as a continuous, protected waterway.

The Parks and Anchorages

There are a few anchorages in Kyuquot Sound, the principal one being at Dixie Cove on Hohoae Island. **Dixie Cove Marine Park** lies on the northeast side of the Island.

At Rugged Point a high promontory offers a spectacular view of the open Pacific Ocean and the breaking surf on the islets and reefs just off the entrance to Kyuqot Sound. But the adjacent nooks where you can drop anchor offer only temporary shelter. They are located between Rugged Point and Robin Point and in **McLean Cove** and **Volcanic Cove**. McLean Cove is the popular one, with some spectacular scenery and no doubt the reason for the area being made into a park. There is some swell action in all of these coves.

Nearby

The settlement of **Walter's Cove**, with fishing lodges, private homes, beach trails, and a general store and post office at the head of the public dock, also boasts a hospital and some other facilities for the general public. Walter's Cove is a worthwhile stop that provides refuge and facilities in an otherwise long stretch of open and undeveloped coast.

About 15 miles up Kyuqot Sound is the settlement at **Fair Harbour** where a launch ramp provides alternative access to this coastal wilderness. Fuel is available at this stop, which is primarily a trailer boat launch facility. There is a small, sparsely stocked store and office on shore. Sports fishing is very active on the west coast. Vessels launched at Fair Harbour can be seen running to and from the fishing grounds off Kyuqot Sound, stopping at Walter's Cove to purchase supplies at the store. Back at Fair Harbour, there is a cleaning station at the fuel dock. If conditions at Rugged Point are not ideal, you will find sheltered anchorage at **Blue Lips Cove** (locally named) in Amai Inlet.

Park facilities

All weather anchorages, beach, kayaking. Rugged Point has toilets, a trail with a boardwalk, fishing, viewpoints and scuba diving in vicinity.

Above: Houpsitas native village in Walter's Cove. Right: Tied up at the public dock adjacent to the store and post office in Walter's Cove. Inset above: Cleaning station at Fair Harbour, Kyuquot Sound.

Tahsish Inlet

Part way up Kashutl Inlet, there are sheltered anchorages at **Hankin Cove** and **Easy Inlet** and a temporary anchorage at Wood Cove. But there are no recommended anchorages to be found up Tahsish Inlet. Note that Tahsis, farther south, derives its name from the same source as Tahsish.

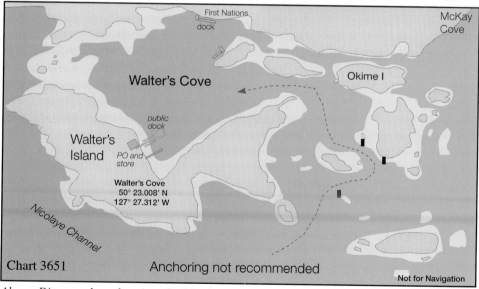

Above: Diagram shows location of public dock in Walter's Cove. Anchorage is not recommended but stopping at the cove is rewarded with a pleasant visit. Diagram on page 268 shows locations of Walter's Cove and Tahsish Inlet in Kyuquot Sound.

Above: Seas picking up on the outside of Vancouver Island. This is typical of the afternoons.

Esperanza Inlet

Charts 3676, 3604

Access

From the open Pacific, **Catala Island** (marine provincial park) lies to the north of the main entrance to Esperanza Inlet. Rolling Roadstead is reached via Gillam Channel although access is also possible by way of a passage around the west side of the island. This passage, however, is strewn with rocks and reefs and should be used preferably only when leaving northbound in fair weather and provided you have a good large scale chart, as well as excellent capabilities of determining the precise passage through the reefs.

The Park and Anchorages

The island has no facilities but is a good place for kayakers to camp. Boats anchored in the **Rolling Roadstead** will feel the steady swell from the open Pacific at practically all times. It is a good place to wait overnight before setting out for an early passage northbound to Kyuquot. But monitor the weather before settling in for the night. This is a good area for viewing wildlife, including otters, orcas, grey whales and eagles. There is a camping area on Catala Island adjacent to Rolling Roadstead.

Nearby

Anchor at **Queen Cove** or on the southeastern side of Nuchatlitz Inlet at **Port Langford** (provincial park) or **Mary Basin**. Not long ago the native village located on the east bank of Queen Cove was a flourishing community, and a few, newer homes still exist in the once-busy little settlement. Farther up Esperanza Inlet are access waterways to the towns of Zeballos and Tahsis with Ceepeecee and Esperanza along the way. It is also the beginning of the inside passage around Nootka Island to Bligh Island and Friendly Cove.

For those who are not familiar with the term Roadstead: This is a body of water, usually located outside of a harbour, where vessels lie at anchor waiting access to the port, such as the anchorage for large ships in English Bay off Vancouver or Royal Roads (as in Roadstead) off Victoria. In the case of the anchorage behind Catala Island, Rolling is an apt description of the almost constant, but usually mild (in summer), sea condition.

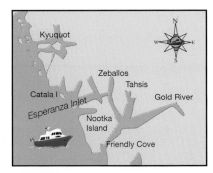

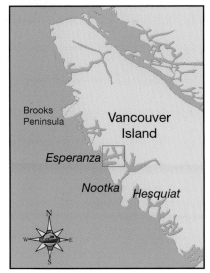

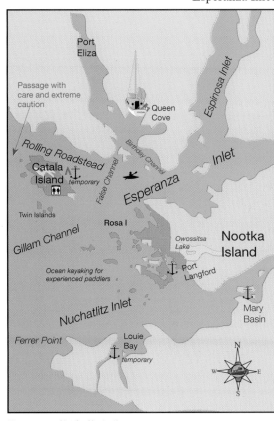

Diagrams are Not for Navigation

Below: There is sheltered anchorage at Queen Cove.

Park facilities Catala Island. Camping, toilets, fishing, viewpoints.

Esperanza Inlet, after departing Queen Cove, en route to Zeballos. Nuchatlitz is to starboard or south of the entrance and if time permits, well worthwhile exploring. Anchorage can be found in Port Langford or at Mary Basin.

Entering Esperanza Inlet from off shore, the safest and preferred passage is Gillam Channel. Once inside, the sheltered waters provide easy cruising along narrow waterways around Nootka Island. This obviates the need to brave the open ocean on the west side of Nootka Island, and provides an opportunity to visit the historic towns of Zeballos and Tahsis, and settlement at Esperanza. Nearby Ceepeecee is a fishing resort. Take in the anchorage at Queen Cove, or go into Nuchatlitz Inlet for its peaceful sanctuary from the open Pacific.

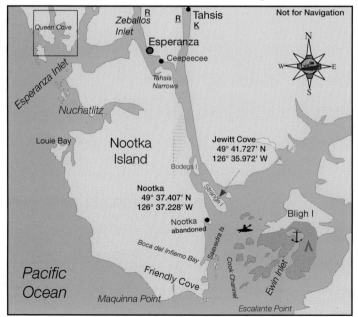

The anchorages in Port Langford and Mary Basin provide spectacular viewing of open water and west coast marine life.

Stop at Zeballos for a touch of history. But there is no anchorage at the town. Gold brought settlers to Zeballos, and although there is still the odd amount of gold remaining, it is largely sports fishing that draws interest in the town today.

Farther along the inlet the settlement of

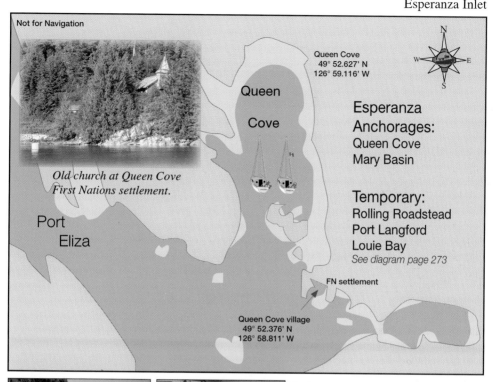

Not for Navigation

Old church at Queen Cove
First Nations settlement.

Queen Cove
49° 52.627' N
126° 59.116' W

Queen

Cove

Esperanza
Anchorages:
Queen Cove
Mary Basin

Temporary:
Rolling Roadstead
Port Langford
Louie Bay
See diagram page 273

FN settlement

Port
Eliza

Queen Cove village
49° 52.376' N
126° 58.811' W

*Below: Approaching the waterfront at
Zeballos. There is no anchorage here.
But the town is worth visiting.
Left: Zeballos public dock and chatting
to the owner at Carrie's Restaurant.*

Above: Launching and retrieving at Zeballos. A fine concrete ramp structure lies alongside the marina at the foot of the town's main street. These boaters in the adjacent waterway are awaiting their tow vehicle and trailer. Below: Passing through Tahsis Narrows. There is little current to worry about in the narrows. The town of Tahsis is just a few miles beyond this point.
Inset right: The boat launching ramp at Tahsis.

Above: A small private dock at Esperanza is used for recreation by youngsters attending the camp. The building in the foreground is the old, still functioning, boathouse and workshop.

Esperanza,which was originally a mission hospital and dental clinic, today serves as a multi-denominational camp for children.

The waters off Esperanza and nearby Ceepeecee are not suitable anchorages for anything other than a temporary stop. Most mariners continue on to Tahsis and southward to Nootka Sound.

Best of the anchorages in the area, apart from Friendly Cove itself, is in Ewin Inlet on Bligh Island. Captain Cook anchored his ships in Resolution Bay and spent some weeks there while replacing masts. Oddly enough, this is not a very suitable anchorage for small craft. Try, instead, Jewitt Cove on Strange Island, although it is too deep for most pleasure boats. **Santa Gertrudis Cove** and **Hisnit Inlet** are more suitable. Hisnit Inlet opens off Hanna Channel. Nearby you will find small fishing camps, and fuel at Critter Cove Marina.

Below: Cathy Daynes runs a good operation at Westview Marina. Don't anchor out. Although small craft of the recreational fishing community dominate, in the lower photograph, the marina has additional, suitable docking for larger craft.

Friendly Cove and San Rafael Island from Yuquot village.

Friendly Cove

Charts 3675, 3604, 3603

Access

Mariners travelling between Catala Island and Friendly Cove usually use the inside passage around Nootka Island rather than the open Pacific. Down Tahsis Inlet, you will pass Jewitt Cove on Strange Island. At the entrance to Nootka Sound is the historic Friendly Cove where the British signed a treaty with Spain in 1790. The comemmoration of this event is seen in stained glass windows of the church in Yuquot village at Friendly Cove.

Anchorage

The anchorage at Friendly Cove is fairly sheltered in the bay beneath the lighthouse and adjacent to the curving beach that fronts the historic village. This is where many early vessels were depicted as having anchored when visiting the area. Members of the First Nations band at Friendly Cove collect a fee for going ashore. Some summers they have a gas barge anchored in the cove. Visit the lighthouse on San Rafael Island, the historic church in the cove and the adjacent beach facing the open ocean.

Nearby

A little farther into Nootka Sound **Santa Gertrudis Cove** opens into Nootka Island. It is a protected anchorage, but mind the rocks and shallows as you enter and search for a suitable place to drop the anchor. The preferred spot is in the north part of the cove.

Across Cook Channel there is anchorage at **Ewin Inlet** in Bligh Island. Anchor at the head of the inlet. Most of the island is a provincial marine park.

South from Friendly Cove, beyond Estevan Point, after rounding Hesquiat Peninsula, either put into Hesquiat Harbour or carry on to Hot Springs Cove. **Hesquiat Harbour** can be easy to enter, or very difficult when seas are rough, due to the shallow bar across the entrance. If it is calm and you have time, anchor temporarily inside at **Rae Basin**. Cougar Annie's Garden in Hequiat is a highly recommended stop. As is Hot Spring Cove.

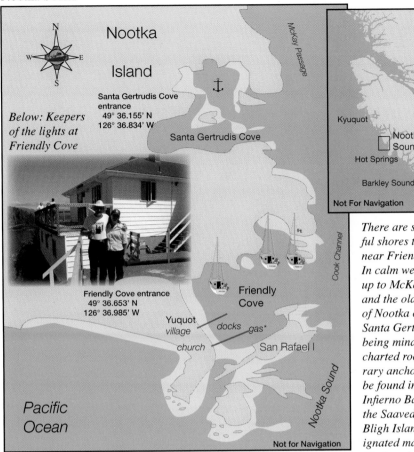

Nootka

Island

Santa Gertrudis Cove
entrance
49° 36.155' N
126° 36.834' W

*Below: Keepers
of the lights at
Friendly Cove*

Santa Gertrudis Cove

McKay Passage

Friendly Cove entrance
49° 36.653' N
126° 36.985' W

Yuquot
village   docks   gas*

church   San Rafael I

Cook Channel

Friendly
Cove

*Pacific
Ocean*

Nootka Sound

Not for Navigation

Kyuquot

Nootka
Sound

Hot Springs

Barkley Sound

Not For Navigation

*There are some beauti-
ful shores to explore
near Friendly Cove.
In calm weather run
up to McKay Passage
and the old settlement
of Nootka or slip into
Santa Gertudis Cove,
being mindful of the
charted rocks. Tempo-
rary anchorage may
be found in Boca del
Infierno Bay opposite
the Saavedra Islands.
Bligh Island is a des-
ignated marine park.
Find anchorage deep
inside Ewin Inlet.
Below: This totem once
stood at Friendly Cove.*

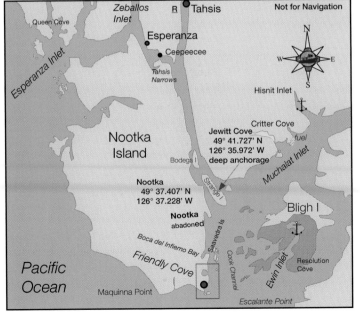

Zeballos
Inlet   R   Tahsis   Not for Navigation

Queen Cove

Esperanza

Ceepeecee

Esperanza Inlet

Tahsis
Narrows

Hisnit Inlet

Critter Cove

Jewitt Cove
49° 41.727' N
126° 35.972' W
deep anchorage

fuel

Muchalat Inlet

Nootka
Island

Bodega I

Strange I

Nootka
49° 37.407' N
126° 37.228' W

Nootka
abadoned

Bligh I

Saavedra Is

Boca del Infierno Bay

Friendly Cove

Cook Channel

Ewin Inlet

Resolution
Cove

*Pacific
Ocean*

Maquinna Point

Escalante Point

Opposite: The church at Friendly Cove. The land belongs to the First Nations people, who manage it and collect a landing fee from visitors.
Above: The anchorage in Friendly Cove. From the beach, a landing extends into the cove. It is available as a dock for visitors. Another, larger dock and a fuel float are located to the left of the vessels (not shown in the photograph–see previous pages). These accommodate visitors as well as the supply ship, MV Uchuck, which visits the settlement regularly.
Right: Stained glass window inside the lobby of the church depicts the signing of a treaty between the British and the Spanish in 1792.
Below: A small recreational pleasure boat trolls for salmon in McKay Passage off Santa Gertudis Cove in Nootka Sound.

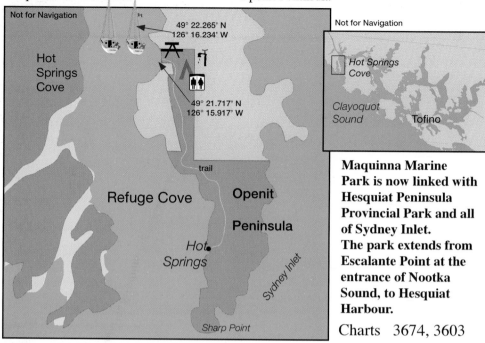

Not for Navigation

49° 22.265' N
126° 16.234' W

49° 21.717' N
126° 15.917' W

Hot
Springs
Cove

trail

Refuge Cove   Openit

Peninsula

Hot
Springs

Sydney Inlet

Sharp Point

Not for Navigation

Hot Springs
Cove

Clayoquot
Sound   Tofino

Maquinna Marine Park is now linked with Hesquiat Peninsula Provincial Park and all of Sydney Inlet. The park extends from Escalante Point at the entrance of Nootka Sound, to Hesquiat Harbour.

Charts   3674, 3603

Maquinna/Hot Springs Cove

Access

Travelling south from Friendly Cove around Hesquiat Peninsula approach Sharp Point, or from the south out of Tofino try the inside passage and exit Sydney Inlet to the open sea. Off Sharp Point turn into Hot Springs Cove (Refuge Cove) being mindful of the shallow reef just off shore. A buoy marks the extent of the reef although it is comfortable for small craft to pass over the shallows unless it is very rough and low tide. Local boat operators use the near shore route constantly, but those unaccustomed to the large coastal swells may find the size of the waves disconcerting at first.v

The Park and Anchorage

There are sheltered and safe places to anchor, as well as a substantial dock in the inlet. There is available camping near the head of the dock. Water and toilets add to the convenience of those staying overnight. A trail made of boards, many with names of visiting vessels carved into them, makes up the walkway through the park in the direction of the hot springs. Carving boat names in the planks is allowed. A one mile hike along this boardwalk through the forest, takes you to the hot springs, a natural flow of steaming hot water that bubbles out of the ground a short distance from the rocky shoreline. The water cascades over a beautiful, low waterfall and runs through a series of small pools. Those pools closest to the tideline, at high water, are subject to a flow of cold seawater washing into them, providing a refreshing hot and cold bathe. A large natural tidal pool in the adjacent rocks is an attractive feature but not much used as a swimming hole. During stormy conditions beware of surf breaking onto the rocks at the water's edge.

Nearby

There is a store at the native village on the opposite shore of the inlet. You will find friendly service and some supplies. It is possible also to purchase fuel.

At the hot springs. A view platform and change room structure overlooks the springs. The inset photo shows one of the pools at the hot springs and the way things were before becoming more popular.

Hot Springs Cove, Vancouver Island

Park facilities

Maquinna/Hot Springs Cove: All weather anchorage, dock, toilets, water, campsites, hiking, hot springs bathing, viewpoint/point of interest.

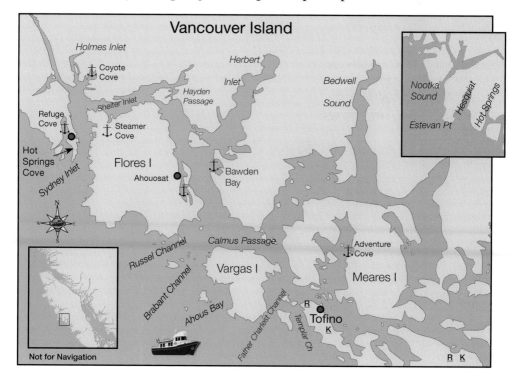

Walking the trail from the dock at Refuge Cove to the hot springs. The trail begins at the picnic and campground sites and ends at the hot pools of Hot Springs Cove. Opposite: Hot Springs Cove dock and anchorage beyond. The blue vessel offers lodging and dining.

Clayoquot Sound

Charts 3674, 3673, 3603, 3685

Access

As you travel southwards from Hot Springs Cove you may take the outside route in calm conditions, around Flores Island and enter the anchorage at Vargas Island off Brabant Channel. Or take the inside passage up Sydney Inlet and find your way to some of the coves that offer overnight tranquility en route to your destination. Many mariners head directly for Tofino and miss some of the pristine shoreline tucked into coves and nooks off Sydney Inlet, Shelter Inlet, around the back of Meares Island or beyond in Tofino Inlet.

The Parks and Anchorages

I recommend trying **Holmes Inlet** or **Coyote Cove** off Sydney Inlet or **Steamer Cove** near Hayden Passage. Try also **Bawden Bay** opposite Matilda Inlet. Call in at Ahousat and visit the warm-water hot springs in **Gibson Marine Park.** There is an anchorage to stop at nearby, and also in the bay opposite Tofino.

Top: We tied up at the dock at Ahousat and stopped for fuel and lunch. A sailboat slips by en route down Matilda Inlet (Ahousat) to the anchorage off Gibson Marine Park.

Above: The store, lodge and restaurant (interior shown centre, left) at Ahousat. Most of the buildings were established by Hugh Clarke (centre, right), son of the early settler who donated the original family property at Hot Springs Cove (Maquinna, page 282) to marine parks.

Park facilities

Gibson: All weather anchorage, beach, warm water hot spring, viewpoint/point of interest.

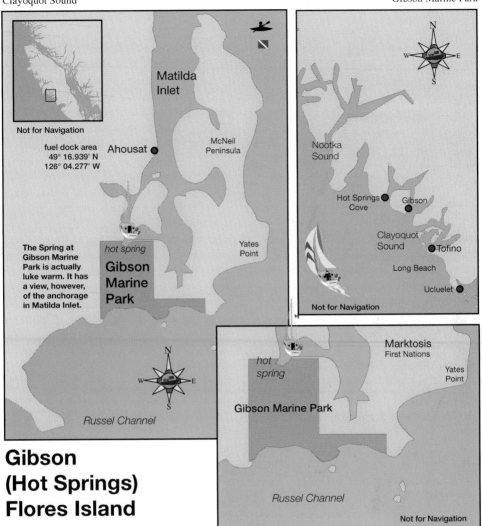

Not for Navigation

fuel dock area
49° 16.939' N
126° 04.277' W

The Spring at
Gibson Marine
Park is actually
luke warm. It has
a view, however,
of the anchorage
in Matilda Inlet.

Gibson
(Hot Springs)
Flores Island

Gibson Marine Park

Charts 3674,
3673, 3603

Access

From Tofino, it is a beautiful cruise to the Gibson hot springs and Ahousat, by way of
Calmus Passage north of Vargas Island and west of Meares Island. From Hot Springs
Cove go via Sydney Inlet, Hayden Passage and Millar Channel to Matilda Inlet.

The Park

A large flat, open stretch of land abuts the shore where the hot springs (warm) are located. There are no mooring buoys, toilets, picnic tables or water. Anchor a short way off
the head of the inlet and row ashore to the springs, easily identified by a low concrete
wall near the water's edge.

Nearby

Store and docks at the settlement at Ahousat. The town of Tofino has all conveniences
and marine services for the transient mariner, including a fine launch ramp.

Kennedy Cove

You may want to continue past Tofino and travel into Lemmens Inlet to **Adventure Cove**. Latest reports state this cove was closed off, probably while archaeological studies were being conducted (check for temporary closure before planning it as a destination).

On the Tofino Inlet side of Clayoquot Sound, preferred anchorages include **Mosquito Harbour, Gunner Inlet, Kennedy Cove** and **Irving Cove.**

Clayoquot Sound is one of the most beautiful inlets on the coast. Its scenic topography makes it inviting and appealing to most mariners cruising the west coast. The sound's convoluted shoreline, like that of Barkley Sound, provides coves and bays in which to anchor, explore, fish, swim, watch whales and birds, scuba dive and paddle. Its numerous islands and islets, which may pose a difficult navigational challenge at places, also provide protection from weather.

Some areas have been designated marine parks, and although these have no facilities they do have a natural attraction that has been preserved for the future. Some offer overnight anchorage. Others are islands or sections of land along the coast, where mostly paddlers and campers will go ashore, beaching their vessels for overnight stays. We stopped at Kennedy Cove on one trip into Clayoquot Sound and swam in the clear waters of the river flowing out of Kennedy Lake. Anchor at the mouth of the river.

Provincial and marine parks abound. They include:

Flores Island Marine Park - west and south shores to Gibson marine park and its hot springs, *Vargas Island Marine Park* - west and south shores - This is a key anchorage, but only for temporary or day use. The anchorage is on the outside of Vargas Island in Ahous Bay off Brabant Channel.

The following offer no anchorage or access for boats other than canoes or kayaks:
Epper Passage Marine Park - Morphee and Dunlap islands northeast of Vargas Island.
Sulphur Passage Marine Park - Obstruction Island and surrounding channels.
Dawley Marine Park - The narrow passage around Meares Island near Windy Bay.
If you are merely in transit down the coast and are taking the inside passage through Clayoquot Sound, with minimal time to stop, consider Ahousat, or anchorage at Tofino for brief stays that are not too much out of your way.

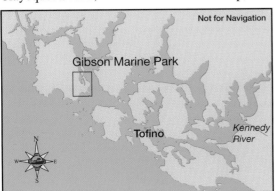

Above: Anchored in Kennedy Cove at the mouth of the Kennedy River. The water was warm enough for swimming.

Anchorages in Clayoquot Sound inlude Holmes Inlet, Coyote Cove, Young Bay, Steamer Cove, Bawden Bay, Matilda Inlet (Ahousat), Quait Bay, Adventure Cove, Mosquito Harbour , Gunner Inlet, Kennedy Cove and Irving Cove.

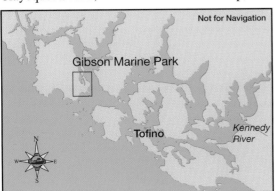

Not for Navigation
Gibson Marine Park
Tofino
Kennedy River

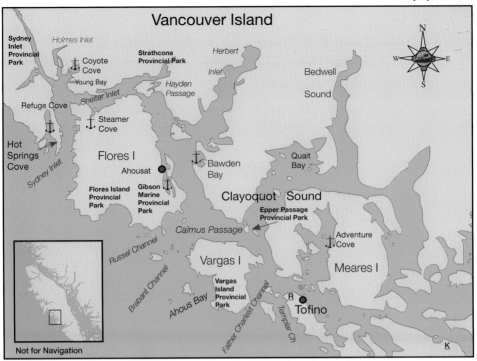

Not for Navigation

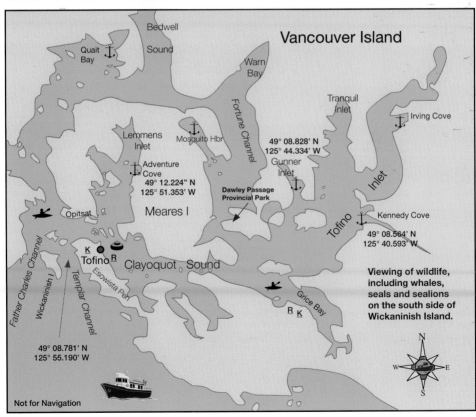

Not for Navigation

Top: Approaching Amphitrite Point from off shore in calm conditions. Above: Amphitrite Point lighthouse at the entrance to Ucluelet. It overlooks Carolina Passage and Alpha Passage, which are separated by Jenny Reef. Use these passages in calm weather, otherwise use Felice Channel south of George Fraser Islands. Below: Anchored deep inside Ucluelet Harbour.

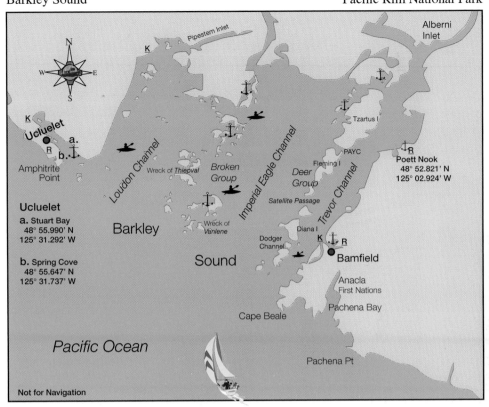

Alberni Inlet

K

Pipestem Inlet

N
W   E
S

Tzartus I

PAYC

Fleming I

Poett Nook
48° 52.821' N
125° 02.924' W

K
Ucluelet
a.
R
b.

Amphitrite Point

Loudon Channel

Wreck of *Thiepval*

Broken Group

Imperial Eagle Channel

Deer Group

Trevor Channel

Satellite Passage

Ucluelet
a. Stuart Bay
48° 55.990' N
125° 31.292' W

Barkley

Wreck of *Vanlene*

Diana I

Dodger Channel

K   R

b. Spring Cove
48° 55.647' N
125° 31.737' W

Sound

Bamfield

Anacla
First Nations

Pachena Bay

Cape Beale

Pacific Ocean

Pachena Pt

Not for Navigation

West Coast Vancouver I

Barkley Sound

Charts 3671, 3670,
3646, 3668, 3602

Access

Boats travelling south down the west coast of Vancouver Island will reach Barkley Sound about 25 miles from Tofino, passing offshore of Long Beach and Amphitrite Point into Ucluelet. Or it can be reached easily from Port Alberni down Alberni Canal, or from the south via Juan de Fuca Strait.

Anchorages

There are several suitable anchorages in the Broken Group and in other parts of Barkley Sound. One of the favourites and easiest to access is at **Effingham Island**. From Bamfield, cross Trevor Channel (we use Satellite Pass) and Imperial Eagle Channel, and enter the anchorage off Coaster Channel.

Good, protected anchorage can be found throughout Barkley Sound, most popularly at **Turtle Island, Jacques Island, Jarvis Island, Nettle Island** and in the **Pinkerton Islands.**

Nearby

The towns of **Bamfield** to the south of the sound and **Ucluelet** at the northwest end have most services for mariners. Sheltered anchoring is possible in the harbours at these towns, and moorage is available at public docks and marinas. Go ashore and enjoy the ambience of two of Vancouver Island's friendliest communities.

N
W   E
S

Quatsino Sound

Nootka Sound

Barkley Sound

Victoria

Above: Anchored in the shelter of Effingham Island, one of the major anchorages in Barkley Sound. It is the site of a one time large First Nations village.
Left: Mid harbour at Ucluelet. There is sheltered anchorage either side of the island in the background.

Activities in Barkley Sound

Kayaking is popular in Barkley Sound. As you cruise through the many islands and protected waterways you will see groups of kayakers making their way to the many camping and park facilities provided. Recreational fishing is an industry in Barkley Sound. The small boats leave their camps early every morning and again in the afternoons for the popular fishing spots. Bird watching and whale watching are popular, and wildlife in abundance includes many sightings of porpoises and sealions.

The area is rich in marine life, and scuba diving is a regular year-round activity with wreck diving being a favourite attraction. Barkley Sound is known for its many shipwrecks including the *Vanlene* at Austin Island and the *Thiepval* in Thiepval Passage.

There is a rich history of settlement in Barkley Sound. While it was Captain James Cook who discovered Barkley Sound in 1778, Captain Charles William Barkley was the explorer-fur trader who gave it its name. His wife Francis Barkley, at the tender age of 17, accompanied her husband on his voyage in 1786, and became the first white woman to see the northwest coast of America.

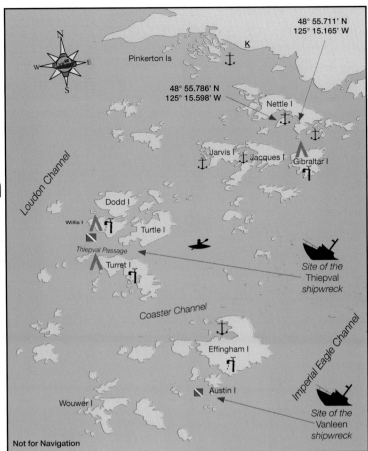

The Broken Group

Charts 3671, 3670, 3646, 3668, 3602

48° 55.711' N
125° 15.165' W

Pinkerton Is

K

48° 55.786' N
125° 15.598' W

Nettle I

Jarvis I
Jacques I
Gibraltar I

Loudon Channel

Dodd I

Willis I

Turtle I

Thiepval Passage

Turret I

Site of the
Thiepval
shipwreck

Coaster Channel

Effingham I

Imperial Eagle Channel

Austin I

Wouwer I

Site of the
Vanleen
shipwreck

Not for Navigation

Park facilities

There are camping facilities at numerous places on the islands. Campsites and drinking water as indicated.

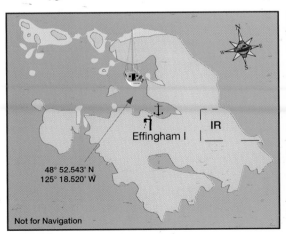

Effingham I

IR

48° 52.543' N
125° 18.520' W

Not for Navigation

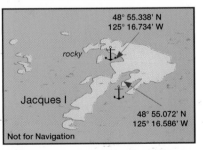

48° 55.338' N
125° 16.734' W

rocky

Jacques I

48° 55.072' N
125° 16.586' W

Not for Navigation

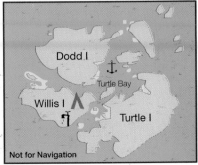

Dodd I

Turtle Bay

Willis I

Turtle I

Not for Navigation

Above: Anchorage in Bamfield inlet is possible at the north side of Burlo Island. In the background is McKay Bay Lodge, a long established sports fishing facility that has a few docks, fuel and some supplies. The nearby public marina on the west side of the inlet has a drying reef running off the outer dock that should be avoided. Check your chart and pay attention to the signage. Inset: The cafe overlooking the community docks. Below: Bamfield Inlet looking north from the community docks. The main road of the west side of town is a wooden boardwalk that runs the length of the shoreline, connecting to the stores.

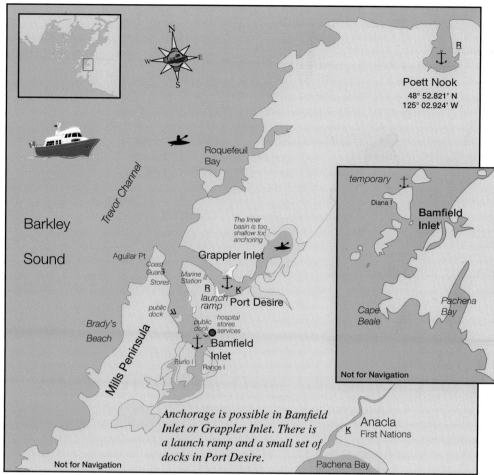

Poett Nook
48° 52.821' N
125° 02.924' W

Roquefeuil
Bay

temporary

Diana I

**Bamfield
Inlet**

The Inner
basin is too
shallow for
anchoring

Barkley

Sound

Aguilar Pt

Grappler Inlet

Coast
Guard
Stores

Marine
Station

R   K

launch
ramp **Port Desire**

public
dock

public   hospital
dock   stores
        services

*Brady's
Beach*

Cape
Beale

Pachena
Bay

hospital
stores
services

**Bamfield
Inlet**

Burlo I

Range I

Not for Navigation

*Anchorage is possible in Bamfield
Inlet or Grappler Inlet. There is
a launch ramp and a small set of
docks in Port Desire.*

Anacla
K First Nations

Not for Navigation   Pachena Bay

Trevor Channel

Mills Peninsula

Below: Temporarily anchored in Satellite Passage, in the lee of Diana Island.

The Town of Bamfield was settled by William Eddy Banfield (the post office misspelled his name and Bamfield has stuck). It was later selected as the terminus for the telegraph cable that would be laid across the Pacific Ocean, connecting North America with Australia and landfalls between. The town also became the site of the Bamfield Biological Station and an important Coast Guard station serving the fabled Graveyard of the Pacific. The rugged Life Saving Trail begins at a campground alongside the First Nations village of Anacla, near Bamfield. Vessels stopping in Pachena Bay will find a long sandy beach and the adjacent campground. The Pachena River flows into the bay, providing a launching area for small boats.

In the early days of settlement, First Nations summer camps and villages were spread throughout Barkley Sound, but little if anything remains to tell of their former existence.

From Bamfield walk across the Mills Peninsula to Brady Beach for spectacular views of the shoreline and ocean.

The Pacific Rim Park ranger's cabin is located at Nettle Island, site of a popular anchorage in Barkley Sound. Anchor at least 100 metres away from the cabin, and well clear of the cabin docks as occasional emergency calls require the ranger to make a hasty departure in his boat, leaving a wash that could disturb anchored boats. Inset: Carla talks to park ranger Darren Salisbury. Below: Kayakers off the Pinkerton Group near Nettle Island.

Port Alberni and Alberni Inlet

Access and Anchorages

From Bamfield, a short distance up Trevor Channel is **Roquefeuil Bay**, formerly known as Kelp Bay. This bight is used as a temporary anchorage and is a popular scuba diving location. About three miles farther is **Poett Nook**, a protected anchorage in a sheltered cove. It is also home to a large marina used mostly by recreational fishermen.

Opposite the north end of Tzartus Island, across the lower end of Alberni Inlet lies **Congreve Island.** A deep cove north of the island provides a good anchorage, as does **San Mateo Bay** a short distance beyond. There are fish farm installations in this bay but lots of room for anchoring. There is also a small public dock just inside Bernard Point.

Uchuklesit Inlet opens to the west. It is an exposed body of water with a post office at Kildonan. Although this was a thriving community at one time, today it is no more than a single building on a float and is run by the family that lives nearby. There are some residents and holiday cottages scattered around the Inlet. Henderson Lake and **Snug Basin** open off its far end. Snug Basin is a protected, but deep anchorage. **Green Cove** and **Limestone Bay** are alternative anchorages at the entrance to Alberni Inlet.

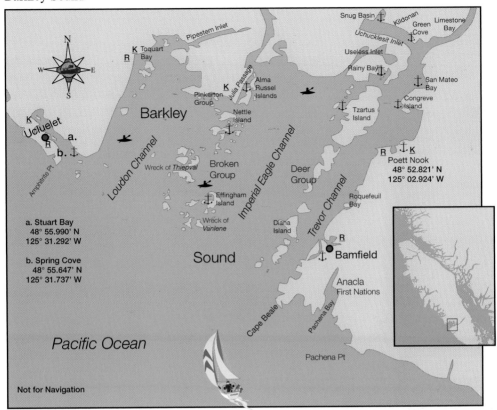

From Uchucklesit Inlet to Port Alberni is about 20 miles. Winds usually whip up a short, steep chop in the afternoon, building as the seas run up the inlet. The only place used as a refuge or temporary anchorage along most of the canal, is at a small dock that has been placed by the Port Alberni Harbour Authority in the tiny nook at **Hook Bay**, immediately beyond **Nahmint Bay**. There is room to anchor in Hook Bay, but anchorage in Nahmint Bay is not recommended as it is deep and exposed. Nearing Port Alberni, China Creek Marina has protected moorage as well as a fuel dock and launching ramp. At the head of the inlet, Port Alberni has a substantial facility at Harbour Quay Marina. Trailerable boats continue past the harbour, and up the Somass River to the launching ramp at Clutesi Haven. Here there is access to stores as well as marinas and fuel.

Victoria Bound

Leaving beautiful Barkley Sound behind, cruise around Cape Beale and make for Juan de Fuca Strait. Check the forecast for fog, wind and tides. If you are powering along the coast, time your passage for calm conditions. If you are sailing, look for the winds that best suit you and your craft. Enjoy the ride home by taking appropriate precautions. I have known boats to encounter rough conditions off Pachena Point despite calm winds. The tides can do that, even out in the open Pacific.

There is shelter along the way. Most vessels put into Port Renfrew. Others make for the more sheltered **Anderson Cove** in Sooke's Inner Harbour. Or continue to Becher Bay where anchorage behind **Frazer Island** provides a tranquil final stop before voyaging on to the British Columbia capital city, or on to the Gulf Islands, or into Puget Sound.

Above: Totems on the banks of the Pachena River at Anacla near Bamfield. Below: The Bamfield Marine Biological Station overlooking the entrance to Bamfield Inlet and the adjacent Trevor Channel in Barkley Sound. Left: Students at the Marine Station.

Above: The supply vessel Lady Rose *calling at Bamfield. Its stop is at the dock alongside the coast guard station and stores. These include a grocery store and a well-stocked gallery and gift shop. Left: The dock on the Pachena River serving the First Nations at Anacla, at the head of the lifesaving trail. Below: The boardwalk at Bamfield. Part of the Pacific Marine Sciences Station seen on the opposite shore.*

Top: Tranquility at Poett Nook on an early Summer's morning in August. Above: Monument to the people of Alberni depicting their ancestral whaling history. Right: A black bear forages along the shore in Alberni Inlet. Right, lower: The post office at Kildonan is all that remains of a once thriving cannery and community. The cannery was established in 1903 and remained in operation until 1960. Anchor nearby in Snug Basin or Green Cove.

Above: Looking down Alberni Canal on a clear, calm morning. This view is from the breakwater at China Creek. The inlet stretches some 20 miles to its mouth at Uchucklesit Inlet and Kildonan with little protection along the way from afternoon winds. There is a small nook at Hook Bay adjacent to Nahmint Bay. A small float is maintained by the Port Alberni Harbour Commission for the use of small craft. Right: China Creek has a marina and a launch ramp. The dock to the right is a fuel dock with access ashore. In the background, the inlet continues a short way to Port Alberni. Right, lower: One of the attractions at Port Alberni is the steam train that takes tourists to the only remaining steam driven pulp mill in the country. Below: Tied up at the Port Alberni Yacht Club at Fleming Island in Barkley Sound.

At Brady's Beach near Cape Beale. Worn by centuries of wind and wave action, monolithic sea stacks like this are a phenomenon of west coast landfalls, and feature prominently in prehistoric folklore.

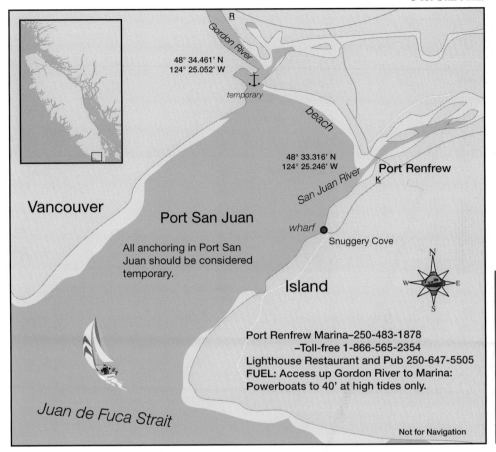

Within the image:
- R
- Gordon River
- 48° 34.461' N 124° 25.052' W
- temporary
- beach
- 48° 33.316' N 124° 25.246' W
- Port Renfrew
- San Juan River
- K
- Vancouver
- Port San Juan
- wharf
- Snuggery Cove
- All anchoring in Port San Juan should be considered temporary.
- Island
- N W E S
- Port Renfrew Marina–250-483-1878 –Toll-free 1-866-565-2354 Lighthouse Restaurant and Pub 250-647-5505 FUEL: Access up Gordon River to Marina: Powerboats to 40' at high tides only.
- Juan de Fuca Strait
- Not for Navigation

Port San Juan

Chart 3647, 3606

There are some tempting escapes from the elements en route between Bamfield and Sooke. These include the entrances into Nitinat Lake (chart 3647) and River Jordan. But these are not easy shelters to enter nor are they always good protection from the seas. They are tricky to enter even in sometimes good conditions so I recommend if you find yourself in a rising storm head for Port Renfrew or Sooke whichever is closest.

Shelter in Juan de Fuca Strait (Port Renfrew)

Access

Port San Juan is a large opening off Juan de Fuca Strait which, once inside, still requires some travel time to reach Snuggery Cove in Port Renfrew.

Anchorage

Shelter can be found either on the east shore behind the breakwater at **Snuggery Cove** that forms a terminus to the roadway from Victoria, or on the west side of the bay behind the cliff that rises over the mouth of the **Gordon River.** Both of these anchorages should be considered temporary, but with a careful watch they will provide conditional shelter and you are probably better off in there than riding out a rough Juan de Fuca Strait. Farther up the Gordon River is a marina and launch ramp for small boats.

Above: Carmanah Point, Juan de Fuca Strait. Below, left: The mouth of the San Juan River at the head of Port Renfrew.

Above: From Sooke Basin looking towards the entrance to Sooke off Juan de Fuca Strait.
Left: Anchorage at Anderson Cove.
Below: Billings Spit from the opposite shore in Sooke.

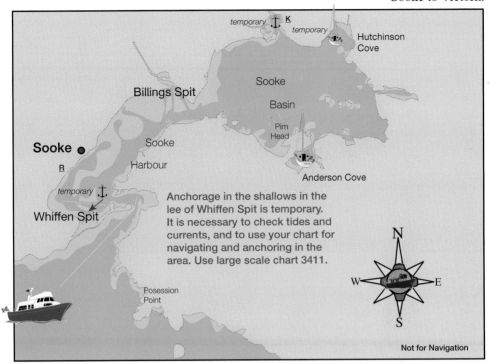

Anchorage in the shallows in the lee of Whiffen Spit is temporary. It is necessary to check tides and currents, and to use your chart for navigating and anchoring in the area. Use large scale chart 3411.

Not for Navigation

Sooke to Victoria Charts 3411, 3410, 3461, 3606

Sooke

When you reach Sooke on your way in from Bamfield and Port Renfrew you are probably already out of the rolling swells of Juan de Fuca Strait, depending on the weather at the time. If conditions are deteriorating you will probably want to take shelter before continuing around Race Passage to Victoria. Travelling from Victoria to Bamfield, Sooke is a good place to stop overnight to await calm weather for the long open stretch to Barkley Sound.

Access

The entrance to Sooke and some of the waterways inside the harbour can be tricky. Use the best charts (3411 and 3410) available for navigation in this area. Enter around Whiffin Spit and follow the navigational markers to Sooke Harbour's usually crowded public docks, where you may find room to tie up.

Anchorage

There is anchorage in the lee of **Pim Head** or inside **Anderson Cove** off Sooke Basin. Other anchorages in the basin include the small cove at the north end or at **Hutchinson Cove** where shelter is limited, due to exposure to some winds.

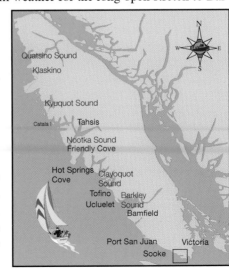

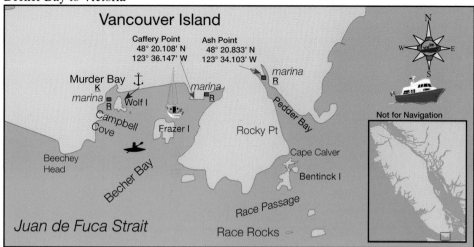

West Coast Vancouver I

Becher Bay

Charts 3410, 3440

Access and anchorage

This convenient bay opens off Juan de Fuca Strait a short distance south of Race Rocks. There is good anchorage at **Wolf Island** in the western corner of the bay. Anchor also off **Frazer Island**. We anchored there once during the Swiftsure sailing race and had a grandstand view of the colourful yachts sailing past.

Pedder Bay

Charts 3410, 3440

Access and anchorage

Pass between Bentinck Island and Race Rocks in Race Passage and enter Pedder Bay between Cape Calver and William Head.

The best place to drop the hook is along the shore off **Rocky Point** where you will probably find shelter from any winds most times of the boating season. Occasionally a southeaster will cause some disturbance in Pedder Bay, and on the rare occasion in summer, if the forecast predicts such conditions, use the facilities at the marina farther up inside the bay. Continue your voyage with the author's **Gulf Islands Cruising Guide**.

We were travelling towards Race Rocks from Port Renfrew in almost zero visibility fog. There was a long rolling swell pushing down Juan de Fuca Strait, which diminished substantially as we neared Sooke. As we kept going we picked up scores of echoes on the radar, denoting that there were boats grouped between us and Race Rocks. It was the fishing fleet.

We heard one tell another on VHF that there were boats (us) approaching and to be wary. We were the ones being wary. At first I decided it might be better to stop somewhere rather than attempt passing through the fleet. So, consulting the chart, I decided to put into Becher Bay. Checking the radar again I realized we would have to pass through part of the fleet to access the bay. We continued into the fleet with great caution, using the shortest radar range available as well as a sharp lookout. Using auto pilot helped substantially, as it allowed me at the helm to keep a sharp lookout without having to monitor the compass constantly. Just as I was about to change course for the entrance to Becher the fog began to lift. We were in the midst of the fishing fleet, all with their nets strung out across the Strait. We had come this far into the fleet, why not continue to Victoria. So we did. And saved a visit to Becher Bay for another occasion.

Above: Anchorage in Sooke. Boats lie in a cove off the inner harbour. The dock serves as access to a restaurant located conveniently on the waterfront.
Below: Becher Bay is open to Juan de Fuca Strait but has sheltered anchorage in the lee of Frazer Island and in Murder Bay behind Wolf Island. The view out of Becher Bay takes in the Olympic Mountains on the Washington side of the strait. It is a convenient place to await changing currents and tides at nearby Race Rocks, when travelling towards Victoria.

Launch Ramps
Gulf Islands, Lower Mainland and Vancouver Island

Vancouver Island South

Becher Bay
Cheanuh Marina 4901 East Sooke Road, RR1,
Sooke, BC. V0S 1N0. 250-478-4880.

Sooke
Pacific Lions Marina and Campground
241 Becher Bay Road, RR1, Sooke, BC.
V0S 1N0. 250-642-3816.

Sooke Harbour Marina launch ramp
6971 West Coast Road, RR4 Sooke,
BC. V0S 1N0 250-642-3236.

Sunny Shores Marina and launch ramp
5621 Sooke Road, Sooke, BC. V0S 1N0.
250-642-5731

Pedder Bay Marina
925 Pedder Bay Drive
RR #2 Victoria, BC. V9B 5B4. 250-478-1771.

Fleming Bay (Victoria)
James Bay Anglers' Association launch ramp
75 Dallas Road, Victoria BC. V8V 1A1.

Oak Bay (2)
Two ramps at Cattle Point on Beach Drive–
good condition. Near Oak Bay Marina, 1327
Beach Drive, Victoria BC. V8S 2N4.
250-598-3369.

Island View Beach
Foot of Island View Road (off Highway 17 at
Keating Cross Roads south of airport turnoff),
Sidney, BC. (concrete-limited use).

Roberts Bay public launch
Ardwell Road, Sidney, BC.
Cartopper launching only).

Sidney Public Launch Ramp
McTavish Road to Tulista Park, adjacent
to the Anacortes ferry terminal.

Van Isle Marina
2320 Harbour Road, Sidney, BC. V8L 3S6.
250-656-1138.

Brentwood Bay
Tsartlip launch ramp, 800 Stellys Cross Road,
Brentwood Bay, BC. V0S1A0. 250-652-3988.

Goldstream Boathouse
2892 Trans Canada Highway, RR6, Victoria,
BC. V9B 5T9. 250-478-4407.

Mill Bay Marina & Public Launch Ramps
End of Handy Road and 740 Handy Road, Mill
Bay, BC. V0R 2P0. 250-743-4112.

Cowichan
Hecate Park public ramp. Cowichan Bay
Road, Cowichan Bay, BC.

Genoa Bay
Genoa Bay Marina, 5100 Genoa Bay Road,
Duncan, BC. V9L 1M3. 250-746-7621.

Maple Bay
Beaumont Avenue, near Maple Bay Public
Dock, north of General Store. 250-746-7621.

Chemainus
Rotary ramp. At Transfer Beach Park. Foot of
Maple Street, Chemainus, BC.

Ladysmith Fishermen's Wharf
Rotary ramp. Foot of Ludlow Road, Ladysmith, BC. Public dock 250-245-7511.

Ladysmith Marina (check availability)
Ladysmith BC. Private facility.
Phone 250-245-4521.

Gulf Islands

Ganges
Salt Spring Island public ramp, Centennial Park, Ganges. Inner Harbour (Fulford-Ganges Road). Dock manager 250-537-5711.

Salt Spring Marina
120 Upper Ganges Road, Ganges BC. V0S 1E0. 250-537-5810.

Ramp and dock at Becher Bay.

Long Harbour
Quebec Drive off Long Harbour Road, Salt Spring Island.

Hudson Point
Off North Beach Road near Fernwood government dock. Salt Spring Island. Cartoppers only-very limited use. Three kilometers north of Walker Hook. (poor).

Drummond Park
Off Isabella Point Road. Salt Spring Island. poor.

Victoria has a good ramp at Fleming Bay.

Montague Harbour
Located at Montague Provincial Park. RR1, Montague Park Road, Galiano, BC. V0N 1P0. 250-539-2115. Limited use–high tide.

Port Browning
Hamilton Road, North Pender Island. Near Marina beach launch. Marina 250-629-3493.

Otter Bay.
Otter Bay Marina, General Delivery, Pender Island BC. V0N 2M0.
250-629-3579. Ramp located at marina.

Thieves Bay
Anchor Way, North Pender Island. (concrete).

Above: The ramp at Port Moody is spacious.
Below: A small ramp serves Maple Bay.

Mortimer Spit
Mortimer Spit Road, South Pender Island. Cartoppers only.

Village Bay public launch ramp
Mayne Island. Adjacent ferry terminal. At foot of Callaghan Crescent via Mariners Way. (concrete).

David Cove
Mayne Island. Petrus Crescent, via Village Bay
Road. (paved).

Degnen Bay
Very Limited use, near Public docks south of
Silva Bay.

East (Central)
Vancouver Island

Brechin Point Launch Ramp
Adjacent Brechin Esso, Nanaimo. Call Stones
Marina 250-753-6122. Info: 250-753-7222.

Nanoose Bay
Snaw-Naw-As Marina and launch ramp. 209
Mallard Way, Lantzville, BC.
V0R 2H0.

Schooner Cove Resort
3521 Dolphin Drive, Nanoose Bay, BC.
V0R 2R0. 250-468-7691.

Beachcomber Marina and launch ramp
RR #1, Box 21, Beachcomber, Nanoose Bay,
BC. V0N 3A0. 250-468-7222.

Deep Bay
Ship & Shore Marine, RR1, S-160, C-69,
Bowser, BC. V0R 1G0. 250-757-8750. Off
Island Highway, Vancouver Island, BC.

Fanny Bay
Pacific Village Motel, 8256 South Island High-
way, RR1, S-29, C-9, Fanny Bay, BC.
V0R 1W0. 250-335-9983.

French Creek
Island Highway, Vancouver Island, BC.
250-248-5051.
Hornby launch ramp
Ford Cove, Hornby Island, BC. Cartoppers
only.

Denman Island
Public launch ramp at Gravelly Road.
Adjacent ferry terminal.

Comox public launch ramp.
132 Port Augusta St., Comox, BC. V9N 8G7.
Ph 250-339-4664. Located at Blackfin Marina,

Pacific Playgrounds Resort
9082 Clarkson Drive, Black Creek, BC.
V9J 1B3. 250-337-5600.

Salmon Point Resort
2176 Salmon Point Road, Campbell River, BC.
V9H 1E5. 250-923-6605.

Shelter Bay Resort
3880 South Island Highway, Campbell River,
BC. V9W 2J2. 250-923-5338.

Lucky Louie Boat Rentals
907 South Island Highway,
Campbell River, BC. 250-923-1242.

Fresh Water Marina
2705 North Island Highway, Campbell River,
BC. V9W 2H4. 250-286-0701.

Tyee Spit Launch Ramp
Spit Road, Campbell River, BC.

Quathiaski Cove
Quathiaski Cove, Quadra Island, BC. Near
ferry landing. 250-624-2222.

April Point Resort
April Pt Road, Quadra Island. 250-285-2222.

Heriot Bay
Antler Road, Heriot Bay, Quadra Island. BC.
Adjacent to public dock.
Marina at 250-285-3322.

Rebecca Spit
Rebecca Spit Provincial Park, Drew Harbour,
Quadra Island, BC.

Brown's Bay Marina and launch ramp
15021, Ripple Rock Road, Campbell River,
BC. V9W 2E3. 250-286-3135.

Vancouver/Lower Mainland

Wards Public Marina
Elgin Heritage Park,
13723 Crescent Road, Crescent Beach, Surrey,
BC. Historic Stewart Farmhouse. Information:
604-574-5744. Open dawn to dusk. Parks and
Recreation 604-591-4426.

Crescent Beach Marina
12555 Crescent Road, Crescent Beach,
Surrey, BC.
Open dawn to dusk. Check with marina
604-538-9666 for additional hours.

Wellington Point Park
3600 Block, River Road West
Ladner, BC.

Bridgeview Marine
8550 River Road, Delta, BC.
Phone 604-987-8566.

Fraser River RV Park
at Brownsville Marine Pub and Bar, Old Yale
Road, Under Patullo Bridge. Surrey, BC.
Turn off Scott Road near Patullo Bridge/Scott
Road interchange.
Open about 7 am to 9 pm.

Rocky Point
Moody Street, Port Moody, BC.
Open 24 hours. Parks and Recreation
604-931-8852.

Macquabeak Park
Burbridge Rd., Coquitlam, BC.
Open all hours.
Leisure and Parks Services. 604-933-6000.

Pitt River
Lincoln Avenue (on Pitt River) Port Coquitlam,
BC. Located at base of Pitt River Bridge.

Pitt Stop
Two ramps: Highways Branch at road end for
car toppers and nearby unpaved ramp for larger
vehicles and trailers. Operates 8 am to 10 pm.

Pitt Meadows Marina
1–14179 Reichenbach Road, Pitt Meadows,
BC. Open most hours.

Ladner Public Ramp
Ferry Road, Ladner, BC. Open 24 hours. Re-
strictions on times of waterways use for skiing.
See noticeboard at ramp. Phone 946-1244 at
Captain's Cove marina next door. Parks and
Recreation 604-946-3293.

The ramp on the river at Courtenay.

Schooner Cove marina and launch ramp.

French Creek ramp on Vancouver Island.

Pitt River at the Alouette River confluence.

Steveston
Foot of #2 Road, Richmond, BC. Try Britannia Heritage Shipyard office 604-272-5539.

Macdonald Beach Marina
3500 Macdonald, Richmond, BC 604-241-0167.
Open dawn to dusk.

Kitsilano Public
Kisilano Beach at entrance to False Creek
Open all hours. Burrard Bridge Civic Marina, at 1655 Whyte, 604-733-5833.
Parks and recreation 604-257-8400.

Cates Park
Dollarton Highway, North Vancouver, BC.
Parks Board 604-986-9141.

Sunshine Coast

Horseshoe Bay
Sewell's Marina ramp. 6695, Nelson Ave., West Vancouver, BC. V7W 2B2. 604-921-3474.

Lions Bay Marina
Lions Bay, 60 Lions Bay Ave., Lions Bay. BC.
V0N 2E0. 604-921-7510.

Sunset Marina
34 Sunset Beach, West Vancouver, BC.
V7W 2T7 604-921-7476.

Snug Cove
Union Steamship Marina 604-947-0707.

Porteau Cove
Sea to Sky Highway, Howe Sound. West Vancouver Parks Board 604-986-9371.

Gibsons
Gibsons Marina next door 886-8686.
Ramp: 604-886-8017.

Selma Park public launch
Highway 101, Selma Park, BC. Turn off, indicated on approach to town of Sechelt.

Cooper's Green Public Ramp
Fisherman's Rd, Redroofs, Halfmoon Bay, BC.

Porpoise Bay, Sechelt
Lighthouse Marina. 604-885-9494.
Ramp adjacent to pub and offices.

Poise Cove
Sechelt Rd. 604-885-2895.

Madeira Park Public Ramp,
Pender Harbour
Take Madeira Park turn-off. Adjacent Madeira Marina 604-883-2234.

Madeira Marina, Pender Harbour
P.O. Box 189 Madeira park, BC. V0N 2H0.
Take Madeira Park turn-off. Adjacent Madeira Park Public Ramp 604-883-2266.

Coho Marina, Pender Harbour
P.O. Box 160 Madeira Park, BC. V0N 2H0.
Pender Harbour. Phone 604-883-2237.
Take road to Madeira Park and follow signs.
(Shopping centre nearby.)

Pender Harbour Resort
4686 Sinclair Bay Road, RR 1 S-15, C-13, Garden Bay, BC. V0N 1S0. 604-883-2424.

Hospital Bay, Pender Harbour.
Located at Fisherman's Resort 604-883-2336.
Take road to John Henry's and Fisherman's Resort, Garden Bay.

Egmont Marina
General Delivery, Egmont, BC. V0N 1N0.
604-883-2298. (unpaved). at Backeddy pub.

Egmont Public ramp
Off Brandwynne Road, Egmont, BC.

Saltery Bay
Saltery Bay Picnic Site, Highway 101. Near Egmont Saltery Bay ferry landing.

Texada
Boat Club Ramp, Sturt Bay, Texada Island.

Powell River
Westview Boat Harbour (municipal). Adjacent ferry landing. 604-485-5244.

Lund
End of Sunshine Coast Highway (101).
604-483-4711.

Okeover
Limited use unpaved launching ramp.
1-800-669-9025.

North of Desolation Sound

Fish & Game Club ramp
Sayward Road (end of Highway 19), Kelsey Bay, BC. 250-282-3792.

Telegraph Cove
P.O. Box 1. Telegraph Cove, BC. V0N 3J0. 250-928-3131.

Alert Bay
Cormorant Island, BC. 250-974-5727.

Port McNeill
Beach Road, Port McNeill, BC. 250-956-3881.

Port Hardy
6555 Hardy Bay Road, BC. V0N 2P0. At Fishermen's wharf inside breakwater. Harbour Authority: 250-949-6332. Adjacent Quarter-deck Marina.

Bear Cove
Bear Cove Road, Port Hardy, BC.

Bella Coolla
Bella Coola, BC. V0T 1B0.

Kitimat
MK Marina Box 220, Kitimat, BC. V2C 2G7. 250-632-6401.

Prince Rupert
Rushbrook Public Dock, Prince Rupert, BC. 250-624-9400.

West Coast Vancouver Island

Coal Harbour
Quatsino Sound. Large unused whaling station ramp. Some seaplane activity.

Fair Harbour, Kyuquot
Enquire–Kyuqout Sound Adventures in Walter Cove 250-332-5225.

Gold River
Downtown public ramp.

continued...

Macdonald Beach on the Fraser River.

Poise Cove at Porpoise Bay, Sechelt.

Serviceable ramp at high tide on Texada Island.

Ramp near the Hornby Island ferry landing.

A popular launching ramp for access to Barkley Sound on the west coast of Vancouver Island, is this one at Clutesi Haven in Port Alberni.

Tahsis
Westview Marina, Box 481, Tahsis, BC. V0P 1X0. 250-934-7622. Launch ramp nearby.

Tofino
Ocean West Marina, 386 Main Street, Tofino, BC. V0R 2Z0. 250-725-3251.

Tofino Public
Fourth Street, Tofino. Located adjacent downtown.

Tofino Public
Located on Clayoquot Sound before reaching town at Grice Bay.

Ucluelet.
Island West Fishing Resort. P.O. Box 32, Ucluelet, BC. V0R 3A0. 250-726-7515. (Foot of Bay St.)

Bamfield.
Kingfisher Marina P.O. Box 38, Bamfield, BC. V0R 1B0. 250-728-3228.

Port Desire
Grapler Inlet, Bamfield.

Port Alberni.
China Creek Marina. Port Alberni, BC. c/o V9Y 7M6. 250-723-9812.

Clutesi Haven Marina and launch ramp.
Port Alberni, BC. 250-724-6837.

Port Renfrew Marina
Launch ramp adjacent. Gordon River Road, Port Renfrew, BC. V0S 1K0. 250-647-5430. Located on the San Juan River.

Above: Port Desire at Bamfield. Below: The public launch ramp at Tofino.

Bibliography

151 Dives. *In the Protected Waters of British Columbia and Washington State (Washington State and British Columbia).* Betty Pratt-Johnson. Adventure Publishing. Kaslo BC. 2007.

A Cruising Guide to Puget Sound and the San Juan Islands McGraw Hill. Scherer.

A Guide to the Western Seashore. Rick M. Harbo. Hancock House, Surrey, BC. 1988.

Best Anchorages of the Inside Passage. Guide to waterways Victoria to the Broughton Islands. Bill Kelly and Ann Vipond. 2007.

BC Cruising Guide Series–Desolation Sound, Gulf Islands, Sunshine Coast. Whitecap Books, North Vancouver, BC. Bill Wolferstan.

BC Marine Parks Guide. Pacific Yachting Magazine 2005. Editor John Shinnick.

Charlies Charts North to Alaska. Charles E. Wood. Margo Wood. Polymath Energy Consultants Ltd. Surrey B.C.

Canadian Tide and Current Tables. Pacific Coast all volumes. Ottawa-Department of Fisheries and Oceans. Annual.

Cruising the Secret Coast: *Unexplored Anchorages on British Columbia's Inside Passage.* Jennifer and James Hamilton. Robert Hale Publishing. Seattle.

Docks and Destinations. Guide to marinas in British Columbia. Pacific Marine Publishing. Peter Vassilopoulos. 2007.

Exploring Vancouver Island's West Coast. A Cruising Guide. Fine Edge Productions. Don Douglass.

Exploring the Inside Passage to Alaska Cruising Guide. Fine Edge Productions. California. Don Douglas.

Exploring the South Coast of British Columbia. A Cruising Guide. Fine Edge Productions. California. Don Douglas.

Exploring the Gulf Islands and Desolation Sound to Port Hardy and Blunden Harbour. A Cruising Guide. Fine Edge Productions. California. Don Douglas.

Gulf Islands Cruising Guide. Guide to the islands in the Strait of Georgia. Pacific Marine Publishing. Peter Vassilopoulos. 2006.

Gunkholing in the San Juan Islands A guide to the islands and waterways of the San Juan Islands. Baily/Nyburg

Local Knowledge Tacoma to Ketchikan. Fine Edge Publishing. Kevin Monahan.

Marine Weather Hazards Manual. A guide to local forecasts and conditions. Vancouver. Environment Canada.

North of Desolation Sound. Guide to the Broughton Islands. Peter Vassilopoulos. Pacific Marine Publishing. 2005/6.

North to Alaska. Hugo Anderson. Anderson Publishing Co. 1993.

Oceanography of the British Columbia Coast. Richard E. Thomson. Ottawa. Department of Fisheries and Aquatic Sciences.

Sailing Directions. British Columbia Coast. Ottawa. Department of Fisheries and Oceans.

Sea Kayak series. Heritage House.

Sea Kayaking Canada's West Coast. John Ince and Hedi Kottner. Raxas Books. Vancouver, BC.

The San Juan Islands. Afoot and Afloat. Marge and Ted Mueller. The Mountaineers. Seattle.

Voyages to Windward. Harbour Publishing. British Columbia. Elsie Hulsizer. 2005.

Waggoner. Robert Hale. Robert Hale Publishing. Seattle. *Annual cruising guide with up-to-date information on marinas and waterways.*

Weatherly Waypoint Guides for GPS and Loran Navigation. Robert Hale. Robert Hale Publishing. Volumes 1–3: Puget Sound, San Juan Islands, Strait of Juan de Fuca. Gulf of Georgia, including Gulf Islands, Jervis Inlet. Desolation Sound to Port Hardy.

West Coast of Vancouver Island. Whitecap Books, North Vancouver, BC. Don Watmough.

My wife Carla and I have cruised the area this guide covers over the past thirty-five years. We have visited all areas described in the book and have stopped at and anchored in most anchorages included in the foregoing pages. Mariners who adventure beyond the known routes and popular areas will enjoy discovering for themselves others I have omitted. There are numerous books on cruising the coast and these along with your charts and reference books should enable you to extend your cruising range substantially and safely.

—Happy boating, Peter Vassilopoulos.

Index

Also available from Pacific Marine Publishing

Docks and Destinations–by Peter Vassilopoulos. $29.95. This is a companion guide to Anchorages and Marine Parks. It is a user friendly guide to marinas and services on the coast. The area it covers, in a south to north progression, includes Puget Sound, the San Juan Islands and all of BC coastal waters. The contents includes fuel stops, moorage, availability of water, supplies, mechanical service, some pertinent distances between fuel stops, laundry facilities, showers available and much more. It contains numerous drawings depicting dock layouts and is illustrated with hundreds of aerial and ambient photographs. It is a most popular publication and is also available from all leading marine stores, marinas and book stores.

North of Desolation Sound Cruising Guide–by Peter Vassilopoulos $49.95 (soft cover). This book, companion to the Gulf Islands Cruising Guide, is one of a three part series. It covers the Broughton Islands and approaches with comprehensive information on destinations, anchorages and marinas and provides suggested cruising routes to reach the Broughton Archipelago, then takes you through them in the most suitable passages. It is large format with hundreds of colour aerial and ambient photographs and illustrations.

Gulf Islands Cruising Guide–by Peter Vassilopoulos $49.95 (soft cover). This book, companion to North of Desolation Sound, is one of a three part series. It covers the popular Gulf Islands with comprehensive information on destinations, anchorages and marinas and provides suggested cruising routes. It is large format with hundreds of colour aerial and ambient photographs and illustrations.

Desolation Sound Cruising Guide to be published in 2008/9. It will be a companion to the above two books and will sell at the same price of $49.95.

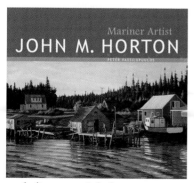

Mariner Artist John M. Horton A popular Heritage House title by Peter Vassilopoulos. $59.95.The publication is a large format, beautifully illustrated, hard covered coffee table book. It depicts scenes of Captains Cook and Vancouver on the west coast, early waterfront scenes in Vancouver and on the Fraser River, coastal views of the St Lawrence and of the Maritimes. It includes a selection of works showing military, historic vessels, events and scenes in the USA and abroad. Order any of these books by contacting the publisher. Please phone 604-948-4618. Or contact Pacific Marine Publishing. PO Box 1312, Delta B.C. V4M 3Y8

website: *www.johnhorton.ca*

or PO Box 984, Point Roberts, WA. 98281-0984. Email: *boating@dccnet.com*

Peter and Carla Vassilopoulos have cruised the west coast of Canada and the waters of Puget Sound extensively for nearly 35 years. Many of those years were aboard their 10 knot converted gillnetter *Balladeer*. Since 1993 they have run their Monaro 27 pictured here. The vessel, built in Richmond, BC, and launched in 1993, is equipped with twin Mercruiser 305 gas engines, Panasonic radar, Lowrance GPS, Teleflex steering and autopilot, a long range fuel tank and additional fresh water storage. Top speed is 45 mph with a cruising speed of 30 to 34 mph. The vessel has served on extensive research trips including places as far afield as Alaska.

The photograph of the boat was taken at Malibu Rapids, Princess Louisa Inlet, in 2006.